Adventures in Gentle Discipline
A Parent-to-Parent Guide

Adventures in Gentle Discipline

A Parent-to-Parent Guide

by Hilary Flower

LA LECHE LEAGUE
INTERNATIONAL

Schaumburg, Illinois

First printing, September 2005

© 2005, Hilary Flower

Library of Congress Catalogue Number 2005927402

ISBN 0-976869-0-7

Printed in the United States of America

Book and Cover Design by Paul Torgus
Cover Illustration by Elizabeth Hannon Fuller

Cartoons by Elizabeth Hannon Fuller
Photo Credits on page 359

La Leche League International
1400 N. Meacham Road
Schaumburg IL 60173-4808 USA
www.lalecheleague.org

To Ben

Contents

Foreword

Sometimes, I really, really feel like hitting my kids. There, I've said it.

It's not something I felt comfortable telling people in my earliest years as a mother. I was afraid that my occasional urges to grab, scream at, shake, or whack my children meant that there was something wrong with me. I was afraid these urges meant that I could never be the kind of gentle, attached mother I wanted to be. And mostly, I was afraid I might lose control and actually do the things I sometimes felt like doing.

Now that I've got some parenting experience under my belt (my children are 13, 9, and 6 years old), I am less afraid of the powerful and angry feelings each of them can sometimes evoke in me. I am also less afraid to admit those feelings. I have come to discover that virtually all mothers, including the ones whose mothering I most admire, sometimes feel the urge to smack one of their kids "upside the head," or at least turn them over their knee.

I knew before I gave birth for the first time that I didn't want to use physical or harsh punishment to guide my children, but when I would tell people this, they would respond with, "Oh, you say that now..." with a knowing grin, assuming that I would eventually give up on this ridiculous idea of gentle discipline. But I didn't give up on it.

Instead, through observation of other parents I admire and good, old trial and error, I created a number of other, more gentle discipline techniques that I can use when needed. Logical and natural consequences, active listening, and breaks from parenting when **I** am not at my best all play important roles in guiding my children's emotional, spiritual, moral, and educational development.

I readily admit that I have not been perfect in my goal of gentle discipline. I have screamed at, threatened, and come very close to hitting my children on more than one occasion, but these behaviors have never found a permanent place in my parenting toolbox.

I will never forget the one time I did totally lose it and hit one of my children. It happened when my daughter was about three years old. I snapped and smacked her on her rear end. Except I missed her very small bottom and my hand instead landed on her lower back, where it left a red, hand-shaped mark.

She stared at me in horror, having never been struck in her life. I stared back in equal horror. Then she said to me in a small, quavering voice I will never forget, "Mama, why did you hit me?" I burst into tears and held her and rocked her and assured her that I was very, very sorry and that she could trust me to never hit her again. I told her that it was never okay for anyone to strike her.

That night, as I tried to fall asleep, I couldn't get the incident out of my mind. I realized that I certainly did not want my daughter to grow up believing that sometimes, under the "right" circumstances, she deserved to be hit by the people she loves. I reaffirmed my vow to myself that I would raise my children without harsh punishment.

Despite several near-misses over the years—times when I have had to leave the room, scream into a pillow, or take deep breaths and count to ten to avoid lashing out at my children— it's a vow I have managed to keep. And wonder of wonders, it's working.

My children are polite, well-behaved (most of the time), thoughtful people. The proof, as they say, is in the pudding, and when people compliment me on the kids' behavior, I always make a point to say that I don't spank them. And on the days when one of them is making me feel like sticking my head in the oven, I find that it helps for me to vent to friends who have children even older than mine—parents who also avoid striking out so these mothers and fathers can remind me how well their kids have turned out without harsh punishment.

This is why I recommend that parents of very young children who want to use gentle discipline methods spend time around parents of older children who hold the same views. On the days when your toddler is making you insane and you feel ready to pull out the wooden spoon for a few swats on a diapered bottom, it helps to see the end product of gentle discipline.

Getting through the days, the weeks, and eventually, the years of parenting without using physical discipline is, in itself, a discipline. I find that having made the promise to myself that I will not resort to hitting provides me with the parenting "North Star" I can use to re-orient myself when I feel angriest. And I have also found that when I am feeling most out-of-control in my parenting, it's a signal to me that something else is going on in my life, something that needs some of my attention and reflection.

In picking up this important book by Hilary Flower, you have taken a first step in finding your own parenting "North Star." In it, you will find many specific ideas and strategies for raising healthy, happy, well-behaved children using gentle discipline that really works.

And remember, on the really hard days, there's always the tried and true method of finding a place in your home where no one can hear you, closing the door, and screaming at the top of your lungs until the urge to throttle your child passes, at least for the moment.

Katie Allison Granju
Author of Attachment Parenting

Acknowledgements

I must thank Judy Torgus at La Leche League International for the gift of this project. Thank you so much for another leap of faith and for getting this project going. I wish to thank Nancy Jo Bykowski for the humor, support, and editorial care she shared with me from contract to publication; her insight into gentle discipline helped bring out the best in this book. What a luxury to have an editor who becomes such a great friend along the way. Thank you also to the many hands at LLLI who will take this manuscript into book form and beyond, including Paul Torgus, Jennifer Hopkin, and Sharon Barsotti.

I want to express my profound appreciation to all of the parents who shared their wisdom and their experiences with this project. Your voices make this book. If ever I got discouraged with the immensity of this undertaking, I only had to read some of the quotes I had saved up from you to get inspired all over again. I must particularly thank Amy Nelson, Beth Cagnoni, Betsy Shepard, Brooke Schumacher, Carissa Dollar, Elizabeth Bonet, Heather Hejduk, Heather Sanders, Heather Petit, Heidi O'Callahan, Jessica Kramer, Lisa Stroyan, Loree Stickles-Noonan, and Rebecca Kasapidis. I want to express my warm gratitude to my personal friends Cheri Riznyk, Kelly Bonyata, Maureen Corbett O'Connor, Missy Ridge Carter, and Sigrid Diane Cartier for their encouragement and insights.

I feel tremendous gratitude to *Mothering Magazine* for the Gentle Discipline forum Mothering.com and to the warm and wise mothers who make up that community. That board was an essential resource for this book.

I can never thank Karen Levy Keon enough for her simply amazing gifts of time, mothering insight, and editorial talent. Her continuous support over the last year has made this book a great deal stronger and infinitely more fun to write.

Closer to home, I must humbly thank my partner, Ben, who has taught me a great deal about empathy and respect. The many mornings and weekends he provided have been a writer mama's paradise. I want to thank my daughter, Nora Jade, and my son Miles, who have given me so many opportunities (and second chances) to grow in my practice of gentle discipline.

Introduction

When I first found out that La Leche League International was interested in publishing a book about discipline, it didn't even occur to me to suggest myself as the writer. When the executive editor, Judy Torgus, first mentioned the possibility, I balked: "I'm certainly no expert on that!"

It's ironic because when my firstborn was a toddler I thought I had gentle discipline all figured out. I could have written authoritatively on how if you just stay in tune with your child you can dance through your days together in perfect synchrony. She was an intense child, and yet I rarely had to say "No" to her. Our days just seemed to flow. Then my son was born. My daughter abruptly changed into a regressive, demanding, unreasonable—and very confused and needy—little girl. I could hardly recognize her, or myself as a mother. I eventually got my sea legs after that initial parenting crisis, and got used to the reality that sometimes I would feel "over my head" as a parent. Few parents of an intense child—or more than one child—get to stay smug about their parenting for long.

Indeed, even as Judy and I spoke, my children were two big and rowdy bulges swishing around behind the hotel curtains,

A word about words

"Gentle discipline"

I chose the term gentle discipline in part to contrast it with "harsh" discipline. The term itself is rather arbitrary. Some parents contributing to this book use other expressions, like "compassionate parenting," "positive discipline," or La Leche League's "loving guidance." I wish to use the term gentle discipline as an umbrella term, including a wide range of parenting philosophies that place empathy and respect as top priorities. Whatever you happen to call your particular approach to discipline, it is my hope that if you wish to place compassion at the center of your parenting, you will find a home for yourself within this book.

"He" or "she"

In an effort to be inclusive, I alternate between using male and female pronouns when talking about children in general. Odd-numbered chapters use male pronouns. Even-numberes chapters use female pronouns. When referring to a parent I use "he or she" to emphasize that both mothers and fathers are engaging in gentle discipline.

We are all in this together

Please know that in an attempt to be as direct and clear as possible, I am speaking to you directly—as "you"—in many places. My intention is to make statements that would be true for most parents wishing to practice gentle discipline, not to make assumptions about or issue directives to the individual reader.

threatening to break out in full mutiny at any moment. I was in San Francisco at the 2003 LLLI Conference where my first book, ADVENTURES IN TANDEM NURSING, was making its debut. My children had been patient during the morning session, but enough was enough. I was torn between continuing my adult conversation for just a few more moments, going over and desperately hissing at my kids to stop playing in the curtains right now, or forcing myself to break off with Judy to take my kids out for some romping and snacking, which was what they really needed. No, I didn't consider myself an expert! I was just another mom getting by as best I could.

"But we don't need another expert telling parents how to do their job," Judy pointed out. "The parents are the real experts. They're the ones in the trenches doing the work. Write it the way you did the tandem nursing book, based on lots of mothers' stories and insights."

Why didn't I think of that? A new possibility began to take shape in my head.

Why do we need another book on discipline?

There are rows and rows of books at bookstores that will tell you how to parent. From horrifying to edifying, when it comes to parenting advice, you could say the bases are pretty well covered.

The expert-driven books promise to give all the answers if you will just follow the authors' advice. And yet so many techniques that are brilliant on paper fall flat at one's own dinner table. What's a real parent to do? On one message board a discouraged mom asked: "When did you first find out that gentle discipline is easier read than done?" A lively discussion followed in which moms gave voice to their frustrations with putting gentle discipline into practice, despite all the great advice they'd read.

It is humbling and a bit odd how often I need to be reminded of the simple truth of what Judy said: It's the parents in the trenches, even the ones waving the white flag (like me!), who really have an intimate knowledge of gentle discipline. What could I learn from them if I spent a year asking questions? What would it be like to assemble an entire book based on real parents' challenges, breakthroughs, stories and wisdom? I wanted to read that book. I wanted, I soon realized, to write that book.

This book is for you

I wrote this book for:

- Any parent who wishes to place compassion at the center of his or her parenting, Friends, grandparents, or other loved ones of parents practicing gentle discipline,

- New parents considering their options,

- Anyone at all wishing to learn more about what gentle discipline is all about, and

- Anyone already practicing gentle discipline who is interested in exploring further.

In order to be most helpful to parents at the very beginning of their discipline journey, I have focused a lot on babies and toddlers who are not yet verbal.

The format of the book

In Part One, each chapter explores one of the fundamental approaches common to parents practicing gentle discipline.

Part Two explores the parent's side of gentle discipline, where we parents strive to put our beliefs into practice.

Part Three comes at gentle discipline from the other direction, starting with classic parenting conundrums, such as whining and hitting, and seeing how various parents apply the basic gentle discipline approaches. You may want to flip to these examples if you want to see how differently various parents approach the "same" problem, or if you are currently facing one of these classic problems yourself.

Part Four delves yet more deeply into the texture of real-life gentle discipline, as ten parents tell their stories in rich detail.

As your children grow, you will have your own gentle discipline story. I hope that this book makes a good companion along the way.

I hope you will find that this book makes several unique contributions:

Celebrating you as the expert on your child

No one can tell you how to parent your child, no matter how many degrees he or she may have or how exemplary he or she may be as a parent. You are the most informed about your child, yourself, and the nitty-gritty situations you face. You are the one who can best navigate your individual challenges and come up with the best solutions available for your family. Gentle discipline takes a different form in each home.

This book aims to help you identify, affirm, and parent from your inner wisdom.

A community in itself

Imagine a lively potluck dinner where a bunch of parents can share their stories with you while the kids play. This book brings you the real-life wisdom of nearly two hundred parents practicing gentle discipline. What have these parents learned that they wished they knew at day one? What skills and insights have other parents developed to work through the conundrums they have faced?

The examples of other real-life parents can be heartening and enlightening as you brainstorm your own options along the way. I am proud to bring you what is, to my knowledge, the first parent-to-parent guide on this topic.

A realistic and respectful guide

To research gentle discipline I collected and analyzed the input of the myriad parents who contributed to this book, looking for patterns. What over-arching ideas or approaches unite parents practicing gentle discipline? I organized the book based on those basic guiding principles, fleshed out with many parents' personal examples. In that way, this book aims to strike the balance between philosophy and practical day-to-day use.

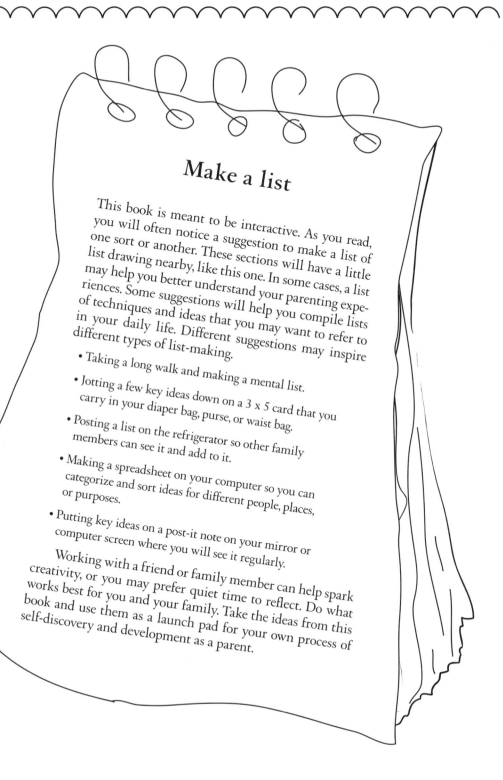

Make a list

This book is meant to be interactive. As you read, you will often notice a suggestion to make a list of one sort or another. These sections will have a little list drawing nearby, like this one. In some cases, a list may help you better understand your parenting experiences. Some suggestions will help you compile lists of techniques and ideas that you may want to refer to in your daily life. Different suggestions may inspire different types of list-making.

- Taking a long walk and making a mental list.

- Jotting a few key ideas down on a 3 x 5 card that you carry in your diaper bag, purse, or waist bag.

- Posting a list on the refrigerator so other family members can see it and add to it.

- Making a spreadsheet on your computer so you can categorize and sort ideas for different people, places, or purposes.

- Putting key ideas on a post-it note on your mirror or computer screen where you will see it regularly.

Working with a friend or family member can help spark creativity, or you may prefer quiet time to reflect. Do what works best for you and your family. Take the ideas from this book and use them as a launch pad for your own process of self-discovery and development as a parent.

Here you will find gentle discipline broken down into its component parts, ready for you to make it your own.

Connecting theory to practice

In practice, gentle discipline means making mistakes, working with your own anger, and growing as a person. What personal challenges of that kind have other parents faced in bringing more empathy and respect to their parenting? How can you best support yourself in your own growth as a parent?

You will find four chapters devoted to a candid, practical, and encouraging exploration of the parent's personal side of practicing gentle discipline.

The missing book

This is the book that was missing for me, the book that would help me honor my own expertise, feel less alone, craft a livable discipline plan, and work with my own personal trouble-spots. Writing this book has helped me to extend my ability to parent with compassion and inspired me to keep working at it. I hope this book helps you meet your own goals.

How this book was written

My role in this book is as questioner, compiler, and synthesizer of the input of as many parents practicing gentle discipline as I could possibly reach.

In order to find parents I posted on online message boards and email lists, solicited for input in magazines, and engaged my friends on the topic.

For my book on tandem nursing, I received a spontaneous outpouring of input from all around the world. My calls for input on gentle discipline yielded more like a trickle. The difference, I was to learn, was that mothers who are tandem nursing know that they are tandem nursing. And, having felt misunderstood or marginalized for so long, they were eager to tell their stories to someone who could appreciate them. When it came to gentle discipline, mothers were reticent. I probed my own friends, who often responded with comments like, "Oh, well, I don't have anything to say on that! I am far from perfect."

The difficulty of recruiting parents to participate underscored for me the extent to which we parents have been taught to de-value ourselves as knowledgeable about parenting. To reclaim gentle discipline expertise for parents, I realized, I'd have to begin with recruiting parents for the project.

For one thing, I had to ask individuals directly to participate and tell them why I wanted them in particular. I became an avid reader of message boards and email lists, approaching many parents by showing them specific quotes of theirs that I found helpful. Many expressed surprise and delight at the prospect that they might have something to contribute, particularly if they were in the middle of a rough patch with their children.

Once on the team, many parents answered a long questionnaire posted on my Web site (**www.gentlediscipline.com**). Some engaged in question-and-answer exchanges with me by email. Others had just enough time to give me permission for a single key quote and to wish the project well.

I also recruited parents to write their stories in essay form. I received many great essays and learned a great deal from each one. It was painful reducing the collection to a mere nine essays, which you will find at the end of this book.

While I took in the input of what turned out to be nearly two hundred parents, I was also working things out in my home "learning laboratory" with my feisty homeschooling five-year-old and rambunctious three-year-old. Indeed, as the writing process began to heat up, so did my home life, when I became pregnant with my third child. Working on a gentle discipline book while doing my best with real-life gentle discipline was a humbling and exciting experience, and it helped me keep this book grounded in reality. Now, as I am striving to crystallize all I have learned in this project and send it off to the publisher, I am looking forward to a whole new parenting relationship, with a baby expected any day now!

Part One

The Components of Gentle Discipline

Based on the input of nearly 200 parents, I have broken the practice of gentle discipline into its basic components. These fundamental approaches and ideas are common to most parents who practice gentle discipline.

Chapter 1

What Is Gentle Discipline?

Gentle discipline means, quite simply, placing empathy
and respect at the very center of your parenting.

Few parents are prepared for the emotional shock wave of
falling in love with their first tiny offspring. You hold your
new child's life in your hands, and through that sacred trust you
open yourself up to new depths of compassion for another person.

When the time comes to provide guidance or limits for this
incredibly important being, you may find yourself rethinking

old concepts of what discipline and parenting are all about. Your baby may have taught you that when it comes to nourishment, sleep, and being held, you can trust his cues and your own inner voice above the many public voices telling you what you "should" be doing. It is amazing to discover that you are the most reliable expert on your own child.

Could the same be true of discipline? Yes. You can trust your heart on this one. If you let him, your child will always lead you to gentle ways. You can place compassion at the center of your parenting.

This chapter will explore the goals of gentle discipline and provide a quick sketch of what it looks like in action, what makes it effective, how to make yourself at home in it, and why it's worth it—for your child, yourself, and the world. The following chapters will explore in detail what gentle discipline looks like in practice, with lots of examples from parents to flesh out the ideas.

What are the goals of gentle discipline?

Many parents who are attracted to gentle discipline share a view of the central importance of empathy and respect in meeting parenting goals. It's probably fair to say that, regardless of their parenting style, most parents want their children to develop the ability to meet their own needs in ways that work well for themselves and others. Parents who practice gentle discipline want other things, too.

Perhaps some of these goals resonate with you.

Safety. We want our children to feel safe with us, so that we can be trusted resources for our children throughout their lives.

 I want my girls to see their relationship with me as a place of refuge, a place they can retreat to for honesty, unconditional love, and support. I want to teach them and have them trust me, not fear me. I want to preserve the gentle souls that I see in them.

Liz M.

Partnership. Gentle discipline is a way to forge a partnership between parents and children. We recognize that our children's behavior will reflect their age and developmental level, and some behaviors will be difficult to face. While we wish to address undesirable behavior, we also want to look below the behavior to our children's underlying feelings and needs, and to help them meet those needs in more constructive ways as they grow. We realize that growing up takes time.

Thus, the quality of the parent-child relationship, more than the presence or absence of particular behaviors, is the best measure of the effectiveness of gentle discipline.

 Most parents want to know what will "work," as if discipline is some kind of magical thing that makes a child never misbehave. Gentle discipline encourages my child to go with me instead of against me, and for me to go with her rather than against her. I truly believe it leads to a happier, more positive relationship in general with my child. It gives my child the feeling that, "mommy and me are in this together," rather than "it's mommy vs. me."

Elizabeth B.

Building better options. By looking for the positive intent behind our children's behavior, we can build better options for the next time—an infinitely more positive approach than simply eradicating the unwanted behavior. As we work with our children to solve problems, we can help them learn to be effective problem-solvers.

To me, gentle discipline is a way of raising children that focuses on building them up instead of tearing them down. This method of parenting shows respect for our children as human beings and teaches them to do the same toward others.

Carissa D.

Is "discipline" too negative a word?

Many parents shy away from a word that conjures up images like an authority figure going for the dreaded belt, or "Little Jack Horner sitting in the corner." Dictionaries tend to be little help, equating discipline with "training," "punishment," and "obedience." From its inception, Western civilization has associated punishment, training, and controlling with the concept of discipline.

But at its root, discipline simply means "to teach." As a parent, you get to create your own family culture in every facet, and that includes your concepts of what teaching and learning are all about. Few of us truly learn best when immersed in shame and blame or when someone else's ideas are always imposed on us.

There is another connotation to the word discipline, and that is as a course of study, a practice. Engaging peacefully with your child is indeed a life-long practice, and one that pays many personal—even spiritual—dividends. By using gentle discipline, you may find that you are learning just as much as your child.

Self-discipline. We want our children to develop their own sense of inner discipline. To this end, we don't want to cover their inner voices with our own, but rather provide lots of good guidance and role modeling. We want them to bloom forth as the beautiful and good people that they are.

 My goal is to preserve my daughter's person, for her to remain "intact" and a whole person, with all of the innate parts of her personality she was born with. I believe that non-gentle discipline tactics teach children to hide, suppress, and even loathe the parts of themselves that cause their parents to hit, belittle, disrespect, or invalidate them. The curious child who is told "no" over and over again will soon shut down his curiosity. The sensitive child who is scolded for crying or protesting unfairness will soon grow to harden himself.

Mariah W.

Nurture respect and empathy. Gentle discipline gives us ways to protect and nurture the more human elements in our children that more traditional discipline methods tend to gloss over.

 Gentle discipline just seems like the obvious route to some of the key elements in real happiness: feeling connected to others, loving oneself, and the ability to express feelings and needs in order to get those needs met.

Dore T.

By emphasizing empathy and respect in every interaction, gentle discipline nurtures these qualities every step of the way—in us and in our children.

 If I want my kids to learn empathy, I have to show them empathy. If I want them to learn respect, I have to respect them.

Michelle N.

What does it look like in action?

If you are practicing gentle discipline, chances are that your

> By emphasizing empathy and respect in every interaction, gentle discipline nurtures these qualities every step of the way—in us and in our children.

approach is as individual as you and your child are. But more likely than not, there are key components to your discipline that unite you with other parents who practice gentle discipline. Each of these overarching components will be explored in the following chapters, with many examples from parents' experiences.

Make empathy and respect number one. You seek to orient yourself to be your child's trusted ally, placing respect and empathy as big priorities even when facing challenging situations.

Track your child's well-being. Because your child will act his best when he feels his best, you strive to stay on top of his basic needs, and you look for unmet needs when things get off track.

Fit discipline methods to your child. One size does not fit all! Your guidance is in tune with your child's feelings and capabilities.

Become a prevention expert. Why react when you can prevent? You set your child up for success as much as you can.

Be a cheerleader. You look for the win-win scenarios, options for your child to meet his needs in positive ways.

Take care with consequences. You don't dish out consequences lightly, but weigh them in light of your child's learning style, the purpose behind them, and any potential costs.

Take care of yourself. You have figured out that the more you are able to meet your own needs, the more patient and positive you can be with your child.

"Gently discipline" yourself, too. Gentle discipline goes both ways. You cultivate ways to keep your cool, while making room for yourself to be authentic, to make mistakes, and to learn from them.

Get support. Gentle discipline can be more difficult when

you're the only one around who is practicing it. Chances are you are able to do your best when you have a support system for yourself within your family and community, while bridging differences as positively as you can.

Can gentle discipline be strong, too?

Initially, the phrase "gentle discipline" may evoke mushy, weak, absent-minded discipline. It may remind you of families with no boundaries, children controlling the parents, or selfish, impulsive children that no one wants to be around. Or perhaps you might think of parents afraid to say no, afraid of their children's tantrums.

This kind of parenting does exist, but it is best described as "permissive parenting." Fortunately, gentle discipline has nothing to do with this ineffective and problematic style of parenting. Gentle discipline is strong and effective.

Let's look at four myths regarding gentle discipline that contribute to doubts about its effectiveness.

Myth 1: Gentle discipline means no boundaries

Being respectful and compassionate toward your child and yourself means having good boundaries. You are not respecting your child if you let him walk all over the people in his life, and you are certainly not respecting yourself or those around you. If you always say "yes" to your child's requests, he won't learn the meaning (and value) of "no." Firm boundaries, where necessary, help children move harmoniously and safely through their days.

As you will see throughout this book, parents who practice gentle discipline put a great deal of thought into which boundaries are important, and how best to help their children learn to meet their needs within those boundaries.

Myth 2: Gentle discipline means passive parents

On the contrary! Because boundaries and respect are important to our parenting, parents who use gentle discipline need to be doubly active. In some traditional discipline methods, a parent

A Quick Comparison

Three-year-old Nathan is throwing a ball around the living room where people are gathered. People or lamps might get hit.

- A passive parent might roll her eyes and commiserate with the person next to her. "Ugh, my son drives me crazy. I don't know what to do with him!"

- A parent of the traditional style might call out to Nathan: "Throw that ball one more time and I'm throwing it in the trash!" or "Get out of here!"

- A parent using gentle discipline might go up to Nathan and touch his arm, saying, "You're having a lot of fun with that ball. It isn't working to throw it in here. I'm worried that someone is going to get hit, or something will break. How about throwing it outside? Or maybe you would like to join

us on the couch. I bet Nancy would like to hear the story of your last soccer game!"

Connection, empathy, boundaries, and options. Parents who use gentle discipline don't have any more access to magic solutions than other parents, but they strive to honor boundaries with empathy and respect. It is an active role, requiring that the parent be observant, emotionally aware, and willing to get on their feet!

can make a demand from the couch and then punish the child for noncompliance and consider that discipline.

You want active? If you are practicing gentle discipline, you seek to take into account what expectations are realistic given your child's developmental level. You take the time to get down on your child's level and communicate with him in a way that reaches him. You try to be proactive, heading off problems when possible. You learn about your own reactions and cultivate peaceful ones. You problem-solve with your child and offer physical help as needed. It's hard work!

From your heart to your actions, gentle discipline calls you to be fully present and engaged.

If my child is hitting in an unsafe manner (as in another person or an animal) and I turn a blind eye, this is not gentle discipline. It is the absence of discipline.

If, on the other hand, I intervene before someone gets hurt to explain to my darling child that hitting or hurting others is not okay, and then let my child know that he can hit a drum or the floor or the bottom of a pot with a wooden spoon. Well then, that's my definition of gentle discipline.

It is every minute of every day. It's repetitive, because children need lots of reminders. It's getting creative and choosing my battles. Is this truly harmful or do I just find it annoying? The bottom line is one of respect and kindness—two very important things I want to pass on to my son.

Mary Beth K.

What makes gentle discipline strong?

It recognizes the need for firm, carefully chosen boundaries.

It calls you to be active and engaged in guiding your child.

It helps you reach your child.

It is the most direct way of teaching respect, problem-solving, meeting your own needs in positive ways, and consideration of others.

Myth #3: Respecting your child weakens your position as the parent

What kind of strength do you want to have? Think of the stern old school marm with the ruler. She's from the fearsome, powerful, and unyielding school of "strength." But look closer and you'll see a puffed-up authority figure, alienated from the children in her charge. The children may obey out of fear or self-loathing, but it is unlikely that the stern school marm will ever bring out the best in them. Is that the kind of strength you want as a parent?

Respect and empathy for your child call you to embrace a different kind of strength: strength that comes straight from your own humanity and connects to your child's. The kind of strength you need to really listen to your child and take his needs into account along with your own. It takes more courage to make yourself vulnerable to your child than to lean on an authoritarian role and superior might.

True respect is a two-way street. There is a pervasive fear in our society that in treating your child with respect, you will erode his respect for you. Some discipline methods insist that respect is a one-way street; parents deserve all of it, children none. We do well to re-examine this belief.

 I inherited the belief that children must show respect to adults, but adults aren't required to show respect to children, that children's needs and feelings are not very important. But in reality, all people, including children, have equal rights to dignity and respect.

Lisa S.

Bear in mind that to say that children are equally deserving of dignity and respect does not have to mean that the relationship itself is of equal power. As a parent, you have a broader view and more life experience to draw from, and these are assets you bring to your child as his adult caretaker. You also bear more responsibility for choices surrounding your child than he does. Your child is looking to you to exercise your authority in ways that keep everyone safe and life flowing as well as possible. The more respect and empathy you can bring to your child, the more you fortify your authority as benevolent.

Respect has the most vitality when it is two-way. You have probably noticed that when you respect someone and feel respected in return, it is much easier to work together. Whenever you treat your child with respect, you make it more likely—not less so—that he will seek respectful ways to treat you and others.

 Gentle discipline doesn't mean chaos and confusion. I simply treat my child with the respect I wish to be treated with. I teach him by setting a good example and being respectful of him as a person. Anyone in "authority" that I have ever respected has not been a dictator or authoritarian, but someone who worked with me and treated me with respect. I think this is true for most people. Also, I strive to be the kind of person I hope my boys will be. In my experience, much of a child's behavior is learned by example.

Laurie D.W.

Empathy isn't mushy! On the contrary, true compassion for your child gives you strength as a parent, calling you to proceed with care. It clears your vision to see the beauty and goodness in your child. From there, you can find the most positive and powerful solutions. Sometimes it may take patience and focus on your part to get in touch with your compassion for your child, particularly if you're in conflict. But when you can do so, it empowers you to make more humane choices for your child and yourself.

> The effectiveness of gentle discipline can be measured more aptly by the quality of the relationship between parent and child, rather than by how quickly a behavior has been made to disappear.

For me, the bottom line is this: gentle discipline is the communication technique with which I wish to treat all humans and the way I wish to be treated. It is all about setting boundaries, teaching respect, and disciplining with love instead of fear. I do not believe discipline is the same as punishment.

When my daughter does something I don't like, I treat her with the respect that I show my husband when he does something I don't like. I try to find gentle ways to express myself. First and foremost, being able to tell her that her behavior makes me angry, sad, or frustrated.

I aim not to criticize the person, but discuss the behavior. In my experience, fear and anger-based tactics do not open the lines of communication. I want to demonstrate to my daughter that she should expect respectful treatment throughout her entire lifetime from me, from her friends, from her future husband.

Jessica K.

Myth #4: Gentle discipline is not effective

Because gentle discipline focuses more on guiding children than on simply eradicating behaviors, it helps you make room for your child to continue to make mistakes as he learns. Once again, the effectiveness of gentle discipline can be measured more aptly by the quality of the relationship between parent and child, rather than by how quickly a behavior has been made to disappear.

By bringing fear into the equation, authoritarian discipline may sometimes be quicker to stop an unwanted behavior. But the implication that such discipline is more effective at reaching this goal seems more fantasy than reality. Often the overtly active nature of the punishment makes it seem as though the parent is being very effective indeed. But look closer: in many cases, the behavior and the punishment keep repeating, even escalating, and around and around you go. If anything, the child is likely to learn how not to get caught, rather than what might be problematic about the behavior, much less how better to meet his needs.

Gentle discipline offers ways to establish and maintain boundaries in ways that encourage the child to become an active participant (rather than a passive or resentful one).

 Since discipline means "to teach," I don't think anything is learned through fear or aggression other than fear and aggression. My goal is to teach my child the ways of his world, his boundaries and what is expected of him in a kind, understanding, respectful manner.

    Lori H.T.

 One of the criticisms I have heard of gentle discipline is "I don't know why there seems to be such a low expectation of a child's behavior." My experience is the opposite. If anything, gentle discipline has a much higher expectation of a child's behavior, which is why we seek to guide, rather than subjugate. I believe that children can learn without being humiliated or "controlled." If I had low expectations, I would simply dictate rather than teach.

    Jessica K.

Am I doing it yet?

Whereas some suffer from the misconception that gentle discipline is non-existent parenting, many worry just the opposite, that it will demand more of them than they can possibly do.

Indeed, lots of parents who believe wholeheartedly in the importance of empathy and respect in their parenting are uneasy about claiming they practice gentle discipline. "Oh, but I'm far from perfect!" is one of the common reactions. What is wrong with this picture? How did gentle discipline become the domain of the mythical Super-Mommies and Daddies?

Let's step clear of that costly misunderstanding, and take a hard look at what gentle discipline is not:

- Gentle discipline is not about doing it "right."

- It's not a list of things to do and not to do

- It's not a lofty standard for us to somehow measure up to.

- It doesn't make adults able to parent in reasonable, calm, and fun ways all the time.

- It's not a way to have idealized children, always cheerful and cooperative.

- It's not an insurance policy against times of struggle.

These ideas are holdovers from a more traditional style of parenting, which places a great deal of emphasis on right and wrong, and tends to have unrealistic expectations of both parents and children. These notions often become mixed up in perceptions of gentle discipline, but they actually have nothing to do with it. Gentle discipline seeks to get past right or wrong dichotomies and embraces a realistic view of both parents and children.

> **If you are earnestly endeavoring to place empathy and respect at the center of your parenting, you can't get it wrong.**

Gentle discipline is at heart a belief: the more gentleness you can bring to your child and yourself, the better. You either believe it or you don't. If you are earnestly endeavoring to place empathy and respect at the center of your parenting, you can't get it wrong.

As you take that belief forward into your family life, there's all the room in the world for you to be yourself, for you to engage in the messy and meaningful art of developing a relationship with your child, to make mistakes, and to feel good about yourself as a parent along the way.

 For me it is better to look at gentle discipline as a philosophy and a process than a "standard." It is a continuum, and children can benefit from every movement toward the gentler, more compassionate side, and away from the punitive, confrontational side. It isn't all or nothing.

Frankly, I still don't know enough to make the best gentle discipline choices all of the time. As my daughter grows, new challenges continuously present themselves, and my parenting strategies have to adjust. So gentle discipline doesn't seem to me to be a bar that I rise above, but simply a philosophy I embrace.

Rebecca K.

It would be a shame for negative and judgmental thinking to prevent a parent from owning his or her most cherished parenting values. If you find yourself getting into a negative space, as most of us do at one time or another, you may do well to identify a key reminder or two that you do not need to judge yourself as a parent. Empathy and respect for yourself will help you stay committed to gentle discipline despite the highs and lows.

 There are times when I'm definitely not doing okay, or when nothing I'm doing seems to be bringing any peace to my home, and I get very discouraged. I think I have somehow developed the perception that if I'm doing gentle discipline "right" then there won't be any conflicts, power struggles, or tantrums. I guess I fall into the trap of viewing discipline more in terms of eliminating inappropriate behavior than in terms of teaching my children how to cope with life.

The one thing that has allowed me to feel a little more successful lately is to remind myself that the important thing is to be a compassionate parent. I want my children to learn the value of their own thoughts, desires, and feelings so that they will learn how to handle their own feelings and make decisions in a healthy way. I have to respect their feelings, their thoughts, and their desires just as I want to be respected. It doesn't necessarily mean we'll struggle less or that there will be total peace in our home.

I try to remind myself that since I wasn't taught how to handle my own feelings or to value my own desires, thoughts, and feelings, I'm learning right along with my children. It's hard to let them have tantrums, say "no," or in any other way express themselves when I wasn't allowed to do that as a child.

Michelle N.

When you consider saying, "I practice gentle discipline," do negative thoughts come to mind? "But my child's behavior sometimes embarrasses me in public." "But sometimes I lose my temper." Bringing these thoughts to light gives you the chance to make room for more of your humanity and your child's in your concept of gentle discipline. Thinking about where any negative reactions might come from, perhaps comparing notes with a trusted friend, may help you come to terms with them and replace them with more positive beliefs about your parenting.

Gentle discipline is not something distant or unreachable. If you want it, it's yours, right now. Like a favorite comfy sweater, gentle discipline is a belief that can nurture you and your child if you let it.

Ahhh, fewer power struggles!

Because you are human, and your child is human, you are going to find yourselves in power struggles. Gentle discipline invites us out of them, giving us insights into brighter alternatives—and showing us how to avoid similar struggles in the future. Each of the following chapters explores ways to reduce power struggles. We can start with our basic beliefs about parenting.

Children are human beings endeavoring to meet their needs the best way they know how

If you look closely at your own growth and your own mistakes, you will probably discover that regardless of the choice you made on a particular occasion, you were nonetheless trying to meet a need in the best way you could at that time. The more skills and support you have, the better able you are to access positive options. The same is true for children.

When you are at odds with your child, he is not your adversary. Your child is still a vulnerable person in need of your utmost compassion and care. Gentle discipline invites you to stay connected to your child when he needs you most.

Society tried to teach me that children are by nature selfish, out-of-control, and demanding, that their goal is power and they are always trying to see how much they can get away with, that you can't let children manipulate you or become too dependent, and that disobedience equals disrespect.

As a mother I have come to believe strongly that my child's primary goals are having his needs met, feeling connected to others, and feeling self-worth. His misbehavior is an attempt to get a need met or to feel significance and connection, done in an inappropriate way. The need might be anything from less stimulation to consistent boundaries. My job as a parent is to help my child identify and meet those needs in appropriate ways.

Lisa S.

Rather than focusing on the tug-of-war of gaining or forfeiting control, gentle discipline is much more about working with boundaries through trust: trusting your child, and earning his trust. The more aligned you are with your child—who he is and what his needs are at the moment—the more effectively you can reach him and help him discover positive ways to meet his own needs.

Trust and goodwill are great parenting tools

When your child feels that you take his needs and ideas seriously, he is more likely to look for your guidance now and in the future.

 Julia (age three) listens to me best when she truly knows that I'm looking out for her best interests. Tonight she really wanted to keep playing with stickers, but it was time to get ready for bed. When I first said, "It's almost bedtime, time to clean up," she protested.

A minute later, I looked her in the eye, and with a calm, caring voice reminded her that she went to bed late last night and woke up early today, so I was taking extra care to help her get ready for bed before she got overtired. When I explained it calmly and empathetically, she just looked at me and said, "Okay, mommy."

> Rather than focusing on the tug-of-war of gaining or forfeiting control, gentle discipline is much more about working with boundaries through trust.

We put her stickers away together and walked to the bedroom hand in hand to get ready for bed. No struggle, no fight.

Karen K.

Gentle discipline also invites you to trust your child with your true self. One of the biggest gifts of gentle discipline is permission for you to be vulnerable with your child, even when things are hard. You love your child more than life itself. When you get worked up into an authoritarian position, even with the best intentions, you may sometimes become alienated from that tender part of yourself that loves your child unconditionally—even from that part of yourself that may also feel confused and scared about the situation at hand.

Gentle discipline is relationship-oriented. It builds a relationship and it draws from that strong foundation to make new things possible.

Discipline is part of your nurturing relationship, not a time when you need to deviate from it.

 The choice of gentle discipline came out of my interest in attachment parenting. I think it just makes sense that when you feel bonded and connected with your child, then you feel empathy and compassion for them; so it makes sense that you would use gentle discipline.

Elizabeth B.

 To me, gentle discipline is a method of raising human beings in a non-humiliating, respectful, and loving manner that does not seek to subjugate, but rather to guide. It is working within the structure of the personality of my child to help her to develop into a responsible, empathic, connected, and loving adult.

Jessica K.

Gentle discipline bears unique gifts

Gentle discipline offers bountiful gifts for:

Your child: fortifying him for the future, providing him with skills he can use for himself over time.

Yourself: giving you many gifts that more traditional methods would not.

The world: spreading the values of empathy and respect from your family outward.

What does gentle discipline offer your child?

Sometimes people feel the need to warn parents who embrace gentle discipline, saying, "Just you wait"—until your child is a toddler, is a teenager, or whatever—"you'll be sorry!" For a society that prides itself on independence, we sure are uncomfortable with the idea of empowering children. Well, what seeds are you sowing when you teach your child that his wants, needs, and perceptions are of great importance?

The very best seeds. The truth is that empowering your child now will serve him—and society—quite beautifully. After all, you want your child to grow up to be an adult who knows his mind, who can think for himself, and make choices that propel him forward in pursuing his dreams and meeting his needs in positive ways. You can't control the future—but you don't have to wait to embrace these goals. You can think about what you want for your child and breathe life into these goals in the present.

The ability to face peer pressure

Most parents want to raise teenagers who can think for themselves, particularly in the face of peer pressure. Well, toddlers are famous for insisting on thinking for themselves! How can you honor your child's independent thinking and help him become increasingly effective at solving his own problems in positive ways?

I believe that teaching children to "obey" encourages them to ignore their own feelings and instincts. I believe that my daughter's fiercely strong will and attention to her instincts could actually help in the teenage years—help her to think for herself and not follow the pack. Sometimes, children break away from their parents in the teen years only to be controlled by peers. I want my daughter to be her own thinking person always, not a puppet of me or anyone else.

Furthermore, and even more importantly, she needs those instincts, the permission, and the skills to say "No!" to an adult who tries to take advantage of her. I'm not saying that I am counting on her to do that. I will take precautions to protect her. But I believe that teaching children to obey adults can make them an easier target for adults who do not have their best interests at heart.

I think that my mother and father disciplined me out of fear for my future. I discipline out of hope for my daughter's future.

Rebecca K.

The ability to follow their dreams

You want your child to grow into a happy adult with a fulfilling life. As such, you will want to nurture his perseverance, his ability to tune in to his inner guidance, and his belief in himself, today. Listening to him and acknowledging his feelings, his individuality, and his free will provides a great start for him.

Loving relationships

You hope that your child will be able to create satisfying adult relationships. And you undoubtedly hope to remain in a meaningful relationship with him all your life. How can you build on your young child's inherent compassion and desire for connection? Treating your child with empathy and respect is fundamental to encouraging him to do the same with others. Similarly, engaging in positive conflict resolution with your child helps him learn how to do so with others.

Gentle discipline is a way to guide your child in relating to others in positive ways. With gentle discipline, you can start now in building a relationship with your child that is sustainable over time.

As my oldest son is now a teenager, I'm finding that my discipline approach of explanation, negotiation, and respect for his feelings is paying off. My son and I have a peaceful relationship and enjoy talking and doing things together.

My husband and I listen to the kids' feelings and are open to changing our requests if they show us good reasons that we are wrong or it doesn't really matter if we do something our way or their way.

My son often comes to negotiate with me about his work, his sleep schedule, his volunteer activities, and time with friends. We spend time talking about why I made my request, why he wants a change, and brainstorming for possible alternatives. We usually come to an agreement that is different from my initial plan but that works just as well to meet our family's needs.

Adria C.

What's in it for parents?

There's no doubt that gentle discipline can be demanding for parents. Thank goodness, the rewards are so palpable and encouraging that it makes parents want to keep on going. When you look closely, gentle discipline gives as much to the parents as to the child. For example:

When to start gentle discipline?

Gentle discipline can start as soon as you realize you want it for your family. Your baby benefits from your empathy and respect when you read his cues and respond accordingly with breastfeeding or rocking. When a baby begins to crawl, gentle discipline takes the form of keeping him safe while he explores. Being in tune with your baby and forging positive communication skills with him as he grows to toddlerhood will serve you well in the months and years to come.

It's never too late to shift over to gentle discipline. Many parents start out in a more traditional path of discipline and later become attracted to the idea of gentle discipline. It's always possible to switch gears. Bringing more empathy and respect can always strengthen the parent-child relationship and unlock new options for moving forward together.

To those who ask: "Is it too late to start practicing gentle discipline?" I say: "No never."

With my first two, I made some choices I look back on with horror. But even though I did similar things with my second, I was also learning other ways. It took some time with them to mend things, but I did it, and we have used gentle discipline ever since. It isn't easy when you change things—not by a long shot—but it is so worth the time and patience to keep persevering with it.

Jennie S.

Lower stress. Remembering that your child is not out to get you can help you feel more empowered and positive about challenges when they do arise.

More insight. By not holding yourself responsible for always knowing best, you make room for a new source of wisdom: your child's. You can learn a lot by observing your toddler, or by listening to your verbal child.

You get to be yourself. You don't have to sacrifice or negate either your own tender feelings or your child's. You can be who you are and go from there.

Adventure. When you make room for your child's side of the equation, you open yourself up to the unexpected. Your first idea may not be the most interesting one.

Connection with your child. Because gentle discipline is relationship-based, you never have to strain your relationship with your child in order to feel you are disciplining him. Steering toward, rather than away from, greater connection to your child is powerful.

Personal integrity. That's not something you can get from a pre-packaged technique! If you believe in treating your child with empathy and respect, it is intensely meaningful to work on putting those beliefs into action.

 One amazing outcome for me from gentle discipline is the ability to have real relationships with my kids. Not the one I grew up with, with the parents doing all the demanding, and the kids doing all the conforming or rebelling. My kids tell me what they think, how they feel, and what they want.

Having forced myself to practice listening to them, I've learned that I can trust them to tell me what they think is best for them. And that sometimes I can let them decide what's best for them, even if I disagree slightly.

Pei L.

I practice gentle discipline because it is the way I can live up to my own morals and values. It is what is right for me. I would not feel right threatening and punishing and doing things because I am bigger and smarter.

Mallory P.

 It is not just the way I treat my child, it is the way I wish to treat everyone. It is also how I wish to be treated. Gentle discipline is my approach to all my relationships, not just a parenting method.

Jessica K.

" . . . because after all, a person's a person no matter how small."

Dr. Seuss

We can change the world

Our society as a whole is in many ways torn apart by a self-perpetuating habit of power and control. This pattern is reversible. Recent generations of parents have been making headway in turning away from the harsh authoritarian models of the past. As it picks up pace, the movement toward more compassionate parenting has tremendous potential.

You can't snap your fingers and change the world in an instant, but you do have power over your own orientation in life, how you treat the people you encounter, and most importantly, you can initiate new possibilities for your family.

You can change the world from your family outwards.

Be the change you wish to see in the world.

Gandhi

If you want to work for world peace, go home and love your families.

Mother Teresa

Chapter 2

Your Child's Well-Being

⌒⌒⌒⌒⌒⌒⌒⌒⌒⌒⌒⌒⌒⌒⌒⌒⌒

Your child is rapidly spinning out of control. You have tried all of your parenting tricks and you're running out of new ideas. Just when you are starting to feel as desperate as your child, a light bulb clicks on: "How long has it been since my child ate something?"

Chances are you've had occasion to notice that a lot of issues that are quite unrelated to discipline can blow up into big behavioral problems. One of the most important questions for a parent who practices gentle discipline is: "Does my child have what she needs to face the day?"

From food to sleep to love, if your child has an unmet need, this can "trigger" an avalanche of behavior problems. A child who is chronically low—or even momentarily low—on any basic needs may be a cranky, easily frustrated, anti-social, whiny wreck. Who wouldn't be? Just think how much shorter your own fuse is after a sleepless night, or how much more likely you are to snap if lunch is delayed into the afternoon. Even for adults, unmet needs can cause an avalanche of behavior problems! Children have smaller tanks—so they need remarkably frequent doses of nourishment for both body and soul.

Tracking your individual child's moods and observing the circumstances may allow you to identify—and head off—potential triggers. "An ounce of prevention is worth a pound of cure." "A stitch in time saves nine." These are clichés but they are also good advice when it comes to parenting.

A great deal of gentle discipline involves setting your child up for success. You want your child to be as resilient as possible. Well-being is one of the main foundations of gentle discipline. Most people don't think of food, love, sleep, and the like when they think of discipline, any more than they think of the sturdy frame underneath a building when they think of architecture. But if it isn't there and solid, you're literally unsupported.

This chapter explores dimensions of children's well-being, ways to maximize it and to restore it when it's flagging. Some of the key needs of children that this chapter explores are:

- Loving connections

- Play

- Engaging activities

- Ways to express their emotions

- Physical activity like running

- Healthy food and drink

- Rest

- Bodily functions (toileting)

What are your child's hotspots?

By experimenting and observing you are likely to identify a few key triggers to look for if your child is out of sorts. They are different for each child, even within the same family.

 My husband and I always try to ask ourselves when problems start whether the child could be (HALT) hungry, angry, lonely, or tired and address that need first.

Patty C.

 My son gets into everything when he is tired. As soon as he starts getting into stuff, I nurse him to sleep rather than discipline him for his behavior. I figure it's partly my fault for letting him get overtired in the first place. My daughter's biggest trigger is hunger and having to go potty. She will insist she is not hungry or does not have to pee. I know what to watch for and insist she eat or go potty rather than disciplining her.

Heather H.

Difficult behavior is a plea for help. Seeing the roots of your child's behavior can help you make an empathic bridge to where she is at that moment—and give you an optimal standpoint to solve the real problem instead of getting into a power struggle.

 I look at Ashley's negative behavior as a symptom, rather than an issue unto itself, and look for clues to the cause. Situations and triggers I've noticed are illness, family stress, junk food (particularly sugary stuff and chocolate), hunger, long car trips, sleep needs not in alignment with amount of sleep she's actually getting, and when my husband is gone at work more than usual. As you can see from this list, most of them are preventable or at least manageable. I try to anticipate triggers and prevent them when I can, and then be empathetic when I can't. Knowing the reason behind the behavior really helps me reduce my own frustration about it.

Sarah M.

Let's look at some very basic needs and how you can meet them.

Connection, connection, connection

One of the most primary human needs—and one of the most powerful ingredients for resiliency—is human connection. It's true for adults as well as children; the more connected we feel to those around us, the more foundation we have to relate to our world in positive ways. The more we feel loved and accepted for who we are, the more optimistic and secure we feel, and the more likely we are to bounce back from temporary set-backs.

A child who is feeling disconnected is likely to act out her anxious and unhappy feelings. She may express her need for connection by provoking an emotional response from you. She may be less able to control her impulses. Her anger may express itself in many direct or indirect ways. Being on the lookout for situations in which your child feels disconnected can give you clues about ways to get her back on track.

 Occasionally I realize that I have been really busy doing "grownup stuff" for too long and I need to just stop for a little while and focus all my attention on my children. When I have that realization and can truly involve myself in whatever they want to do for 30 minutes or so, the turn around in their behavior can be amazing. They've been acting out to get my attention. When I give it to them completely and in a positive way, it's often as if a big switch has been thrown that corrects the negative behavior.

Carissa D.

Try to always bear in mind the impact of consistently and abundantly communicating your unconditional love for your child. Your ability to guide your child is as strong as your relationship with her.

Finding ways to immerse your child in your love on a daily basis fortifies her for any challenges she may face throughout her day.

Ideas for maximizing connection

Little doses, given frequently. When your child wants to talk to you, try to stop what you are doing and make eye contact. When driving, take the opportunity to talk to her about her thoughts or sing favorite songs with her. When your child falls, take the time to snuggle her until she is ready to romp away. These little doses of love add up to a childhood of feeling seen, heard, and valued.

Chunks of time. What are the activities that you most enjoy doing with your child? What activities does your child most crave your attention for? How can you build a time for these activities, these sacred rituals, in your day or week?

Some parents set a timer for a manageable amount of time—as little as 15 minutes or as long as an hour at a time—and say that they will do whatever the child wants. Make a name for it like "Mama Time," "Papa Time," or "Rainbow Time." Be it tag, drawing, or reading a picture book, your child will be grateful to have your full attention for that sumptuous stretch of time. Whether it is long or short, it doubles in significance because your child knows she has full claim on you for that time.

When there's a lot to be done around the house, setting a time limit can make it much easier for many busy parents to give themselves over—it makes it a lot easier to say, "Yes." When the timer "dings," you are free to get back to the taxes or the dishes—but you may find you are having too much fun to stop. Connection can be contagious if you open yourself up to it.

Cranky child checklist

If you are facing a child who is having a difficult moment, day, or month, take a step back and consider what underlying triggers may be behind the rough patch. Ask yourself:

- Does my child feel disconnected?

- Is my child over-stimulated or bored?

- Is my child feeling emotions that need to come out?

- Does my child feel restless and cooped up inside?

- When is the last time my child had a drink or ate something sustaining?

- Could my child be overwhelmed or stressed? Is this a time of great change for my child?

- Could my child be tired?

- Does my child need to use the toilet/potty or have a diaper change?

Yesterday, Friday, I had a splitting headache and both of my girls were extremely needy that morning. I proposed the idea of spending the first hour with three-year-old Daisy, the next with my six-year-old Gayle, and using the third for cleaning the house. It went wonderfully. Each one picked a great activity and were more than happy to share their special "mommy time" with each other, as long as they were the one calling the shots. We liked it so much we are going to try it every Friday.

Beth R.

Go on a date! A "Daddy Date" or a "Mama Date" may consist of eating out at your favorite sandwich spot, going to a favorite playground, or even just taking your child to the grocery store. Everyday activities take on new meaning when done with focus and love.

Small daily rituals of connection help enormously. Morning can start with a gentle touch, a favorite rising song, a silly game. If there are times during the day when you separate from your child, remember to hug her or tell her you love her. When you reunite make a point of reconnecting, perhaps sitting down to cuddle with her in a particular spot. For some families, mealtime is a special time for the whole family to connect and share their days. Ending the day with loving rituals helps everyone put the day behind them and get ready for a new day tomorrow.

You will be rewarded. Setting a strong foundation of connection in the home will help your child feel safe to explore her world, be herself, make mistakes, and trust you to guide her along the way. Reinforcing your connection to your child can help her get back on track when she's feeling low.

 We've been traveling non-stop this month. Travel is fun for my daughter, but it makes her need me 110% when we get home, just when I have more to do! She's like the Velcro kid. Today a friend called and asked for parenting advice. Her infant seemed to be needing her even more than usual. I found myself telling her the following things:

- let everything else go,

- carry your baby in a sling as much as she wants,

- ask for help,

- take a bath,

- relax,

- nurse,

- concentrate on yourself and your baby.

And, at first, I thought, " That wouldn't work for Julia now. She isn't a baby. She's two years old! I can't just carry her in the sling, nurse her, and make her my world." But really, I can. Okay, she doesn't nurse any more and I sure can't carry her in a sling, but I can let the answering machine get the calls, make a simple dinner, do puzzles, read books, listen, and be there for her.

It feels much harder to do that when I know that she can wait, entertain herself, spend time with her father, even though what she really needs right then is Mommy! It's major harvest time in our huge garden and I'm finding myself feeling impatient to complete a task like hauling in all of the green beans at once when Julia really needs me to stop and pay attention to her more than she normally would.

It feels like a vicious cycle. So I'm making a huge effort to get off of it, enjoy her, love her, let other stuff go. All hard for my "Type A" self! On the whole, this week aside, I feel myself really cherishing my time with Julia. I need to get back into that fun, easy-going space and hope that better parenting flows from there.

Karen K.

Connection to others

As your child grows, so does her need to connect with others besides her parents. Social skills take time! Some of the most challenging behavior can occur when a guest comes to the house or when a child is feeling uncertain in a group of peers.

When your child is acting up in a social setting, consider the possibility that she is having difficulty connecting. I once saw a three-year-old boy knocking down the elaborate sandcastle that a group of older children were making, and they were getting angrier and angrier at him. In desperation, his older sister suggested that they make a few decoy sandcastles that their nemesis was allowed to knock down. Soon everyone forgot about building the big castle because they were having too much fun making piles for the little guy to pounce on with a flourish. You could see the pride and joy on the face of the three-year-old who found his role shifted from "outsider" to "service provider." Harmony reigned.

Children need to play!

Adults tend to think of play as frivolous. But for children it is how they process what they are learning about the world. Play is children's work.

A child who spends an hour sudsing her hands is a scientist learning about the textures, properties, and nature of a fascinating substance. A child who claims to be a superhero for weeks at a time is learning about power, what it is like to be big, and the joy of self-invention. The little one who loves to dump the basket of Tinkertoys off the couch to hear them "laugh and party" as they tinkle and roll around the floor is learning about sounds, and, for better or worse, creative arrangement of things in the house.

Now, does that mean you should have to buy cases of soap, let your resident superhero jump on the new couch, or clean up the Tinkertoys a dozen times a day? Of course not! But it never hurts to take a step back and really see the value of the play your child is engaged in. It's impressive how perfectly children tailor their play to their developmental needs of the moment.

Even as you respect your child's need for play, you still have a full range of options for how you will respond. However, looking at it from this perspective may give you a new idea for how your sudser, jumper, or dumper might meet her needs in a different way. When does your child's need for play create friction between you? If your child is verbal, try to talk with her about it, searching for a mutually agreeable way to meet both of your needs.

The biggest set-up for misbehavior is an environment in which children are expected to rein in their need to play. For instance, expecting a small energetic child to sit still, be quiet, and keep her hands to herself is like expecting a fish not to swim or a frog not to hop. It's just not an age-appropriate expectation.

In many cases, feeding a child's innate love of play can help you meet your own goals.

Minimize situations in which your child must curb her healthy instinct to play, and try to carve out as much freedom to play as you can. In many cases, feeding a child's innate love of play can help you meet your own goals.

> Cole loves to roll around in the covers when I'm making the bed. I flop on the bed with him and we play for a few minutes. When he runs off, I make the bed quickly. I find that if I acknowledge his need to play as a real need, and incorporate that into our activities, things go more smoothly and I actually even get more done than if I were putting him off all day.
>
> *Jennifer K.*

Sometimes seeing the value in your child's play can shift your own parenting priorities in the moment. As your child grows you can expect her to be able to play without you more and more. Even so, taking time to be silly or play games together can help both your child and yourself.

Children need engaging activities

"Good grief, more activities? But my child is already over-stimulated! I am already exhausted! Plus I am out of ideas!"

In our fast-paced world, it is easy to confuse the notion of "engaging" activities with ones that are really just stimulating (lots of bells and whistles), entertaining (when the child is barraged with input but needs to take it in passively), or momentarily gratifying (such as a new toy before it breaks or ends up tossed by the wayside). These kinds of activities tend to create a cycle of more-more-more, requiring ever more work/money (and batteries) from the parent to provide them, and seeming to result in a less and less satisfied and grounded child. All this outward focus can leave both parent and child exhausted and frustrated.

Indeed, buying lots of toys and spending time in toy stores sets parents up for either extra boundary setting or unwanted purchases and more toys to clean up. Many parents find that television creates its own set of behavioral problems, too.

What about boredom, that mood so notorious for producing irritating behavior? Ironically, one of the most active things you can do in meeting your child's needs for engaging activity is to streamline:

- Reduce activities that are over-stimulating, passively entertaining, or too-fleetingly gratifying. Instead, help your child maintain and build her ability to be an active participant in her play.

- As your child becomes old enough to play by herself, ask yourself: What activities truly light up my child, so that she is engaged for an hour or more at a time? What activities or toys does my child come back to again and again?

- Brainstorm with your child about activities that she loves

Put your energy into supporting the engaging activities while limiting the time and space allotted to the less meaningful ones.

and that help you to connect with each other.

- Put your energy into supporting the engaging activities while limiting the time and space allotted to the less meaningful ones.

- Engage your child in the daily goings on in the home, from meal preparation to gardening to cleaning.

It is also helpful to set your house up to maximize favorite activities. If painting-time is a rarity because the easel is near the white kitchen curtains, could you move the easel to the porch or take the curtains down until your child is a little older? If the train set is a big hit but the playroom is too cluttered, are there toys you can put in a closet or give away? Can a regular clean-up routine yield more play space?

How can you help streamline your household to make the most of activities that engage your child?

 There are no toys in the house that either play by themselves or require only minimal interaction. Definitely no batteries. I want to eliminate those things that would probably serve to reduce her attention span in these early years. I rotate the available toys, which seems to keep them interesting longer. I make sure there's a lot of "down" time during the week.

As my daughter is approaching three, she seems less interested in toys except as props for imaginative play. Since her toys don't inherently limit the terms of her play, she has to create her own worlds (most of which mirror ours in some way) and resolve the actions of her characters which are based on her own life and the stories she has heard.

One day she played with bits of ripped up paper for over an hour; they were cats, frogs, lily pads, and footprints in turn. Another time it was her baby sister's hat; she was the fox come to stuff the little red hen in a bag, then it was a purse, then a boat for her stuffed penguin. Slippers worn on hands, a paper skateboard, surfboard, sleigh. It's easy to see why kids can so easily believe in magic and transformations. Art supplies and paper for cutting are always available.

Moira N.

Remember, far less than being merely entertained, children

often want to be included in the meaningful activities of the family.

 When my child is bored and needs a way to keep busy, chores can help her feel like a contributing member of the household. When I started asking Abi (three) to do chores such as watering the plants, setting the table, picking up laundry, or putting away laundry it was like she grew in stature almost, and accepted the new responsibility with pride.

Darshani S.

Be active! It is easy to forget some of our most satisfying activities in the hustle and bustle of family life. Make a list of favorite activities—some that your child can enjoy without you and some that are fun for you and your child.

 My three-year-old and I connect when we make muffins, do puzzles, and watercolor, not so much because of something inherent in the activities but because those things relax us and put us in proximity for talking, cuddling, and connecting. She gets something different, but also a valuable connection, from jumping on the bed with her father and playing with his motorized trucks.

Karen K.

Children need to express their emotions

In the same way that children need to get their energy out, they also need to get their emotions out. Children's emotions are just as powerful as our own. Yet they have fewer options for releasing them. A two-year-old enraged by having a toy taken away is unlikely to pop out with, "I am angry that you took that away. Please give it back."

As you work to fortify your child's foundation of well-being, remember to respect the power of your child's emotions and her need for a true outlet.

A Diagram of Emotions

happy   sad   mad   excited

scared   glad   upset   worried

angry   jealous   elated   super dooper happy

It's not always easy to recognize feelings.

I find that by labeling emotions with my three-year-old daughter she is able to curb her frustration better by expressing to me what is making her angry, sad, hurt, or frustrated. Instead of just having a tantrum, she is really getting good at telling me how she feels. It makes life easier for me. We can sit down and work out solutions that way.

When I empathize with her first, and let her know that there is no such thing as a wrong feeling, she feels empowered and more willing to listen to me when I offer alternatives and solutions.

I find it's win/win. I also appreciate it when adults are

I put words to her emotions and reactions when I can: when a friend hits her or grabs a toy away from her, in addition to comforting her with a hug and attention, I suggest "That really hurt your head, didn't it?" "You're really frustrated that Sally took your doll."

Not only am I validating her feelings, I am teaching her how to express herself, so even at two years old, my daughter was (occasionally) able to say things like "I'm not happy!" or "Mark is frustrating me!" or "I'm scared, Mommy, protect me!" instead of simply crying and running to me.

Kathy E.

 I think it's important to separate behaviors from emotions. My daughter is 21 months old, and we use lots of feeling words around here. She can identify when she feels happy, sad, or scared. I find myself saying things to explain and validate her feelings: "Oh, you feel really sad that you can't play with that sharp stick. That's very disappointing. Let's play with this leaf instead." Or, "I know you're angry that you have to sit in your car seat, but it's not okay to kick Mommy. Put your feet down. Would you like a snuggle to help you feel better?"

Rachel S.

Model effective ways to express emotions

The best way to teach healthy emotional release is to do it yourself. Many adults still struggle with finding outlets that are both appropriate and satisfying for releasing emotions, especially ones like fear, anger, and disappointment. (This is discussed in Chapter 8.)

Explore age-appropriate ways to let feelings out

Unexpressed emotions don't go away. Instead, they tend to seep or explode out, often indirectly, in ways that are disruptive to others and unsatisfying to the person feeling them. Many apparent behavior problems are really the result of emotions that need a better way to come out.

The key is that the outlet has to be the right fit for the child, so that the strong emotion is truly moving out. There is no magic formula; each child will have a unique emotional style. She needs to find expressions that feel authentic to her and that genuinely help to move the anger through. You can help her practice different ways.

 In discussions with other parents I've concluded that some children need to work through anger physically (hitting a pillow is the classic example) and some do not. My son is one who does not: physical experssion seems to escalate his anger.

I tried a plastic bag filled with cotton balls to throw (it just frustrated him), pillows to hit (he wanted to hit me with them which I didn't want though this could have been a way to make it playful instead). I did not have much luck with any of these options.

One thing I've done effectively is to turn aggression toward me into play. When he was four, he would try to hit or throw things, and it would turn into a struggle. Finally I started getting out of the struggle with playfulness, getting him to try to push me to the other side of the room. I would say I bet he couldn't do it, as I was slowly letting him do so. After about a month he finally got to the point where he would say, "Mom, I need to push on your hands."

Lisa S.

It may help to role-play with toys or directly with a child, as you and your child explore her feelings about options and the consequences of certain behaviors.

My nearly three-year-old daughter loves to play with figures of her favorite cartoon characters. When she asks me to play with her, I often take the opportunity to role-play situations with her through the toys. We talk about hurt feelings or actions that physically hurt and how the characters can handle the situation. I know some of it sinks in, because when she plays on her own I often hear her act out similar stories with them.

Carissa D.

Play is a natural way for children to explore difficult issues, because they are in control and there is no risk.

 Ashley received a beautiful wooden dollhouse with wooden and cloth dolls for Christmas. We had just been through a week of her hitting and kicking me. I heard her using one doll to tell another doll how hitting and kicking hurt and that's why we don't do that. I was delighted! They are now a tool to explain important concepts to herself.

Sarah M.

Encouraging your child to express her emotions can help keep your relationship on track in many ways.

 My daughter, Accalia, will be five in a few months and has taken to "writing" or drawing to show me how she feels. There are times when she's given me a picture that shows her with a sad face or with tears streaming down her face. There are times when she's "written" me a note telling me I need to be nicer to her.

It's one thing when you have a small child who may just start crying or become sullen if you discipline in a punitive manner, but when your child becomes able to eloquently state her feelings, you realize how important each action of yours is and how closely your child is watching you.

Amy N.

Run, jump, throw!

Many children need running around time to let off steam and flex those growing muscles. If that is happening in your kitchen, you may spend the afternoon setting boundaries—how aggravating for all concerned! This is a classic case of the environment being the problem and not the child.

When you can, ideally once a day, make a point of getting outside. This can provide the space for "outside voices," running and jumping, and boisterous play. As children know instinctively, something about breathing fresh air and taking in an expanse of grass, the intrigue of a forest, or the wonders of a beach is deeply satisfying. Just a walk around the block or looking for bugs in the backyard can be a helpful outing for little ones.

It is no surprise that small apartments or rainy/cold months can be times of increased parent-child conflict. When going outside is not an option, are there indoor errands like going to the grocery store that you can make interesting for your child and productive for you? How can you make your home a more hospitable habitat for your wild thing? Can you allow jumping on—or even dismantling of—the couch? Can you set up one room as a safe romping room, even if it has to be the living room? A plastic play-structure, an inflatable ring bouncer, or a small trampoline can be a much-needed way for children to release some of their pent-up energy indoors.

 I used to get uptight over my two-year-old daughter being energetic and climbing or jumping. However, when I thought about it, I realized that it really wasn't that big of a deal as long as she wasn't hurting herself or other people.

Now, she can climb on any furniture except the tables as long as her shoes are off. When she starts to climb on the table, we get her down and tell her she can climb on the couch, and so on. She can jump on beds as long as I'm there to make sure she doesn't jump off. We kick balls outside.

If she acts like she's going to hit, or starts play hitting, I tell her the things she can hit—the floor, a stuffed animal, the bed, the pillows, or any other inanimate object— but she may not hit people or the dog. She also loves it if I offer a hand for a "high five."

Sometimes I think she just needs an outlet. And me demonstrating hitting the floor is always good for a laugh! We also frequently turn on music really loud and do silly dances until we are laughing and sweaty.

Since I stopped getting frustrated with her trying to release all the energy she has inside, things have been easier. Now we spend lots of time outside and at parks and playgrounds where she can climb and jump to her heart's content!

Stacy S.

The balm of healthy food and drink

 Another thing that has helped is keeping snacks with us, and making sure Gabriel eats regularly. I know he'll get crabby if his blood sugar gets low.

Beth C.

 A child with low blood sugar: it just isn't pretty. (Neither is a parent who has missed a meal! More on that in Chapter 8.)

Children have little tummies, expend lots of energy romping around, and need extra energy to grow bigger muscles and longer bones! No wonder they seem to need a constant stream of food. No wonder the biggest meltdowns have a way of occurring when it has been a while since the refueling.

One of the important things to realize about blood sugar is that by the time it's low, even a healthy high-energy meal may not have the power to improve the person's state of mind immediately. Once a child's blood sugar is low, problems like irritability and temper tantrums may interfere with her ability to actually identify or accept the food she needs. Staying ahead of the blood sugar roller coaster is well worth your time and attention.

You may find yourself well rewarded for taking the time to prepare sustaining snacks and a water bottle that your child can reach throughout the day. Pack enticing options for outings. An insulated bag or small cooler can provide a wide range of healthy and refreshing options when you're on the go.

Similarly, dehydration can make a child irritable. Windy, cold, hot, or active days are particularly risky. Keep drinks handy. One way to monitor your child's hydration is by paying attention to the color of her urine. It should be a pale yellow; darker yellow is an indication of dehydration. You can also note whether your child is urinating frequently or rarely.

Just as important as the frequency is the quality of the nourishment you offer. A sugary snack or drink is unlikely to provide much sustenance for an active growing child. Indeed, it may lead to a spike and plunge in blood sugar, a classic recipe for hyperactivity or crankiness soon thereafter. As you may have noticed, many "fruit" drinks marketed to children have very little fruit and very much sugar, and many processed children's snacks are laden with added sweeteners with little of substance to offer.

The type of food that best fuels activity and growth is quite simple: whole foods. Offer your child plenty of healthy options, such as whole-wheat pita with hummus, a whole grain rice-cake (hold the sugary flavoring!), a cheese stick, a juicy peach, beans, or a piece of chicken. Some parents note that protein snacks are particularly sustaining and there's no drink better than water. WHOLE FOODS FOR BABIES AND TODDLERS, published by La Leche League International, includes many recipes to entice even the pickiest eaters.

What snacks help keep your child's engine running?

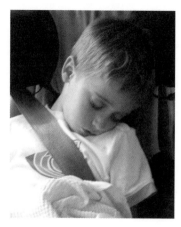

Rest

Nighttime rest is vital—rest for those tired monkey-bar muscles, a chance for those growing bones to stretch, and time in the world of dreams to sort through the surprising emotions and experiences of the day. Some say that young children need upwards of 12 hours of sleep a night. You are likely to find that each child—and each developmental phase—requires a different amount of sleep.

Working with your observations of your child's changing needs for rest can pay off huge dividends. Sleep deprivation may be the culprit behind a child seeming to "get up on the wrong side of the bed," or becoming listless, unusually emotional, or prone to frustration in the afternoon.

Keep track of your child's sleep needs by noting: how much sleep she seems to get when she is able to get up whenever she is ready to; how her mood and energy levels seem to be after various amounts of sleep; and what time the first signs of yawning or tired crankiness start to appear in the evening. (For ideas on working with bedtime, see Chapter 12.)

Naps or quiet time can be very important for different children at different stages. Sometimes the need for a regular nap is so palpable and inescapable that you have little choice but to reserve that time of day for rest, no matter how inconvenient. Other times the signs may be more subtle.

Bear in mind that a child may go a year or more without needing a nap, and then may suddenly need a regular nap again. Returning to a naptime could be just the thing to help your child bounce back for the rest of the day. Sometimes children simply need quiet playtime to absorb more active experiences from earlier in the day. If your child's behavior is a bit out-of-sorts after school or another stimulating activity, see if a quiet time helps her regroup.

To encourage daytime rest, you may want to designate a predictable time each day. See if it helps to make yourself available for reading or other quiet shared activities. If your child benefits from being alone to regroup and recuperate, set up a quiet room with a favorite book on tape, drawing materials, or perhaps a favorite blanket, stuffed animal, or pet to snuggle with. Some parents set a timer so the child can see how much time they need to rest.

Bodily functions

Poop happens. And sometimes it doesn't. Who among us is happy when we are not, well, regular? Sometimes a diapered child has a great difficulty in taking care of business. And many potty-trained children go through a phase of "pee avoidance," preferring to squirm and squeal and hold their hands between their legs rather than interrupt their play to go to the bathroom. If a child is having trouble eliminating, odd behavior can result. Sometimes the connection isn't obvious until after the child "goes"—and her disposition improves immediately!

If your child is often constipated, post a list of helpful foods on your refrigerator and offer them often. For the toilet avoider, keep a potty in the playroom, or offer companionable escorted trips to the bathroom frequently. Have songs or stories that you reserve for time on the toilet or potty. Brainstorming ways to make it easier for your child to perform these bodily functions can help keep your child more comfortable throughout the day.

Young ones in wet or dirty diapers can get cranky, too. It can be easy to lose track of how long it has been since the last diaper change when you are out running errands, just as you can sometimes lose track of when the last nursing was. No matter where you've spent the day, changing diapers promptly can help keep your child feeling more cheerful.

Children need routines

To feel secure, children need their lives to feel somewhat predictable. Having a good idea of what to expect from you, from their home life, and from life in general gives children a comfortable home base. Some children particularly thrive with routines and schedules. It gives them a sense of control over their day.

Of course, it is not always in our control to keep things on that steady path. There are so many life-changing events in childhood. If your child is learning to walk, becoming a big brother or sister, starting school, moving to a new home, experiencing a death in the family, or dealing with other monumental shifts in her world—just think of all of the reorganizing, processing, and redefining that must be going on inside her mind and heart.

Like a trapeze artist in flight between one swinging bar and the next, your child is often mid-flight, hurtling through space in a grand leap of faith that a new source of security is just within reach.

Not surprisingly, big times of change—even when they are welcome and exciting changes—tend to be times of upheaval for a child. And her behavior shows it. Your child may seem particularly demanding, moody, or irritable. Your child also may be determined to test limits, to see just where the security lies. Providing firm limits can be just the thing your child needs, even as she fights it. As with any underlying problem that can't be fixed all at once, you may need to have a plan to get through the rough patch.

Getting through rough patches

When a child is out of sorts, you can sometimes identify the well-being issue at the root of the problem—but—it can't always be remedied on the spot. Life-changing transitions, such as moving to a new home, will go on whether a child is ready or not. More mundane issues such as illness or lack of sleep can make a child cranky for a few days. Even transient issues, such as running out of snacks while running errands, can leave you and your child both feeling hungry with no immediate solution in sight. Regardless of the cause, you have to keep parenting through rough patches even when you can't do much about the underlying issues.

What can you do to help?

- Convey your confidence that your child will indeed make it through to the other side of this adjustment.

- Provide the security of your solid relationship, offering extra nurturing and closeness.

- Help your child process what is going on for her through conversations, drawings, or play.

- Listen to her distress, including the distress embedded in difficult behavior.

- Re-double your efforts to keep all other aspects of her well-being on track, providing extra rest, good food, and opportunities for emotional connection.

- Provide as much consistency as possible in her routines and preferences, with firm boundaries as needed.

Stay aware of the true problem. When the problem can't be fixed right away, awareness of what the true problem is can save a lot of flailing around trying to eradicate an endless array of behavioral symptoms that spring from the same root problem. It can also de-intensify the potential parent-child conflicts because you know that it's a no-fault situation. Your child is no more able to make the problem go away than you are, and in that sense you are in it together, both suffering. Like someone on a

What forms of love is your child most hungry for?

As your baby grows into a toddler and your toddler grows ever taller, you will get to know what forms of attention most help your child feel connected to you, loved by you, and valued by you.

Each of us has certain ways of showing love that are easiest for us, and sometimes we may inadvertently limit our expressions of love to these ways. We also may receive love more fully in some ways than in others.

In *The Five Love Languages of Children*, author Gary Chapman describes five basic ways of expressing love:

- Acts of service (like packing a special lunch),

- Words of affirmation ("You are so special to me."),

- Quality time (curling up together with a book, or going to a baseball game together),

- Gifts (a new paint set or a flower from your morning walk)—although be careful not to overdo the use of gifts to communicate love,

- Physical touch (from hugs to a gentle hand on the shoulder).

Be a love detective!

You may find it helpful to copy out this list of five ways of expressing love. Jot down ideas for versions of each of these that might be particularly meaningful to your child. It's great to be able to offer your love in a variety of ways.

You may observe that your child particularly hungers for or values one or more of these ways of receiving love. Such observations can help you put your energy into offering your love in the ways your child can most deeply receive it, even if it isn't your typical way of expressing it.

"cranky drug," your child may be "under the influence" of the underlying problem until it is resolved.

Cut slack and be consistent. During the rough patches, you may do well with a two-pronged approach. On the one hand be particularly careful to make lots of room for your child to express her emotions, even if it is somewhat annoying. Any time you see that your child is off balance, dig deep in your own reserves for patience and love. Your child really needs you. Do all you can to keep her tank full so that she can get through as best she can.

 I'd have to say that one of my favorite gentle discipline "instincts" is to really focus on my son (two years old) when he's going through his "punchy" periods. That is to say, when he's doing those things he knows he shouldn't (presumably to gain my attention). Many would tell me that I'm "rewarding bad behavior" and therefore reinforcing it, but in my experience, slowing down the pace of life to focus on his needs, whatever they may be at the time, has always resulted in a happier, more secure, and naturally well-behaved child.

Mary Beth K.

Pick your battles: you don't want to have to confront your child any more than you need to, and your child may benefit from a little more leeway.

On the other hand, bear in mind that boundaries do confer a sense of security, even—perhaps especially—for the child who is testing them. So convey clear strong boundaries for the important things. The predictability and routine can help your child recognize that you are still there to keep her safe.

One mother juggling a toddler and newborn described this two-pronged approach simply:

 I feel like what is working for us is more routine and consistency, and more compassion and empathy, too.

Karen K.

Some of the very hardest parenting times are situations when something is bothering your child, and yet there's nothing you can do at the moment to make the problem go away.

We've all been there. Once you've been through a rough patch, you can take strength from it as you move ahead.

 The times when I've grown the most as a disciplinarian are the hard times when it seems as if Gabriel is acting up all day every day. It really tests my patience and makes me have to be committed to gentle discipline.

I've also found that I'm even more attached to my toddler, and even more patient, when those hard times have passed. Bad days don't seem quite as bad when you've been through horrible days.

Beth C.

Deeper underlying problems

If you find yourself facing a long period of difficult behavior from a child, you may wonder if something more significant than basic physical and emotional well-being is at the root of it. Might this challenging behavior be a symptom of something larger, something with a diagnostic label? It's so hard to know, because, of course, many children do go through months or even years of challenging behavior as part of their normal healthy development, and they simply grow out of it. Careful observation and consulting your child's pediatrician may be in order.

Food-related problems

Some parents examine their children's diets more closely and discover problem foods. The classic one is sugar. Sometimes a little detective work can reveal the culprits.

 My four-year-old is very even-tempered by nature, so we have really tried to analyze situations where she acts out of character.

Food is a huge issue for her. She would often return home after a special outing with my mom only to act wretched the remainder of the evening. We soon discovered that she and my mom had a special candy store they would go to in the mall where she would get red jelly beans—bad news!

Now that we all realize how much sugar and dyes affect her, we are very careful about when and where those treats are provided (only after a well-balanced meal and/or right before she is going to be engaging in physical exercise, such as swimming). That has really helped.

Liz M.

In relatively rare cases, even healthy food can cause problems if food allergies or other sensitivities are present. Your pediatrician or an allergist may be able to help you. A small number of children react strongly to certain additives and naturally occurring chemicals in certain foods, such as salycilates. The Feingold diet is based on identifying and avoiding what additives or salycilate-containing foods might be a problem for a particular child (see **www.feingold.com** for more information).

 We realized that when our son had any sort of artificial coloring (or other salycilates) he would always have a tantrum and "go crazy." Seriously, it was like he got 100 times stronger. It was scary! Once we did the Feingold diet with him, *poof* his behavior magically got better. The food coloring Red #40 is the worst. The preservatives BHT (butylated hydroxytoluene) and TBHQ (tert-Butylhydroquinone) are close seconds, as are tomatoes and citrus (which contain salycilates). Even coloring in certain cleaning products (bath bubbles, laundry soap) affect him.

Beverly E.

One mother found that difficult behavior at mealtime had a treatable physical cause, severe reflux.

 His defiance at mealtimes, his power struggles over even touching a new food, the entire picture could have easily seemed to be a discipline problem—but instead, it was a normal reaction to a lot of highly negative associations built up about eating. When he ate certain things, or more than a small quantity, his body said stop. So he listened, and he listened well.

We were told later that if we had treated it as a discipline issue, the odds were great that we'd have ended up with a far worse feeding situation than we had already.

Heather P.

Developmental problems

You may find it helpful to consult your child's pediatrician and read up on your child's expected developmental abilities (see Chapter 3 for a list of resources). Sometimes a delay in developing skills can create apparent discipline problems.

 I spent about a year (from ages two to three) trying to figure out why all of the great suggestions that I was reading from the great sources at La Leche League and at Mothering.com weren't working with my son.

I would say things like, "Tyler, you need to stay where I can see you." He would reply, "Okay, Mom," and then run into the street. I thought I was failing as a mother.

When Tyler was three, his pediatrician calmly suggested that I might have him tested for receptive language issues. We had him tested and he was one year to 18 months behind. What his diagnosis means is that although he was speaking at an almost normal level (he was very slow to speak) he didn't have a clue what we were saying.

After two months of intensive twice-a-week speech therapy, my son went from a frustrated, regressive, and aggressive child who used language in an inappropriate way, to a happy, loving child who was willing to sit at a desk and do work with the therapists.

At this point, he still obviously has issues, but the seven months of intensive speech therapy helped us get to the point where all of the gentle discipline ideas could actually work.

Genevieve C.

Other conditions

As you consider the possibilities of underlying problems, you may find yourself exploring diagnostic terms, such as Attention Deficit Hyperactivity Disorder (ADHD) or autism. If you are considering such a possibility, make sure you get as much support and accurate information as you can, and take it step by step.

If your child receives a diagnosis that accounts for some of the behavioral problems, you may find a great relief in seeing not only that it's not your fault (or your child's) but that you now have a wealth of options and information for helping her work with her condition in constructive ways. Remember, too, that you still have all of your options open. You can choose a treatment approach that is right for your family. Regardless of the label, your beloved child is still infinitely precious and whole.

> Regardless of the label, your beloved child is still infinitely precious and whole.

 Both Brendan and Gabe have both over-sensitive and under-sensitive sensory integration processes. So, when they are over-stimulated, they both tend toward behaviors that are high-impact, high-muscle-use, high-force activities. They have to increase stimulation in their under-responsive systems, to counteract over-stimulation in their more sensitive systems.

The report from the occupational therapist for Gabriel was enlightening. It listed dozens of activities that we could encourage Gabriel to do to reduce his stress reaction to over-stimulation. Many of them were things he already did—burying himself under pillows, jumping up and down—things we'd been trying to put a stop to. Oops!

He had been using those behaviors to self-manage his own system, and doing so effectively. We just had to find activities that were within our tolerance that satisfied his body's need for over-stimulation of large muscle groups. Again, if we had continued to treat his "out of control bouncing" as a discipline issue, we'd have ended up with a child who had no resources for de-stressing his physical systems when he was over-stimulated, over-excited, or just plain over-stressed.

Heather P.

Meet those needs!

If an unmet need is at the root of a behavior problem, taking the time to deal with that may save untold aggravation and heartache, because until the need is met you are likely to be facing even more difficult behaviors. Indeed, once a child is already low (tired, hungry, traveling) it is important to realize that little real disciplinary headway is likely to be gained on any front until the child is feeling like himself again.

Meeting your child's underlying needs is a powerful parenting technique because it gets to the root of the problem and it makes it a no-fault situation. It's a great way to remember that your child is not choosing to act in a difficult way, but needs your help before she can access better options.

Chapter 3

Tailor-Made Discipline

 Observation is my greatest tool. I "read" my children, because they are the only and greatest book on themselves. If I want a manual, I have one, right in front of me. My job is to learn how to read it.

Heather P.

Childhood is an amazing time in each of our lives, as we emerge from the womb into greater and greater connection to the world around us. Each child is born with an individual personality, an urge to connect, and a rapidly growing curiosity about the world and his place in it. As a parent, you have the privilege of nurturing, supporting, and witnessing this remarkable process of emergence.

As your child grows, you can tailor your discipline approach to let your child be a child, to be himself, and to thrive in each stage of his development. This chapter explores three main aspects of tailoring discipline to your child:

What it means to be a child: giving your child space to be childish, to take risks and to make mistakes.

Temperament: working with your child's personality and learning style.

Developmental level: Taking into account your child's developmental level when setting your expectations and choosing your approach to discipline.

Let them be children

It is important to remember that children are every bit as complex, important, and human as adults. Childhood can be magical, joyful, tender, and also intensely challenging. Children's brains and bodies are growing at a staggering rate. Their world is expanding fast enough to make your head spin. Growing up is hard work.

How do children grow? We tend to think of "growing up" in terms of inches gained, lessons learned, and milestones passed. But those are all measures of growth that has already been completed. Learning to walk comes from a hundred tumbles, lengthening of limbs is accomplished by nights of growing pains, learning to share comes from experience with a whole range of interactions. Growth is a process, and few of life's real lessons or skills are learned by hearing about them. To facilitate our children's growth we need to make space for them to

> Growth is a process, and few of life's real lessons or skills are learned by hearing about them.

explore, fall down, ache, be surprised, make a mess, and, well, be childish.

Children are supposed to be childish

It is telling that in our society, the expression "being childish" is tinged with disapproval, even when applied to children! It is time to reclaim childishness for children, and reserve adult-like expectations for adults. If discipline is guiding children to maturity, then we need to make room for them to be immature along the way—to be child-like. After all, on the road to knowing better is not knowing better, and the road to better choices includes many regrettable ones.

What is the job of the child? While growing into greater maturity, children tend to:

- Have more impulses than control, so sometimes it's hard to stop themselves from doing tempting things even when they know better;

- Be self-centered, first tending to their own self-interest before being able to consistently consider the feelings and needs of others;

- Need a lot of autonomy, generating their own ideas and seeing them through helps them experience their own self-hood;

- Be dependent, needing a great deal of interaction, help, and empathy from caring adults;

- Be exuberant, needing to get the silly wiggles out a lot; and

- Crave exploration, touching, tasting, changing, and learning about their world in physical ways.

These are the raw ingredients for thriving children. Accept these traits and watch your child reach for greater and greater maturity as he grows. Seeing these traits as necessary steps on a path can help us celebrate (or at least tolerate) rather than stifle them. Making room for childish energy is a wonderful way to let your child be himself.

Children aren't adults and when their spirits are left intact they can be very gleeful, energetic, even obnoxious at times.

Alecia I.

Notice your own reactions. Some childishness involves behaving in a way we adults are not allowed to (but how many of us have wanted to have a temper tantrum now and then?). Sometimes childish behavior triggers memories from a parent's own childhood of when his or her childishness resulted in a harsh response. For these reasons, watching your child manifest immature characteristics may trigger an urge to push your child to act with more maturity than he is truly capable. You may find yourself feeling anxious, worried, irritated, or embarrassed. Tune into these reactions, and notice that they are not a true reflection of your child's behavior. If you can let the feelings come up without making it your child's problem, you are taking a bold and important step in support of your child.

The gift of childishness. When you create a non-judgmental framework to view your child's immature behavior, you give the gift of unconditional love, accepting your child for who he is right now. Then you can support your child in growing greater skills at his own natural pace.

It is not necessarily acceptable to throw and hit certain things, however these are very common behaviors for children. They are learning about how their behavior affects their surroundings (among other things).

I would rather be patient with these behaviors while I help my son to understand why these things are inappropriate than to teach him that you don't do them because "mama said so."

I guess that sums up gentle discipline rather well for me, helping my child to do "the right thing" because it is the right thing, not just because he fears the punishment if he doesn't.

Laurie D.W.

By making room for your child to be himself, you get to know him so much better.

With gentle discipline I am interested to see how much the texture of my children's personalities comes through. They don't hide their hearts from me the way I hid mine from my mother. It is okay for them to be angry, disappointed, afraid, and also for them to be passionate, joyful, and silly. There's not even a flicker of a sense that they feel I'd be unable to understand how they feel. That, for me, is a huge gift, and one I didn't even know to expect.

Heather P.

Children learn through risks

Children need to take risks—and to be kept safe. It may be tempting to spare your child some of the bumps and bruises, and ideally some of the messes, of learning as he goes. Indeed it is your job to protect him from harm. When you think it's safe, it can be very meaningful to step back and let your child stick his neck out a little. Doing so requires your assessment of your child's needs and abilities at this particular stage.

Sometimes a child will take risks in his relationships with people. "What happens if I_____?" As a parent, you may sometimes need to put boundaries around his options, or give him feedback about the effects of his choices on others. At the same time, you will want to recognize that his quest for experience is a noble and important one, for a person so new to the world. When your child tests boundaries in his relationship with you, it may really trigger your own defenses. It can help you stay centered if you remember that it's all part of his job.

Mistakes are important

Instead of "I can't believe he did that!" you can say to yourself: "Ah, so he's still working on learning that." Mistakes are part of learning. They are how one can test out various options, see for oneself what the outcome is, and learn the nature of good and effective choices.

> Mistakes are part of learning. They are how one can test out various options, see for oneself what the outcome is, and learn the nature of good and effective choices.

 No one is perfect, and that includes me. I think it's great for my children to see me make mistakes and to see how I handle making mistakes. When I grew up, I was ridiculed for making mistakes, and it has taken a long time for me to get over the fear of risking and trying new things. I want my children to not be afraid to make mistakes. As the teacher in the popular television and book series, *The Magic School Bus*, always says, "Make mistakes and get messy."

Rachel J.

There is a lot you can do to support your child around mistakes. Mistakes often speak for themselves, and your child can learn from direct observation. When your child is not able to make the connections, you can offer a brief explanation in a helpful tone. Help your child see his mistakes not as failures, but as interesting experiments to learn from. You can support your child when he make mistakes, show him that your love for him is unconditional, help him rectify the problem if possible, and convey your trust in his ability to learn better options and move on.

Your unique child

Children are born as individuals. Take into account how your individual child processes and responds to the world around him.

> For me, gentle discipline means working within the structure of the personality of my child to help her develop into a responsible, empathetic, connected, and loving adult.
>
> *Jessica K.*

Each child will have needs—and face challenges—that reflect his own unique personality.

> What brings out the worst in each of my children is unique to each of them. My older son (seven) is sensitive to disrespect. He requires that we respect him, and that we respect others. If he is not listened to, responded to, and regarded well, his whole life tangles up and becomes a mess. My three-year-old is sensitive to autonomy, which is appropriate for his age. He needs to feel that he is treated as himself, as an individual, rather than being lumped in with others.
>
> *Heather P.*

Fit discipline to your individual child

It is no wonder that formulaic advice has a way of falling flat in practice. What sounds good on paper, or what worked wonders with your friend's child, may be a poor fit for your particular child. Parents of more than one child often notice that the dis-

> What sounds good on paper, or what worked wonders with your friend's child, may be a poor fit for your particular child.

cipline their second born needed from them was drastically different from what their firstborn needed.

 I enforce our house rules differently for each of my children. My oldest son is very self-aware and verbal. I can ask him to think about why he is upset about something and what would fix it. He will go away, think, and come back with an insightful response.

My second child does not respond to requests in the heat of a disagreement. If I point out natural consequences or create penalties he sees it as both persecution and challenge. I have to convince him that something is a good idea before it becomes a conflict and then he does it thoroughly and independently.

My third child hates conflict and is loving, cuddly, and absent-minded. He is happy to cooperate. I just need to gently step him through the things he needs to do. I have to remember to leave time to work with him because he doesn't avoid work intentionally, and he just falls apart if I scold him.

Adria C.

Every child benefits from as much respect and empathy as you can bring to him. The precise form of gentle-discipline-in-action will depend on your child. By attentively observing your child, you will become sensitive to what your child needs from you in the way of guidance and support, and what approaches help keep him on track. Tailoring discipline to your unique child is a creative and loving act, requiring that you be tuned in to your child and observant about what is working and what is not.

All temperaments have a bright side

Some temperaments are more challenging than others. Traits that will serve your child well in the long run may make for some difficult parenting situations in the short term. What are the challenges of your child's temperament? Can you see the positive aspects of these same traits?

My son is so picky about his body. He hates having his nails clipped, his hair brushed, or doctors looking in his ears or listening to his chest. He is a very affectionate, loving kid, but is so particular about who touches him and where and how. It can be a real pain sometimes.

However, I am also glad he has such clear boundaries about his body. Even though I hate it when he screams bloody murder when the doctor just tries to gently look in his ear, I'm secretly proud of him for standing up for himself.

Ginger F.

 The screaming is challenging to me. When he's upset he flips, but when he's happy, his laughs are so joyful, enthused, loud, and contagious! Also, he never stops talking. That can be quite draining, but he is such an interesting conversationalist that it's all worth it.

Jessica O.

 I have a nine-year-old dreamer. Peter lives in a world of imagination and mind play. He forgets to eat because he's busy reading. He forgets to put his clothes on because he's singing a new song. He doesn't get his schoolwork done because he's folding new paper airplanes with pages he tore from his notebook. Yet he spends hours creating art. He's a natural at math. Peter notices that sweet potatoes can look like torches. My little dreamer finds humor and beauty in everyday processes. He finds them when I have forgotten to even look in my hurry to accomplish my goals.

Adria C.

Seeing the positive side of your child's challenging character traits can help you weather the downsides in the short term.

 His creativity is entwined with his risk-taking and what others might call "destructive" behaviors. He loves taking things apart. He will disassemble anything he can. However, if we always stopped him in the middle of that, we'd never have discovered that he does so in order to build something new from those materials. He's not destructive. He's a deconstructionist, an architect of recovered materials. Knowing that enables us to set limits that protect certain things (including himself), while leaving room for him to explore his love of building.

Heather P.

Check in with yourself. How does your child's temperament compare to your own? Sometimes the traits in your child that drive you crazy may be ones that are strikingly different—or strikingly similar—to the difficult side of your own personality. Noticing this—and finding a positive side to it—can help keep it in perspective.

Seeing the positive side of your child's challenging character traits can help you weather the downsides in the short term.

Parenting a spirited child

One of the disadvantages of having a strong willed or intense child has nothing to do with your child—but with bystanders. You may receive judgment or criticism from others when what you need is support. Some parents may even look at you struggling with your child and try to tell you that if you just parented the way they do, your child would be as well-behaved as their (milder) children. Such messages can leave you feeling inadequate, as though there's something wrong with you or your child. Only parents with equally intense children really know what it's like.

 I have had my share of spirited children. When my children were each four years old, it was a tearing-out-my-hair stage of development for me. It really tried my resolve but it did pass every time. I learned that I couldn't compare my spirited children with the average ones. They were operating on all thrusters and were much more of a handful. They were learning their limits. They needed boundaries and would (even in a relatively calm stage) test those boundaries repeatedly.

Debra B.

Intense children can be exhausting to be around sometimes. It is important to remember that they are no less in need of empathy and respect than other "easier" children.

> My daughter is three-and-a-half and is very spirited. I really don't want to put the stubborn flame out, just help her to cultivate it into healthy confidence.
>
> *Shireen F.*

Reach out to other gentle parents of children like yours. It can be such a relief to see that other smart and loving parents also struggle in the face of their intense offspring. It can be immensely encouraging to hear that they found ways to guide their children without resorting to harsh discipline. Hearing other parents' experiences can make you feel less alone and can give you new ideas for working with your child. (For ideas on support networks, see Chapter 11.)

If you can find some parents of intense children who are now grown up it can be inspiring to see that these children are often highly successful and happy adults.

You may also find key insight and ideas from books like *Raising Your Spirited Child* by Mary Sheedy Kurcinka, and *Easy to Love, Difficult to Discipline* by Becky Bailey, PhD.

> It can be such a relief to see that other smart and loving parents also struggle in the face of their intense offspring.

Changing development, changing discipline

To tailor discipline to your child, you will need to find ways to celebrate—and accommodate—his need to be immature and to be himself. As you move forward in time there's one more dimension to fitting discipline to your child: gauging and responding to his changing developmental level.

It takes time to grow up

Messages from mainstream society often imply that children should be much "better behaved" or more "obedient" than is realistic for their developmental level. Be on the lookout for this wishful thinking in your own parenting responses, and you will save yourself many unnecessary power struggles and disappointments.

Yes, it would be nice if all children would share toys easily and use their inside voices all the time—but clinging to unrealistic expectations like this won't help you reach a flesh-and-blood child who is still working on learning these skills. Starting with where your child really is, and helping him move forward at his own pace, requires that you tune out a great deal of misinformation about how quickly children should mature.

Once you get the long view of how child development unfolds, it's easier to relax a bit more as a parent. For this reason, parents of more than one child may sometimes worry less about the bumpy stages of their second and subsequent children. They have the reassurance of having seen that their eldest really did learn to share, listen without interrupting, and clean his room. All in good time.

 I became frustrated when it seemed my son should know better, when he was around two years old. Now that I have a daughter this age, I realize my expectations were completely unrealistic. Even though she is more of a handful, I am more gentle and patient with her because I respect her immaturity.

Kathleen P.

What is normal?

Fortify yourself with accurate information. Just what is normal? A two-year-old who grabs toys? A three-year-old who won't dress himself? A four-year-old who has a temper tantrum in the store? A five-year-old who can't clean his room without someone right there with him helping? Normal, normal, normal, normal.

Bear in mind that each child's developmental rate and style are unique to him. While one two-year-old may be quick to master the social art of sharing, his playmate may be busy mastering something totally different, like the gross motor skills required for climbing and jumping. Instead of comparing your child to another, get a sense of the wide window of normal development for skills.

Other parents may be your best resource. Sharing developmental woes with others can provide great relief and even laughter.

A good way to help redirect myself away from frustration is to use some humor. My partner and I will often say "You're acting like a one-year-old!" (actually, "two-year-old" now) when we start feeling frustrated. It's like a reset button.

Anna-Liza H.

You may also want to check out child development books such as:

- The aged-based series by Louise Bates Ames that starts with *Your One-Year-Old* and continues through age ten;

- *Innovations: Infant and Toddler Development* by Kay Albrecht and Linda G Miller;

- *The First Three Years* by Burton White;

- *Your Baby and Child 1-5 Years* by Penelope Leach;

- *The Child Under Six* by James L. Hymes Jr.; and

- *The Discipline Book* by Martha and William Sears

All of these books contain both developmental information and parenting advice, and sometimes the advice may not mesh with your own values. As always, take what you c.an use and leave the rest.

If it's normal then it's not anyone's fault

When you take a step back, it can be a profound relief to recognize that a difficult behavior is developmentally appropriate. Now you don't have to take it personally, as a reflection on your parenting or your child. This reality check can diffuse the tension that a difficult behavior could otherwise create between you and your child.

When my child's behavior is really difficult, I try not to take it personally, and I try not to hold it personally against him. I look at it more like an unfortunate but necessary aspect of his development. It is as if he is compelled by forces beyond his control. Plus he's still in the process of learning things like cooperation and has no sense of delayed gratification.

I find that if I keep looking at it like this, I see it more as just a psychological stage and am able to disassociate both of us from it a little. Then, when it's over, I just try to forget about it.

It's like a sunny afternoon after a rainy morning. You don't spend the rest of the day being sad about the morning, right?

Jennifer K.

Finding patience for normal development

When confronting an age-appropriate—yet unacceptable—behavior, it can take a great deal of parental fortitude to maintain perspective. With presence of mind you can stay on your child's side—the side of him that wants to grow up. From there you can help him find better solutions for his strong feelings and impulses.

 At the library yesterday, my tired two-year-old son pushed his sister. This is an age-appropriate way for him to handle his stress, but not acceptable. I was pretty furious, so I told myself over and over in my head, "I will not lose it! I will remain calm until I am at home and can sort out why I am feeling this way."

So I removed him from the situation, went home, got myself in control, took care of his needs, and then, when I was a little calmer, addressed what I could do to make changes for the long term.

Tara W.

Sometimes, your response may be more of a stop-gap—your way of responding to the problem at hand while understanding it won't go away overnight. Sometimes the much-needed breakthrough comes on its own with the gift of time.

When a behavior is age-appropriate, then almost by definition you may need to be patient while your child grows into better options. Development can't be rushed. That can be daunting sometimes, but it means there is light at the end of the tunnel.

Your child will move out of this developmental stage and leave the old behaviors behind.

Paying attention to normal childhood behavior from the beginning saves parents from later regret.

 My biggest problem with parenting at first was not knowing what was normal exploration and what they'd outgrow. (It never occurred to me to get a child development book series until the conflicts got so bad I couldn't stand it any more.)

I feared that many behaviors that seemed anti-social to me would go on forever if I didn't communicate consistently and clearly that they were wrong, bad, dangerous, or what-have-you.

I wish I could go back and do over those first three years with my daughter. I would allow myself to just redirect, use playfulness to defuse conflict, and not feel as though I had to be teaching a lesson every time she did something that made me worried about her future character. That's how we learn as parents, I guess.

Susan S.

Keeping up with changes

Tracking your child's changing abilities is a dynamic process. With young and curious babies, many parents choose to focus on indirect methods of maintaining boundaries.

 As Grace became mobile, we "disciplined" her undesirable behaviors (for instance climbing on furniture, handling breakable objects, throwing toys in the toilet, and emptying kitchen cabinets incessantly) with a combination of flexibility, changing expectations, constant surveillance, strategic redirecting, and babyproofing to make frustrations less frequent (for her and for us). In other words, we didn't try to shape her behavior so much as just keep her safe and keep us sane.

Kathy E.

As your child grows, what he needs from you shifts, too.

My 18-month-old is still very much at the age where he can be distracted from what he's doing, whereas my four-year-old really only responds when we discuss and explain our actions. For instance, if both children were handling our dog too roughly, Cole would simply need to be shown how to be gentle with the dog, whereas Accalia would want to be told why it's important to be gentle with the dog and what could happen if the dog becomes upset with the rough treatment.

Amy N.

It is important to be on the lookout for opportunities to scale up your expectations when you see your child is ready.

Requests from a child

If a young child were to have the opportunity and language to express his thoughts to parents, he might say something like this:

Remember that I am a child, not a small adult. Sometimes I really don't understand what you are saying.

Let me have fun out of little things, no matter how foolish they may seem to you.

I know very well that I shouldn't have everything I ask for—I'm only testing you. Be firm. It makes me feel secure. And if you're not consistent, you add to my confusion about "right and wrong."

Let my manners grow out of an understanding heart and good examples.

I am very busy living. I need healthy food and sleep to keep me going. And I need you to keep yourself fit and healthy, too.

Try to give me a home where I will always want to bring my friends—not a rich, fancy one, but one where children are respected and mistakes are not treated as sins.

Let me explore my universe. Don't slap my hands when I touch something bright and pretty. I love experimenting and couldn't really learn without it, so please be patient.

Try to give me at least a little corner in our home that is all my own. I need to learn about respecting privacy.

Help me to develop standards by which to understand my own conduct, as well as others. If I don't understand limits, I'll never learn to get along in the world.

Don't ever think that it is beneath your dignity to apologize to me when you have erred. An honest apology makes me appreciate you and teaches me how to do it when I make a mistake.

Let me question. Give me as honest an answer as you know. If you put me off when I ask questions, I may stop asking you and seek my information from others who may not have the same ideas.

Don't correct me in front of people if you can help it. I'll remember much better if you talk quietly with me in private.

Let me feel that I am wanted, that I am important to you. Don't be upset when I say, "I hate you." I love you and need you to love me just for being me—not just for the things I can do.

From a column entitled "Speaking For Children," by Fran Morris, published by the Oklahoma Gazette from 1985 to 2003.

 Yesterday, my two-year-old decided that she was all done riding in the grocery cart at the food co-op. Really done. Adamant. I knew this was a good opportunity for my daughter and me to work together on changing expectations. She's two years old and we go to the co-op a lot. I like it to be a positive experience, and she needed to know that I respected her getting older and more capable.

Before I let her grab the child-sized cart and take off, I took her back outside where we could concentrate on talking. We worked out an agreement: She could push the small cart instead of riding in my cart if she didn't touch everything. If I said no touching, she needed to not touch—even those tempting bulk food bins. If I said that we didn't need something, we weren't going to get it just because she could touch it. We decided that if those things were too hard for her to do, she could get back in the cart and we could try again another time.

She did great! Hands off everything, and no begging to get stuff. She even unloaded her own cart onto the counter. The rest of the day, she bragged about helping me at the co-op. It was a really neat moment, seeing her growing up and asking to change her limits. She knows what she can do.

Karen K.

Sometimes developmental leaps can happen so quickly that it's hard to keep up. Depending on your child, you may encounter unexpected behavioral challenges at certain ages, or at other "coming of age" stages like talking, becoming a big brother or sister, or starting school. Sometimes it may be hard to recognize—much less guide—this strange new person before you. You may find yourself a bit out of sorts alongside your child as you adjust to a new stage.

 Taylor is three. He was mostly a "dream" child until the last six months or so. Most of the time I find myself looking at him as if he is some alien who came and took over my adorable son.

Sandra L.

Each parent is likely to find his or her own growth accelerated at one point or another.

It seems that as a child grows up, the challenges for gentle discipline become more frequent. It's easy to say a gentle "no" to a baby reaching for something, and to create as much of a baby-friendly environment as possible in order to decrease the number of No's. Then they grow to the age where they understand completely, but don't want to do what you're requesting.

 My son is emotionally exhausting for me. I have to step back at times, as I think every parent does, and give myself a break before I respond.

Elizabeth B.

As your toddler grows into an older child you may start to recognize a rhythm to the challenges and their resolution.

 Dylan and I used to find ourselves puzzled by new behavior challenges. We found it easier to stomach when we could recognize that Julia had outgrown some other behavior that frustrated us in the past. We started to see it more as trading one challenge for another, not adding them up all the time.

I feel so proud of Julia when I see that she has worked hard to change and grow. She used to hate people talking about her curly hair so much that she wouldn't want to leave the house sometimes. "Mom, if I go there, people will say 'I like your pretty hair' and I don't want people to talk about my hair!" The other day, someone said, "I like your pretty hair," and she looked them in the eye and said, "Thank you," just as politely as can be. I was pleasantly shocked!

We try to notice and celebrate their progress, even the baby steps.

Karen K.

Some stages are easier than others

Even when you have a good grasp of what is age-appropriate, the fact remains that some stages are easier than others, and some are spectacularly difficult. And each stage is unpredictable. Because each child is different, your child may skip the terrible two's only to throw you for a loop at four.

The best thing about hair-raising developmental stages is that they do pass. However, a great deal of love and patience may be required for you to survive to tell the tale. As with any crisis, hunker down, take on as little as possible, and get as much support as you can.

 My daughter is almost four, but when she was three, she went through a phase when she was unhappy or melting down about anything and everything. It was extremely emotionally draining at the time.

Carolyn J.

Childhood is a long and exciting journey

Rowdy, giggly, boisterous, dreamy, loud, messy, or cuddly—here's to letting children be children. As your child grows up it is exciting to get to know him better as an individual, and it is an intimate act of relationship to tailor your discipline techniques to his needs. It will certainly be intriguing to see how your child's special individuality plays out across the many metamorphoses of his emergence from babyhood to adulthood. What a privilege—and a challenge—to be his trusted guide along the way.

Chapter 4

Preventive Discipline

For many people, the word "discipline" conjures up a parent reacting to a child's problematic behavior. The child acts and the parent reacts, a daunting cycle that threatens to leave the child and parent forever out of synch. One of the exciting things about gentle discipline is that it helps you prevent that cycle from getting started in many cases. Instead, you invest more of your energy into helping each day proceed more smoothly in the first place. Whenever you can set yourself and your child up for greater harmony you save untold effort and heartache chasing after avoidable problems.

The previous chapters examined two key ways to prevent unnecessary problems: fortify your child's emotional and physical well-being as much as possible, and have expectations of your child (and approaches to your child) that are in tune with her age and personality. This chapter explores more basic ways to be proactive about discipline:

- Be clear about your rules,

- Be prepared for positive follow-through,

- Seek structural solutions,

- Anticipate and troubleshoot challenging situations, and

- Model the behavior you want to see.

> Used with respect and empathy, the right rules increase fun and well-being.

Know your boundaries

Do you have rules?

For many of us the word "rules" conjures up childhood memories of seemingly arbitrary restrictions imposed upon us. The way they are sometimes used, rules can be like the bars of a cage, restricting and oppressing the person being "ruled" over. Not surprisingly, many new parents are uncomfortable with the idea of establishing "rules" for their own households.

It is worth taking a step back and re-examining what rules can mean. In the simplest sense, rules are just a system of boundaries. Boundaries are ways that you can help your child stay "in bounds," maximizing the good you can offer her, and minimizing the risk of problems. Used with respect and empathy, the right rules increase fun and well-being. Basketball would not be fun without rules. Driving would not be safe without traffic laws and practices such as defensive driving. Life for a small child would seem out of control to her and those around her if she were not helped to avoid harming herself, hurting others, or damaging property.

As your baby turns into a toddler and beyond, you will increasingly seek to balance her needs and wants with those of others. In time your child will internalize the boundaries that help her meet her needs in positive ways.

Rules don't need to be arbitrary, spontaneous, or oppressive—in fact the more predictable, consciously chosen, and considerate they are, the more readily they become part of the rhythm of the household.

It may help to think of it this way: Are there things that are important enough to you that you will actively follow through on them each and every time they arise?

Positive follow-through

There are plenty of positive and active ways you can support even a pre-verbal toddler in working with family boundaries, from holding her hand to cross the street to showing her how to touch the cat gently.

As your child's judgment and problem-solving abilities become more mature, less and less is needed from you. Gentle discipline is, after all, the process of helping your child develop inner self-discipline. However, in the earliest years, maintaining the rules will require an active role from you.

The first thing to do is take a step back and look at rules from your child's perspective. When your child is small, the rules usually make a lot more sense to you than to her. To a baby, the world appears to be her canvas for creative expression. It will take time for you to share boring adult ideas (e.g., walls are best left unmarked by crayon or pesto) with your more free-form little family member. It only makes sense that initially you need to take more responsibility for follow-through.

Being prepared to follow through on a boundary makes some key things possible. Consistent follow-through:

- Helps your child see that this concern really is worthy of action.

- Lets you relax a bit, because you know the rule will be honored in some way.

- Encourages you to be deliberate and positive in how you follow through.

• Motivates you to whittle down your rules to the most important ones.

Some people call active and positive follow-through "Get Off Your Butt" (GOYB for short).

 I'm of the "Get Off Your Butt" philosophy to get things done. When I find myself repeatedly asking her to stop something, I realize that I need to make that happen. For instance, if my toddler is banging the glass stereo doors open and shut, I have to go over there and help her stop, sometimes physically moving her hands (not roughly, just helping her) while explaining what I need.

Meghan S.

You are likely to find that summoning up consistent follow-through is well worth the trouble.

 A good way for me to tell how big of a deal it really is, is to see if it's worth going over there. If I'm telling him what to do or not do all day when only part of it even matters, he'll start disregarding me. However, if I only speak up and follow through when it's important, he'll start learning that Mommy will protect him, and that when I talk, it's worth paying attention.

Anna W.

Once you have a manageable, age-appropriate, and predictable set of house rules, you will almost certainly have to do that physical follow-through less and less.

Make your own list of rules

If you don't already know exactly what your rules are, try this exercise. (It's more fun with a friend or your co-parent.)

Get out a pad of paper and pen. Write "Things that are important enough to physically get up and go over to my child to make sure they happen or don't happen." (Or simply "GOYB.")

Now make columns, headed: "Always" and "Sometimes."

Under "Always" you might write "No running into the street," "No hitting," and other things that you find that you consistently take immediate action on.

Under "Sometimes" you may write things such as, "No jumping on the couch (unless it's been a long day)." These are things you prefer to happen or not happen, but that you do not enforce consistently for various reasons.

"Always:" Your bottom-line rules

Your "Always" list is basically your bottom-line family rules. What do you call them in your house? You may be surprised to see them tumble out onto paper. Chances are that most of these are not sources of conflict, because you are so confident that they are important and you send a clear message about them.

Our Family Rules

1. No hitting
2. No biting
3. Use nice words
4. Say please and thank you
5. No jumping on the bed
6. No feet on table
7. Wear clean underwear
8. No running im hmm——
9. Take care of younghys...
10. hmm—— ll~—~—

 With regard to letting things slide, we have biggies and smallies in our house and we just never let biggies slide, ever. Good thing is, we have precious few biggies. Before I say no to something I ask myself, is it really damaging (to himself, others, or my furniture), or is it simply annoying? If it's the latter, I let it go. This can cover a lot of territory. The less I say no, the more responsive he is when I have to say it or need him to work with me.

Mary Beth K.

If a rule on your "always" list is often a source of conflict, you may need to look at it more closely to identify the problem:

- Is it age-appropriate? Is your child ready to work with the rule?

- Is the rule clear to you and to your child?

- Are you consistently following through, thus sending the message that this is important?

- Is your follow-through positive and helpful?

- Does your child need more help from you in meeting your expectations?

If any of the above ingredients are not in place, you are likely to find that the rule is associated with resentment or conflict. Both you and your child are likely to work with it better when you have had the chance to give more consideration to the nature of the rule and to planning how you can positively implement it.

 We had a dinnertime issue for a while. I felt that my daughter should be able to sit in her seat and eat dinner with us without food throwing, crying, or playing.

One day I yelled at her, took her out of her seat none too gently, and told her she would help me clean up the mess on the floor.

Which she immediately did, willingly, at 13 months.

I realized at that moment that it was my dinnertime issue, not hers. She was unaware of the concept of people sitting together to eat at the same time. She hasn't been conditioned to eat to make other people happy or because she is "supposed to." She eats when she is hungry. She doesn't know that food is "supposed to" stay on the plate or tray.

These are all my rules, not hers. Since then, I just ask if she is done, set her down, and she usually winds up in my lap eating off my plate. I don't yell or handle her roughly; she doesn't cry. A few months ago this would have made me crazy (she's not "supposed to" do that!) but I've realized I regiment my life way too much, usually for no reason at all except "that's the way I've always done it." I won't accept that reason from other people so why do I accept it from myself?

Nancy V.

Some items on your rules list may well be age-appropriate for your child to begin working on, and yet it may still take a great deal of time for your child to grow into them. It may help to avoid thinking of it as an "obedience" issue and embrace it as a learning experience. Your role is to support your child and have reasonable expectations along the way. Giving your child permission to be a learner can take some of the pressure off, and help you be affirmative in your follow-through.

 My daughter is currently participating in preschool and one of the songs is the "Rule Song" that includes "We never hit or kick or push" and if one of our kids forgets that rule, we sing the song together to remind them.

Heather H.

Your "Sometimes" list

Some of the items on the "Sometimes" list may be there because you have been uncertain that they are important enough for consistent follow-through. These may be sources of conflict between you and your child, in part due to confused expectations. After thinking about it, you may decide to move some to your "Always" list because they deserve more consistent or helpful follow-through on your part (which may in turn reduce the conflict by reducing the confusion).

You may decide that some items really belong on a "Sometimes" list. There are many kinds of boundaries that you may have good reasons not to enforce all the time. If you explore your reasons for only sometimes following through on a rule, you may learn something about it that will help you work with it positively.

Some rules are situational, such as whispering in the library (but not at home), wearing underwear in public (but in the home may be optional). You may need to help your child to

Unrealistic expectations

Sometimes negative or unrealistic ideas may get in the way of your thinking of or using rules in positive and helpful ways. Some of the concepts you may need to *unlearn* include:

• Children should be able to remember a long list of rules.

• Parents don't need to be clear about all of their rules in advance—they can just make them up on the fly.

• Telling a child to do something should be enough.

• If a child does not follow the rule, she is being defiant.

• Rules must be enforced with punishment.

As you consider your relationship to rules, it may be worth noticing what negative images and ideas come up for you about what you or your child should be doing, where these notions come from, and what positive messages you can replace them with.

No fishing in the toilet

Children have a way of inspiring us to create rules that are more interesting than those that we might originally have thought of. What are your wacky rules?

No fishing in the toilet.

Anno B.

No wiping your nose on the couch.

No spitting in the house.

No playing with Daddy's nipples.

When we tell you to stop licking us, it is time to stop.

Wait until the person is looking at you before throwing the ball at them.

No jumping on mommy's back when she is bent over trying to change the baby's diaper

Ginger F.

No licking the furniture.

Wipe your nose on your own shirt.

No pouring or sprinkling your drink on your sister or brother.

Nicole C.

Don't lick the dog.

Don't drink from the dog dish.

Jamie N.

Don't lick strangers, even if you are playing "puppy" when you meet them.

Catherine F.

Do not put food in daddy's boots.

Do not chase or bother our old dog. She is old and doesn't feel good. (However, you can chase or bother Mommy, even though she is old and sometimes doesn't feel good.)

If you insist on taking seven toys on a hike, you must carry them. Mommy is not a sherpa.

Merrill F.

Don't take food off other people's plates (as she tries to swipe some stranger's fries).

Amelia B.

No sitting on the baby's head.

No throwing your shoes at people while in the stroller.

Leila W.

No licking something so no one else will eat it.

No building forts around me so I can't see what you are doing (so you think).

Jen L.M.

No pulling daddy's finger, especially when he asks you to.

Patty C.

No jumping from my dresser to my bed while I'm sleeping in it! Please wait until I get up.

Christy H.

understand how these situational rules are consistent in their own way. Sometimes you can redefine your boundaries in such a way that the sense of consistency becomes more obvious on its own.

> At one point, I was thinking that the whole consistency thing was baloney, because we don't have any consistent rules. Eventually, I learned that it's just external consistency that is baloney: rules like "No jumping in the tub" or "No throwing sand at the park." What is important to me is internal consistency: rules like "We keep ourselves and others safe," and "We learn and have fun."
>
> So I am being consistent if I let my son jump in the tub when I hold his hand, or when I let my boys throw sand if no one else is near the sand box, because they (and others) are safe and they are learning and having fun.
>
> *Mallory P.*

You may realize that some items are preferences of yours, things that you would like to see happen, but that do not lend themselves to being enforced all the time, at least for now. It may work better to request but not require that your child meet your expectations when it comes to your preferences. Realizing that you are flexible about it can reduce your own tension around dealing with it. For instance, you may wish that your toddler would clean up her toys but notice that she often has trouble doing it. Upon reflection, you may decide she is not ready to do so consistently. You may find that by placing "clean up toys" on your "preferences" list, you can bring more positive energy to any difficulties your child might be having. It may also bother you less on days when you decide it will work better for you to just do it yourself.

Knowing what is negotiable and what is not can help you maintain the territory that you feel is important, and honor your child's freedom as much as possible. Each parent will make his or her own judgment calls about things he or she can hold as a "preference" rather than a "bottom line rule." These assessments will have a lot to do with the parent's perceptions of his or her child and what is working. Every family is different.

Realistically, what choices will my child make that will be detrimental to him later? I mean a couple of days of no teeth brushing will not make all his teeth fall out and a week without a bath will not cause irreparable damage. I feel that showing him that we trust him to make decisions now, when the decisions are small and safe, will help him to have the ability, experience, and confidence to make the bigger decisions later when it will really matter. It works (so far) and all of us are happy, healthy, and relatively clean.

Laurie D.W.

Some of the items on your "sometimes" list may be behaviors you don't think need to be stopped at all costs, but over time you are trying to nurture better options. These fit into your long-term goals for your child. You may find that many daily problems that do not have fixed responses can be dealt with by working with your child in the moment, sharing perspectives, brainstorming ideas, and coming up with a creative middle ground. Working with boundaries can be dynamic! What a great opportunity to hone your child's and your own skills at creative problem-solving.

There will always be someone to tell you that you are being too strict, and someone else to say that you are being too lenient.

In our home, not hurting each other is a bottom line rule. We pull out all stops to enforce that.

Then I think of the things I wish to change—long-term goals such as teaching my three-year-old how we like to be the best people we can be.

Last night at dinner, Julia said she didn't want a napkin at the table. I thought it was no big deal and she was just figuring out what she wanted. But then she threw it down on the floor. Throwing napkins bugs me, but I realize it isn't terrible. If Julia or I were maxed out, I might not make a big issue about it. Maybe I'd just say, "Let's pick it up together."

Last night I had more time and energy. I explained to her that it's okay to not want a napkin, but it isn't okay to throw it. Before even talking about picking it up (because she probably would have just thrown it again), we brainstormed how she could handle that feeling of not wanting a napkin. She could put it back in the drawer. She could hide it. She could say "no thank you" to the napkin when we set the table.

Once we came up with ideas, she was ready to pick it up. I needed to kindly and supportively take her by the hand though. She then proceeded to sit on the floor and work intently at folding her napkin back just the way it should be so she could put it away in the drawer.

It's this kind of teaching about feelings and manners that is a whole other level of gentle discipline for me!

Karen K.

You may use this rules exercise as a basis for compiling a list. Taking some time periodically to clarify where you stand with boundaries or rules in your home may help you communicate more effectively with your children.

 I use different language and tone of voice when he's climbing onto something (he could potentially get hurt) than when he's throwing food off his chair (making more cleanup for me).

Sohee P.

How many rules are enough?

Some families have many rules. Some try to keep them to a minimum. Some people prefer to be organized and systematic about their rules. Others prefer to be loose and go with the flow. It's very individual, and there is no right or wrong way to go about it. There will always be someone to tell you that you are being too strict, and someone else to say that you are being too lenient. It's one of the joys of parenting to always fall on one point or another along the continuum.

The important thing is that you work with boundaries in a way that fits your personal style, parenting philosophy, and observations about what is working in your home. What are rules like in your family?

 My older daughter is three-and-a-half. We don't really have set rules or consequences. Our basic rule is "no hurting." My daughter loves to tell others "Hey, we're a no hitting, no pinching, no smacking family."

We have safety rules, but I don't call them rules, or present them as such, just as logic. For example, "This is a car park (parking lot) here. I'd like you to hold my hand until we get in the store."

If something happens like throwing or spitting food, we just give a reason why it's not acceptable, and clean it up together.

If she speaks rudely, I ask her to speak kindly as it hurts my feelings. She always corrects herself immediately. I don't see it as what Americans call "back chat" or "sassy," just as a normal three-year-old learning how to express herself when feeling challenged. I gently model back the gentler way to express things.

If they make too much noise or are too boisterous, they need to go somewhere where they are not bothering others.

Nicola C.

One of the reasons that boundaries and rules are so personal is that very often it takes energy on your part to either make room for your child to do something—or to help keep her from doing it. Members of families are interconnected, and your feelings about limits are likely to reflect that. You may find layers of interdependence that influence how you formulate and enforce some of your rules.

 If I tell my toddler not to climb on the table, I ask myself if it is because it is inconvenient for me to supervise her because I want to be finishing up the dishes, or because it's really a safety issue. I might decide it's the former. I could help her get up on the table and explore it. If I allow her to take care of that urge, she'll probably move on.

A safety issue would be for her to try to do that on her own when she is not yet capable of doing so safely. Then I wonder if she is at a place developmentally where she can judge when she needs help or not.

As much as I would love to be able to supervise all her explorations, we need to eat and function in the house, which means I have to tend to those things and can't be supervising her forays every second.

Kelly C.

Adjust as you go

When circumstances intervene to make you less available, you may need to adjust your rules accordingly.

 My daughter was two when my son was born. I often asked her to do something or to stop doing something, and then just hoped she would comply because I was tied up with the baby. It didn't work well, and I believe it set us up for some battles when she became three and even now that she's four (although it's getting better).

I basically taught her that she didn't have to listen to me if she didn't want to. As a consequence, I later felt I had to raise my voice more or threaten consequences to get her attention.

I find it is so helpful to physically intervene almost immediately. Now that my son is two, I try not to wait until I've said something five times. It's hard with a baby, but it's worth the effort later, in my experience.

When it's difficult to intervene, I've learned to take a second to consider whether or not to say anything at all until I can. If it's a safety issue, I must intervene right away, even if that means a crying baby or a burned dinner. But if it's just spilled applesauce or dawdling, I try to bite my tongue until I can back up my words with action if need be.

Stephanie C.

Your boundaries may need to grow with your child. With small children, things can happen quickly, and it can be hard to tell just where the real boundary lies and how best to enforce it. After all, it's always easiest to identify a rule when it has been turned on its head.

 We bought a whiteboard for our 11-month-old daughter. I showed her how the pens mark on the whiteboard and then you can just wipe them off. At first, it was great watching her "draw." But then she wanted to roam all over the room with the pens in her hands, and the second I put the lids on, she would screech, cry, and wail. She was not able to understand the complexities of, "Yes, you can draw here. No, you can't draw there." To make it worse, she wasn't even trying to draw on

Boundaries for babies?

Yes! Babies need boundaries, too. You are providing gentle discipline to your baby when you take the time to get to know her unique personality, identify and meet her needs so that she feels cared for and learns to trust you, and any time you help her explore her world as harmoniously as possible.

Without an active parent, even a baby could get into some troubling situations. Chances are that before your child learned to crawl, you started looking for gentle ways to prevent her from unwittingly harming herself or others, or damaging property. Perhaps you steered your crawler away from an electric outlet, took a biting baby off the breast, or placed Auntie's crystal vase out of reach. If you can see tricky situations from your baby's perspective, you can find positive ways to support your baby in learning and having fun from the start.

other things, but just holding the pen as she went around the house playing with other things. If she accidentally got it on my mother's carpet or furniture, my mother would have a fit.

At first, I repeatedly put the lids on. She would then wail in frustration and misery, and I would take the lid off, thinking, "I'll just follow her around." Then I'd tire of that and put the lids back on. Soon, I felt like the world's worst mother. I was being completely inconsistent and totally unfair to my daughter. I seemed to be "rewarding" her for screeching and crying. It was awful.

So what did I do? I put the pens away where she can't find them. I held her while she cried, gave her lots of love and nursies, and apologized to her. I realized that the pens and whiteboard were not age-appropriate for her development. I chalked it up to a learning experience, and moved on. I learned a big lesson that day about not being "perfect" and just having to deal with it. I ate my humble pie, and hopefully I'm a better mama for it.

Mariah W.

Remember that you can always adjust as you go. A large part of parenting involves identifying, re-evaluating, and shifting your boundaries and family priorities as time goes by.

Avoid the avoidable

When you are clear about your boundaries, ask yourself: "How can I make my boundaries as easy as possible to stay within?"

Two of the most important approaches are to seek structural solutions and to anticipate challenges in your day.

Seek structural solutions

With a "structural" solution, you are not trying to get your child to see the problem and react according to your ideas. Instead, you endeavor to arrange objects or activities to reduce the likelihood of your child crossing the boundary.

Babyproofing. The more child-friendly you can make your child's environment, the fewer boundaries you need to set with words or actions. This is a particularly big part of gentle discipline for crawling babies and exploring toddlers.

My attitude with my 16-month-old is to keep her environment as much of a "Yes!" environment as I can. This means childproofing as much as possible and redirecting her gently when she's doing something I'd rather she didn't.

Mariah W.

The time and effort of childproofing your house can pay big dividends for your happy explorer and eliminate a great deal of unnecessary disciplinary actions for parents.

We babyproof well. All electrical outlets are blocked by furniture. Knives, cleaners, and medicines are all high out of reach. There is hardly anything downstairs that my kids can't touch.

Patty C.

Later, you can teach your child about safety and considerations of property. The art of teaching, after all, requires readiness on the part of the pupil.

Ashley (18 months) just couldn't stay away from the house plants. So, we moved them outside or to another room where she couldn't reach them. We are not avoiding an opportunity to teach her. We are putting the issue on hold until she is at another developmental stage and can better understand why she shouldn't do something.

Sarah M.

As your child grows older, there will still be ways to child-proof your environment. If she is likely to be tempted to do something problematic, take responsibility for taking care of it for both of your sakes.

 I find that many incidents of apparent "intentional misbehavior" can be "fixed" by adjusting my expectations and acting accordingly. For example, it's too much for my three-year-old son to handle if I leave laundry around. His impulses tell him to jump on it and he doesn't really have enough impulse control yet to resist the urge. If I don't want the clean clothes to be jumped on or knocked over, I need to put them out of his reach. Expecting him to not jump on them is just too much.

Amber S.

Some destinations and activities are more easily managed when you can go all out to help your child make it work, such as errands with a boisterous toddler, or situations that your child is temporarily unable to handle safely.

 If we are rushing around and running late, my son gets very anxious and is less likely to handle the outing well. Knowing this, I try to run errands when I can spend the extra time it takes to shop with a three-year-old. I know it's hard (he often tells his toy cars to hurry up, we're running late), but it is worth it to avoid the stress on everybody.

Laurie D.W.

When you can't or don't want to support your child in that way, it is

Rules and the older child: A collaborative effort

One of the great rewards of having an older child is getting her help in devising and working with rules.

Consider calling a family meeting to discuss rules. Begin by listing together the rules that you each feel are important. You may want to note as you go along which rules apply to everyone, and which don't (and why).

Discuss contentious rules and try to find ways to find common ground. Encourage your child to share her feelings and perceptions, and share your own.

Work together to devise a list of family rules and priorities that everyone can feel good about and stand behind.

Brainstorm positive ways of helping the rules happen. You may be surprised at how creative and involved your child can be about rule enforcement.

ideal not to bring your child into such a loaded situation. Sometimes it helps to take a hiatus from trouble spots.

Personally, we just don't go places that aren't childproofed. It's no fun for baby, and it sure isn't a pleasant visit when we are running around taking everything from her hands.

Mariah W.

You can phase these things back into your life when your child is more ready to work with the challenges.

When he was 18 months old, Gabriel went through a biting and hitting stage. He was hurting me and other children at playgroups. We avoided playgroups for a few months until Gabriel was old enough to understand that it hurts when he bites or hits.

When we did resume seeing other children, I stayed right behind him the whole time, even when he climbed all over the jungle gym. If he went toward another child, I could prevent him from hurting them. I reminded him repeatedly for months that biting and hitting hurt, and he grew out of it. It was a really hard time for me and I got emotionally and physically exhausted, but it was so rewarding to see him stop and now he is so gentle and loving to other children.

Beth C.

Anticipate challenging situations

As you plan your day, think ahead to what problems tend to arise in various situations and troubleshoot them in advance. With an older child, you can talk about challenging situations with her before you get there, walking through options, feelings, and consequences. Role playing new skills and difficult situations can be a safe way for your child to explore her options and feelings.

By acting out scenarios ahead of time, I can guide my children into knowing what is appropriate before we are in that situation.

For example, the kids were having a lot of trouble behaving during church. Who wouldn't have trouble being good during a one-hour meeting that isn't very fun for a little kid? So at our weekly family night activity, we practiced being reverent. We talked about why we should be reverent and how to be reverent. We practiced walking and sitting reverently. Now, if we say, "Time to be reverent!" they sit still (or walk nicely) with their arms folded.

Heather H.

Talking about events in advance can prepare your child for what she might feel and experience, what might be expected of her, and what her options are for meeting her needs.

 We prepare our four-year-old for big changes whenever we possibly can. We talk about trips to the dentist, moves, out-of-town visitors, and make a game out of imagining such things. She likes and needs these preparations to be repeated right up to the event. It gives her something to relate to when the event occurs. We often re-enact the event afterward, too.

Nicole M.

Sometimes situations are challenging because your child's needs are not being met. Brainstorming and planning in advance can sometimes help you set your child up to meet her needs more adequately. This comes up frequently with babies, but can also be a very important consideration for older children, especially in adult-oriented settings.

 It often helps if I plan and prepare my son for the situations he is likely to face in our day. If we are going to a meeting where I will need my five-year-old Keithen to play on his own so I can focus on something else, we will often pack a backpack full of quiet activities for him. If we are going to a playgroup and I know a child he often has conflicts with will be there as well, it may help to talk with him about how I expect him to handle himself.

Carissa D.

Working with your child's individual needs helps you set your child up for success.

One of my children is very shy around new people. He tends to act out in these situations. While we can't avoid new people, we do have a way of dealing with it. I let him decide when he will or will not join the group. He can watch from afar if he wishes. If he feels comfortable later, he can join the group.

One of my children gets very over-stimulated and needs down time. I try to respect that and give it to her. I space errands and playdates to allow enough time for her to have her down time and fun time, too. It makes things much more enjoyable for all of us.

Amy E.

Model the behavior you want to see

One of the most powerful ways in which parents can influence their child's behavior is by their own behavior. Children learn by example.

 As a mother, I have learned that children learn mainly by modeling. Actions speak louder than words.

Lisa S.

 I try to set a good example. Our job is to give her the tools she needs to grow up and become a centered, compassionate, well-adjusted adult. I get to see myself at my worst when my child starts imitating me. She watches everything I do. I've been telling Kathryn (three) that she needs to teach little Francesca how to be a good sister. I say, "Teach Francesca how to treat you by treating her the same way." Now I've realized that I can take the same advice. I have to teach Kathryn and Francesca how to be a mother, how to be a woman, how to be a wife. It's a heavy responsibility but if I take it one day, sometimes one hour, at a time, it's not so bad.

Sharon G.

We choose to lead by example and trust that our three-year-old will follow that example. He is learning manners because we are polite to him. When he gives us something, we say "thank you." Now he says it too because he has grown up with it being a natural part of interacting with others. If we make a mistake, yell, or are disrespectful to him, we apologize. He learns that when he is disrespectful to others, he should say he is sorry.

Laurie D.W.

Sometimes parents may model a behavior very deliberately to solve a particular problem.

 We play together a lot. When we play "house," I model the behavior and reactions that I like to see. It really makes a difference.

Kati S.

 My favorite gentle discipline technique is to change my own behavior. If I notice that my kids are driving me crazy by not responding when I say their names, I work on responding the first time they say my name. Do I wish everyone would talk more quietly and say "Please," more often? I probably have not been as polite as I could be. I have control over what I do, so I get to see at least one person changing immediately. And it doesn't take long for my children to follow my example.

Mallory P.

Body boundaries

Many parents find it best to avoid or minimize rules regarding a child's bodily functions. These are never in our control—and trying to control another person's bodily functions can lead to power struggles. You can nurture your child's ability to read and respond to her own cues so that she learns to eat, eliminate, and sleep in synch with her own body's natural rhythms. Parents who minimize rules about bodily functions still have bound-aries—they just choose different boundaries.

 I believe a child knows best what he wants to eat and how much. It starts with breastfeeding.

I stopped spoon-feeding about a month after they started solids. I used many "finger foods" so they could put food in their own mouths. They learned to use a spoon and fork very early. It was messy sometimes. It worked well for us, though.

I believe my job is to put quality food in front of them at meal and snack times, but I do not force them to eat any of it. I especially avoid insisting that my children should clear their plates or finish their drinks. The amount of food on their plates is often due to my choice. It has nothing to do with how hungry or thirsty they are.

Now that they are two-and-a-half and almost five years old, we pass the serving bowls, and let them put their own food on their plates. Sometimes they choose not to put a food on their plate. However, they are great imitators. When they see us putting a food on our plates and then eating it, they often ask for it again and end up at least trying it. I watch for "too much" when I know they are just putting more on the plate for the fun of scooping with the big tongs or spoon.

We have no battles about what they must eat. In a day, they eat a variety of foods, and none of them is over- or under-weight.

Brooke S.

 If he does not want to eat what we cook, he can choose something else. I don't cook something separate, but he can have anything he can get for himself. We only keep healthy options, so anything he chooses is okay. If we only buy healthy things, and we only eat healthy things, then he will have that example to fol-low. Most importantly, he will have practice in making healthy choices.

Laurie D.W.

Parents can also adopt a relaxed tone about using the toilet. Bodily functions can't be forced, but you can support your child in taking care of business without trying to actually make her pee or poop.

In order to entice our three-year-old Clio to stay on the toilet long enough, we have to tell or read stories. Otherwise, her bottom would be on the potty for about three seconds. Usually, after the story, she gets excited and starts tearing around telling her own story on a similar theme.

Cheri R.

You can also set limits about when bathroom time needs to happen (for instance before bedtime or outings) without controlling whether your child actually "goes" or not.

 As Meara (three) learned to use the toilet and was wearing underwear during the day, we added a new part to her bedtime routine. We told her that all we want her to do is sit on the toilet, and give everything a chance to come out. We told her that if nothing comes out, that is okay. Usually, she does pee.

The first few times, we explained our reasons. We wanted her to be comfortable during the night. If she gave herself a chance to use the toilet before going to bed, then her body might not need to wake her up in the night to go to the bathroom.

This approach has also helped overcome her reluctance to interrupt more interesting daytime activities for the bathroom. After all, just sitting on the toilet is pretty quick.

Maureen C.

Parents' feelings and ideas about children and sleep can often be complex. Some parents find it's possible to stick to a bedtime ritual and gently encourage sleep, without putting pressure on their child to fall asleep at a particular time or even in a particular place. Sleep is explored more in Chapter 12.

Proactive transitions

Let's examine preventive discipline through the lens of one of the classic parenting conundrums: transitions. At some point or another, you are likely to need to help a reluctant child move from one place or activity to the next: from home to the store, from playgroup to the stroller, from playtime to bath-time. Transitions can be hard, in part because children have a different sense of time than we do. Also, changes can trigger emotional upheaval; your child may have many feelings aroused by the activity at hand, the activity ahead, and the whole idea of letting go.

Transitions are a prime opportunity to pull out your prevention tools. Rather than correcting your child for not changing gears, what can you do to make it as easy as possible for her to do so?

 My daughter is three, and transitions are very difficult for her. She even gets freaked out when I come home from work, and has to hide under her covers to calm down enough to greet me.

I try not to see her inability to cooperate in the midst of a transition as defiance. I try to see it as an honest-to-goodness difficulty for her. She'd like to, but it is just too hard.

So, instead of focusing on her behavior during a transition, we try to make transitions less difficult for her. We have fewer activities in a day, and provide plenty of reminders about what will happen next and when it will happen.

Rebecca K.

Finding ways to help your child anticipate changes can help her feel more in control.

 My two-year-old son could get pretty intense around transitions. What worked for me was using a timer and saying several times that when the timer went off, then this and this were going to happen. For a little while I had to carry the timer with me everywhere we went just to get him to transition from one seemingly minor thing to another. It worked very well and he seemed to grow out of it quickly.

The timer seemed to help him by giving him three to five minutes to adjust to the fact that something new was about to happen. We literally had to use it to get him to eat, take a bath, get out of the bath, change his clothes, oh the things you wouldn't believe. Now all I do is tell him that soon we are going to eat, leave to go shopping, or whatever.

While he still becomes anxious sometimes, he seems to be going with the flow better.

Jen R.

Some find that a countdown works well.

Because I know Gabriel (18 months) so well, I'm able to avoid the situations that are triggers. For example, when we're getting ready to leave the playground or a playgroup I always remind him, "Five minutes. Four minutes. Three minutes." I have him repeat what I said so that I know that he heard me. After one minute, I tell him, "last time," and he gets to choose his last thing to do. Then we leave together, happily. He usually runs for the door or the stroller before I even have a chance to.

Beth C.

Help your child bring closure to the current activity.

We are task-oriented people, so I might ask my three-year-old, what she wants to accomplish (at home), touch (somewhere new and inviting), or play with (at the playground) before we leave.

She's quite a negotiator now. She knows what is reasonable because it's been an active process for her. She knows that three times on the slide will be okay, but not slide and swing and sandbox. She can plan.

Karen K.

Help your child look to the next activity.

When my children have something to look forward to—a favorite snack or a fun thing to do—it makes us all feel more cooperative.

Amy N.

Developing fun rituals around transitions can help, too.

I have found success with singing loudly as a transition is happening. "Old McDonald Had a Farm" is the standard, but any song used consistently works.

Nancy V.

Some children do best when they know what to expect out of the day.

We plan what we are going to do today and tomorrow and talk about things in sequence. "First, we'll go to the library to get mommy from work. Second, we'll go to the thrift store. Third, we'll buy some groceries. Last, we'll go home."

Nicole M.

If your child has serious problems with transitions, you may find yourself gaining quite a bit of expertise.

My daughter has always had profound difficulty with transitioning. I have established about a million tricks to get her from A to B.

When I am transitioning my daughter, I give her as much control over the situation as possible. Saying, "Ten more pushes on the swing and then we'll leave," worked better than a minute-by-minute countdown. I think it was more concrete to her than talking about "minutes." Then I would ask her how she wanted to leave. Did she want to crawl like a bear, run like a doggy, or hop like a bunny? Her favorite was, flying like a bird, which involved my carrying her through the air.

I also would say things such as, "It's time to go. Who's the leader?" She would yell, "I am!" and run in front of me. If she was hesitant to leave, I would simply say, "It's time to go. I'm the leader!" She would react by saying she was the leader and run in front of me. Sometimes I'd announce it was time to go and that I was going to dance out. I would do the craziest dance to the door. She would usually laugh and follow me when I did things like this.

Sometimes I give her jobs when we need to leave the house. For example, I'll ask her to hand me her coat, hat, mittens, sippy cup, or whatever else she will need during the trip. I might also ask, "Can you hold the door with me?" "Can you help push the trike?" "Can you hold mommy's sunglasses?" "Do you want to wear mommy's sunglasses?" "Do you want to hold the car keys and push the button to unlock the door?" Like many toddlers, she loves that last one!

When I give choices, I make sure none can be answered with "no." In other words, I don't say, "Would

you like to fly like a bird?" Instead, I say, "Do you want to fly like a bird or jump like a frog?" If she doesn't want either, I say, "I'm going to hop like a frog," and just start going. She usually joins in the game.

Because I have many ideas to try, I don't feel I have to limit her activities to avoid trouble with transitions. I need to give her some control over such times. At this age, my daughter may act as if she wants to control me, but in fact, she would find that very scary. It works best for me to give her control within certain boundaries so that she feels secure in making a choice that I have set up for her.

Jessica K.

Chapter 12 includes ideas about managing four classic situatons related to transitions: car seat avoidance, cleaning up, bedtime, and getting out of the house.

Make it easy

The key to preventive discipline is having clear and realistic family rules, knowing your child's trouble spots, and taking action to make it as easy as you can for your child to meet your expectations. The more preventive discipline you practice, the more you are able to support your child in meeting her needs in positive ways. After all, you both want the day to go smoothly.

 To me, a lot of gentle discipline is setting my children up for success. I think that other forms of parenting are punitive and set parents and children apart, as if parents are waiting for the children to fail so they can punish them. I practice gentle discipline because it seeks to create successes for children and parents who are on the same team.

Karen K.

Chapter 5

Getting Back on Track

$\sim\sim\sim\sim\sim\sim\sim\sim\sim\sim\sim\sim\sim\sim$

Being proactive helps parents avoid avoidable problems. But what about the unavoidable ones? No matter how proactive you are, you can count on parenting, childhood, and life in general to be messy anyway. Everyone has his or her needs, desires, and ideas, and sometimes they are in conflict. Each incident offers parents an opportunity to guide and support, rather than oppose, their children.

This chapter will explore key ways to deal with problems in positive ways, from effective communication, to helpful follow-through, to problem-solving. In many ways, this chapter is about developing new skills to replace the traditional ones.

More often than not, we come into parenting knowing what we don't want to do, and not able to put a finger on what it is we do want to do.

Mariah W.

You can't have too many positive options. Each parent will create his or her own set of positive tools and will need to develop new ones as time goes on.

When I initially adopted gentle discipline (when my son was three), I found that this new set of beliefs leads to an entirely different set of tools. I would use some of my new tools, get frustrated if they didn't "work" or if I couldn't operate them properly, and fall back on my old tools.

Having clarified and strengthened my set of beliefs I can now evaluate my tools and hone them continually. I can also trust that they are going to be effective even if a particular behavior is not immediately controlled.

Switching away from punitive discipline required a huge mind shift for me, and still does on a daily basis, but I'm seeing positive effects on my son's behavior and especially his self-confidence.

Lisa S.

Gentle discipline is not all or nothing.

At the same time as it explores the many ways to be positive, this chapter also encourages you to remember that you can always say "no" firmly when you need to, that you can't always make your child happy, and that you don't have to be positive and creative all the time. Gentle discipline is not all or nothing.

Let's begin by looking at ways to remain connected to your child when problems arise.

Positive communication

Get connected

If you want to reach your child, you must first make sure you are connected to him. Lessons offered within a cloud of disconnection are likely to be lost. Boundaries set without connection may feel like battles.

Ask yourself:

- Is my child ready to listen to me?

- Am I ready to listen to my child?

- Am I ready to speak to my child as a person?

- Is my child ready to share his or her thoughts and feelings with me?

By making eye-contact, getting down to your child's level, offering a touch, or using a tone of voice that conveys a desire to genuinely connect, you disarm yourself. You make it possible to reach your child more deeply and truly move forward together.

My husband went out of town for the day. I was very nervous about parenting my four-year-old Carter and six-month-old baby by myself for not only the day but also the nighttime routines. To make it extra challenging, Carter's best friend and his one-year-old brother were going to come over in the afternoon!

I told myself to make it a goal all day to connect first. Wow, what a difference! When things got a little dicey with two four-year-olds playing alongside a one-year-old, instead of yelling from the deck, "Careful of the baby, guys," I used an idea from Becky Bailey's book, *Easy to Love, Difficult to Discipline.* I went down, took Carter's hand, and said, "There you are." Then I explained my concerns about the baby's safety.

I asked both older boys how they could play and still keep the baby safe. They came up with great, safe ideas. Carter and his friend enjoyed a long afternoon of playing amicably together.

In the end, active and connected parenting worked better and afforded all of us more relaxation than techniques that might appear "easier." There were moments when I really didn't want to be a single parent, but in the end, it was a very pleasant day.

Amy M.

An upset child can't listen

Helping your child move through his emotions and calm

down can be an important first step to talking about the problem. Depending on your child, he may need to be alone to blow off steam and come back to you when he is ready. Or he may need your support—or at least your presence—to work his way through his strong feelings.

 Sometimes my child has been so beside himself with emotion that not only can he not communicate what is wrong, he cannot focus well enough to listen. This was my son when he was around two-and-a-half years old.

I discovered a wonderful little trick that worked well to calm him, even when he was too upset to hear me speak. He was very agreeable to this technique and cooperated willingly. I would take him into my lap, facing each other chest to chest with his legs straddling my hips. I would hold him close with my face near his and calmly talk directly into his ear, telling him to take deep breaths. While I talked, I would take exaggerated deep breaths myself so he could really feel me breathing. I would also rub his back, stroking upwards when I inhaled and down when I exhaled. Sometimes I would count while we breathed. Other times I would talk about blowing bubbles or blowing out candles.

When he was beyond using or hearing words, I think the close contact of our little ritual helped him begin to focus on calming himself so that he could communicate again.

After several months of repeating this ritual, we could just tell him that he needed to take some deep breaths, sometimes counting for him as he breathed. As he got older, he learned to tell us when he needed a few moments just to breathe and calm down.

Carissa D.

You may be able to find a nonverbal language to help your child when he is not able to hear you. Communication is so individual, doubly so when emotions are running high.

 We have known for a long time that when Bella (now three) is at all emotional, she needs physical reminders of things; words just don't work. She needs to do something or be physically shown something.

When she was two years old and less verbal, she seemed to have a lot of tantrums. We showed her how she could jump up and down to get her frustration out.

Even though she is more verbal now, she still has times when I know she has trouble hearing what I say to her. So we have developed a game where we pretend that she has a whining button (her nose), and a volume button (her ear) that I can just touch. These serve as a reminder to her that she is doing something that people around her have a hard time dealing with. She loves to test how well these buttons work on my husband and me as well, by touching our noses or ears. This gives us a good opportunity to model the negative behavior, so she understands what we don't like. She also sees us stop ourselves from doing the things that we ask her not to do.

The touch gets through to her when nothing else will. Usually, we are able to move on in a calmer manner so I can actually understand her needs and not feel frustrated and stressed myself. Sometimes she tells me she wants to cry, yell, or whine. When she tells me that, I trust that she knows what she is talking about.

Physical interventions such as these work well for our family, and Bella picks up on and internalizes them very quickly. I feel proud when I see her remembering these coping mechanisms and using them on her own.

Jeanette L.

Sometimes it is best to meet your child's basic needs first and address the behavior at another time, when he is in a better position to learn.

 Sometimes I put a thought on hold and talk about it later. For instance, one night my three-year-old threw her toothbrush. It wouldn't have helped to scold her when she threw it. She needed to go to sleep. I just picked it up for her.

In the morning, I said to her, "You were really tired last night. I felt angry when you threw the toothbrush. How can we do it differently tonight?"

Will she learn from the experience? Yes. Did she get away with something? No. We talked about it the next day.

Karen K.

Be real

Using gentle discipline doesn't mean you should never express a negative emotion to your child. It just means doing it respectfully whenever you can. You can communicate authentic displeasure and point out the consequences of behavior and still be respectful. This is all useful information for your child. Give yourself permission to use a firm "I mean business" tone with your child when the situation warrants it.

Playfulness speaks to children

Playfulness can cut through would-be power struggles.

 One time, I was driving home from gymnastics in the evening. My daughter spilled her water all over herself in the back seat. She was on the verge of hysterics and was insisting that I change her into dry clothes immediately. I was about to pull onto the freeway, had no dry clothes for her, and had nowhere to change her if I did. Also, I'd had a long day and was close to flipping out myself. I could taste the words, "Just shut up!" on my tongue.

From somewhere very deep, somewhere divine, I said something really random: "Well gee, Bonnie, if your wet leotard is bothering you, just take it off and throw it in the clothes dryer. There's a clothes dryer back there isn't there?"

She giggled. "No, mommy!"

"What? I know I put a clothes dryer back there. Well, if you can't find it, just hang your clothes on the line."

She giggled some more. "There's no clothesline back here, mommy!"

From there we went on to suggest more and more goofy, impossible solutions to the problem: buy something new at the clothing store in the back seat, order something new on the Internet, or sew something dry to wear. We were home before we knew it, giggling the whole way.

Catherine F.

Explain why

When a child asks "Why?" it may feel as if he is challenging you. When you are sure of your position, you do not want to get into a debate, defending the reasons behind your decision. But giving a clear explanation of why you are insisting on something can be important. Sometimes things that are obvious to an adult are not obvious to a small child.

 The situations that make me lose my cool the most are the ones when I have to ask her repeatedly to do or not do something. It is helpful to remember that explaining why can quickly halt the cycle.

Sarah M.

Slow down

Positive communication sometimes means calming yourself down and getting your thoughts together before you try to talk. It may help to take a deep breath and consider your options.

Improve your communication skills

Positive communication enhances connection and builds a cooperative atmosphere. Your skills will improve the more you practice communicating with your child with empathy and respect. It can also help to have good role models, such as your friends or your co-parent, to get new ideas for listening and speaking around difficult situations.

To build their skills in communicating with children, many parents turn to the classic book, *How to Talk So Kids Will Listen, and Listen So Kids Will Talk*, by Adele Faber and Elaine Mazlish. This book is full of suggestions for streamlining your speech with children so that you hit the main points in a way that children can best receive them.

Positive follow-through

There is a place for "no." Setting boundaries doesn't have to leave you feeling as though you're being mean. Often the most effective no's are the ones that have a yes attached to them. Try finding a way to say "yes" to something that your child can do instead of "no" to something you don't want him to do. Think of one door closing and others opening.

Emphasize what you want more of. Try to focus not on the unacceptable behavior, but on your child's positive alternatives.

Taking the time to think of a positive alternative for my daughter works much better than telling her what she shouldn't do. For example, saying "feet on the floor" gets quick results, while "do not climb on the table" gets none.

Replacing the words "don't touch" with "one finger touching" has made a big difference in many situations. This little trick first became useful when Bella, at 15 months, was entranced with the Christmas tree ornaments and was pulling things off the tree.

We were frustrated for days because no matter how many times we said "no" or redirected her, she just went right back and pulled off another ornament. Then we decided to show her how to touch with one finger. Every time she went for the tree, we repeated "one finger" while showing her how to touch with her index finger only. Much to our amazement, she understood after only a few tries. She was overjoyed to be able to explore the tree.

Jeanette L.

Finding a way to say "yes" is sometimes referred to as "redirecting." Take your child's needs or impulses as a cue, and think of a better way for your child to meet that same need.

With my nine-month-old daughter, redirection is often the key to eliminating problem behavior. If she wants to climb on the fireplace hearth, I redirect her to a safer, more appropriate place that she can climb, such as the couch or a pile of pillows. Patience certainly comes into play here. It can take several attempts to redirect her before she figures out that she's not going to be allowed to do something.

Carissa D.

> Take your child's needs or impulses as a cue, and think of a better way for your child to meet that same need.

Show your child how he can meet his need within the boundaries and many would-be power struggles disappear.

Recently at a playgroup, we had one craft table for adults and one for children. Gabriel went up to someone at the adult craft table and tried to use the supplies there. She said "no" very sternly and my son started to get upset. She was very stern with him and said, "I'm sorry that upsets you, but I said no." I could see she wasn't seeing the situation from a two-year-old's point of view.

He came running to me crying and I said to him, "What happened? Tell me what happened." And the other mom answered for him, "He's just mad because I said he couldn't have this."

So I asked Gabriel again, "Tell me what happened." He told me what he wanted and I simply said, "You can't have that, but there's a craft over here for you." He happily ran over to the children's craft table to do a craft. If the other mom had just pointed out what he could have, instead of what he couldn't, the whole situation could have been avoided.

Beth C.

Sometimes the alternative can be very different from the original idea.

Last night my daughter (almost 17 months) was having a breakdown over not being able to carry a glass. She did not want to carry her own cup but rather my glass. I said, "I know you want to carry mommy's glass but it is dangerous." She didn't really care and seemed to only want to carry the glass. So I said, "Instead of carrying the glass, would you like to play with ice?" She perked right up, we put some cubes into a bowl, and she played until they melted.

We totally changed the direction of what we were doing and she was still not allowed to carry the glass.

Valerie P.

Give choices. If your child is having trouble with a boundary, it may help to give him choices: "Do you want to clean up the blocks with your dump truck or should we have a race to see who can clean up the most?" "Do you want to do it now or after a snack?" "Do you want to put your shoes on by yourself or do you want me to help you?"

If you're trying to offer choices, make sure that the choices are real ones. Saying, "Do you want to clean up your toys right now or not go to the park?" could be more of a threat than a choice.

When/then. You can encourage your child to move forward by stating things positively. Instead of "Don't talk to me that way or I won't help you," you can say, "When you talk to me in a nice voice, I am happy to help you." "When you get your shoes on, we can take a walk."

Offer to help

The younger your child is, the more likely it is that he will need you to do more than use words to direct his actions. You may often need to physically help to get him moving in the right direction. When you can do this in a positive spirit, you win, because you see the result you'd hoped for. Your child also wins, because he meets your expectations without feeling coerced.

Ask your child to change his behavior. Be very specific: Instead of "No throwing sticks," say, "Please keep your stick low."

Tell him why: "Sticks can hurt people, and there are lots of kids around."

Let your child know that he can do it himself or you can help.

Go over and help. Remember: help feels helpful, not punitive.

 Let's say my son is grabbing things off of the counter. I might say: "I can help you look at those things. If you grab them off the counter, they (or you) might get hurt."

If he does not respond, I would go over and physically stop him from grabbing them while saying the same thing.

Amber S.

Giving help is great modeling, because it shows how to do the job and that the job is worth your effort, too.

 I keep in mind that children are great imitators. When I want them to do something such as picking up toys, or lying down to go to sleep, I start doing it myself. They almost always join in and quiet down.

Brooke S.

Problem-solving instead of power struggles

When there is a conflict between you and your child, it is easy to get into the mindset that you are right and he needs to get with the program. The more you can approach conflicts from a problem-solving perspective, the more you can avoid power struggles and strengthen your relationship.

Here are some key ways to remain your child's ally when facing conflict. Each one will be explored in more detail in this section.

Assume there is a reason. Assume that your child is trying to meet his needs in the best way he knows how at that time.

Empathize with your child: Using a caring voice, label his emotion: "You're feeling—"

Identify your child's needs. What need is motivating your child in this situation?

Get creative. How can you work with your needs and your child's to move forward together?

Assume there is a reason

A powerful thing you can do to solve problems with your child is to step out of your own shoes and imagine his perspective.

Don't take his behavior personally. Society encourages parents to judge children's behavior and even to take it personally.

This sets parents up for a battle with their children. Even when a child is directing negativity at you, you can look below it for a deeper cause. There is something amiss that is causing this reaction—and that is your connecting point.

Initially I reacted to my child's misbehavior as if it was more about me than about him. "Why are you making me so mad?" "What will others think of me as a parent when he misbehaves?" and "He's testing me." When I examined these reactions more closely, I realized they were based on a set of inherited beliefs about children and parents that I no longer agree with.

Lisa S.

What feelings arise in you when you are at odds with your child?

I admit to feeling as if my daughter has won if I don't get her to do exactly what I want her to. And that's about me. I don't feel like I'm winning very much at the moment. I think I need to work on my self-esteem and valuing myself and what I do.

Kirsty C.

Taking negativity personally does not feel good. It can be a relief when you can let that go.

I do most of my trying-to-figure-her-out thinking in quiet times, not when we are interacting. But the second she does something that's bugging me, I start telling myself that my daughter (16 months) is not intentionally trying to work against me.

Somehow, knowing that she is not trying to work against me makes it better, even as she is having a tantrum in a slobbery heap on the floor because I am not going to let her dump her frozen peas on the kitchen floor for the third time. It's not less aggravating, just easier not to get angry about it.

Jen M.

By extending the benefit of the doubt to your child, you

begin to see that you are two imperfect but decent humans who are, together, in a bit of a pickle. This is a productive starting point.

Look for a positive intent. However challenging the behavior, if your child could access a better option he probably would. It is your job to support your child in that developmental process. For instance, a child who is hitting may be trying to get his anger out, an intention you can validate, but one for which he will need better options.

Your child's point of view has its own validity, indeed its own internal logic. Sometimes understanding your children's reasoning can actually lead you to re-evaluate your own priorities in the moment.

 Sometimes, whatever my daughter is doing is more important than what I think she should be doing (for example, cleaning up) even if it doesn't look important to me. Play is work for kids that age.

Hannah T.

 We encourage "cooperation," and not just from our daughter, but from all of us equally. If our three-year-old really doesn't want to do something, I am teaching her to respectfully refuse. Sometimes she has a really good reason for refusing and even I don't want her to do it anymore!

Rebecca K.

Empathize with your child

Emotions can be easier to relate to than difficult behavior, and they can give you new insight in how to support your child. Identify the emotion behind your child's behavior. Say it, either out loud ("You're frustrated!") or to yourself ("She's screaming because she's frustrated").

Figuring it out. An older child can tell you how he feels. With

> By extending the benefit of the doubt to your child, you begin to see that you are two imperfect but decent humans who are, together, in a bit of a pickle.

a young toddler, you may need to read his nonverbal cues.

 The other day, my daughter refused to go through a greenhouse. I asked several questions before I hit upon, "Does this scare you?" and she said, "Yes! Plant scary!"

Nancy W.

Some families find that "baby signs" make communication easier in the pre-talking stage.

 Our daughter learned many baby signs before she could talk, so she rarely got frustrated that she couldn't express herself. She could sign for "nurse," "eat," "water," more," and lots of animals, but the most useful sign at that age was "all done." When she was done in the high chair, she could sign "all done" and we'd get her out. She didn't have to throw food before we noticed that she was through.

The benefits of signing hit home with me one day when I took 14-month-old Julia to a puppet show at the library. As we approached the hour mark, Julia looked at me and signed "all done." I signed it back to her, neither of us making a sound, to make sure that I "heard" her right, and she nodded yes. So we quietly got up and left without a tantrum, without interrupting the play, without making a scene, both of us happy as could be that we got to watch the puppet show.

Karen K.

Sometimes, your own reactions may give you the clue you need.

 I started paying attention to my own reactions to things my son did, and then responding to him as if he were feeling the same way I was. Much of the time, the problem ceased instantly!

If he was having a tantrum and was completely out of control, I would feel scared, powerless, frustrated, and angry. Turning that knowledge his way, I could offer him comfort, opportunity, commiseration, and support.

Often, the most powerful feeling he had was simple

frustration. He wasn't able to do what he wanted (either physically or due to some safety rule he didn't comprehend), or he wasn't able to communicate what he needed. Just commiserating with that—letting him know that I understood how hard it could be, that it didn't seem fair, that it would make me want to scream, too—was enough to help him grapple with his feelings. It also comforted him to understand that other people have these feelings, too—even grownups.

Heather P.

Empathy can be the solution. Sometimes, your child may just need your empathy as he struggles with his emotions, and no further problem-solving is required.

 My daughter was about three-and-a-half and my son was an infant. My husband had gone to bed early. Both children were still awake and it was getting late for all of us. I was tired and definitely not at my best for patience and understanding. I think I had just nursed my son, Cole, to sleep and suggested to Accalia that we all head to bed.

She made it up to the top of the stairs and suddenly fell down on the ground screaming and kicking. I was able to get from her that she wanted Daddy to read her a story or take her to bed, which wasn't possible since he had long since fallen asleep. Accalia kept kicking and screaming, but I managed to get her back downstairs where I just sat with her until she grew quiet. Then we were able to talk a little about how she was feeling: "You must be very tired, and you feel very sad that Daddy isn't awake to read you a story and carry you to bed."

It was such a powerful moment for me especially because I was able to ride the rage of her meltdown with her while remaining calm myself. Then I could clearly see that she just wanted someone to be right there with her while she got her emotions out. The last thing she needed was someone to tell her to be quiet or to send her away.

Amy N.

There is something positive about staying calm in the face of chaos. We can really set the tone for our children, holding a calm space for them to return to when they are ready.

Deeper feelings. When dealing with anger, try to get at the underlying feelings. Anger tends to come after a more vulnerable emotion, such as fear, sadness, powerlessness, or hurt feelings. An angry child who pushes another child might also feel lonely or left out, unable to connect with the other child. Being empathetic includes identifying and working with these soft and tender feelings as well as the loud and angry ones.

Empathy gives you a powerful connecting point, even when you are the target of your child's intense emotions.

 The other day, my six-year-old was mad about something, and was making ultimatums and demands and basically not speaking at all nicely to me. I commented that he seemed really upset and asked if he wanted to snuggle on the couch. His aggression melted as we snuggled.

After empathizing with his feelings, and apologizing for my part of the conflict, I was able to share how I felt when he spoke to me that way. I told him that when I was talked to disrespectfully, it made me not want to do what he needed because I was angry about how I was being treated. He gave me a big hug and said he would try to talk to me respectfully the next time even if he was mad. He seemed to understand more than he had at other times, when I've tried to get my point across in the moment of conflict.

Lisa S.

Identify your child's needs

Children, like adults, are always trying to meet their needs. A big part of discipline is identifying what those needs are and helping your child find positive and effective ways of meeting them.

Ask yourself:

- What need is my child meeting through this behavior?

- How can I support my child in getting this need met in a way that works better for everyone involved?

- What does my child need from me right now?

Look for basic needs, too, lurking below the subject-at-hand: does your child need to eat, to go to sleep, to explore, to connect? If your child's well-being is lagging, behavior is likely to be rough until the underlying need is met.

> When my daughter deliberately acts inappropriately, that is her way of telling me that something is wrong in her world. She has a need. She feels anxious, bored, tired, hungry, or something. When she feels right, she acts right. When she acts inappropriately, I become a detective. What is going on here?
>
> *Rebecca K.*

Get creative!

Creativity takes energy, and sometimes we parents are too tired, overwhelmed, or stressed to think out of the box. But when we do have just enough mental bounce, problem-solving can be such a welcome way to avoid power struggles. Think of problem-solving as an option you can use when you're up for it. The more practice you—and your child—get with it, the more easily it will come.

Problem-solving helps parents meet goals such as helping children better understand their worlds, keeping the lines of communication open, and helping children learn to deal with such things as anger, disappointment, or sharing.

Some basic steps to problem-solving are:

- Identify the problem.

- Think of several possible solutions.

- Try a solution that sounds good to everyone.

- Evaluate the results.

Problem-solving is a great skill to model. Just about everyone can use some practice with it and our children give us plenty of opportunities. Every time we brainstorm with our children to find mutually agreeable solutions, we are giving them a precious gift. What better way to teach problem-solving to our children than to give them lots of practice in solving problems that they care about?

 I very much want a thinking child. We have worked out a strategy for this that so far seems to be working for our two-and-a-half-year-old daughter.

First, we lay the groundwork. We think aloud a lot so that she has a model of how problems are resolved. And we talk her through resolutions to her problems, such as getting her shoes and socks off or doing a puzzle.

Second, when she gets frustrated or angry, we get down to her level and help her tell us what is wrong. Then we repeat back to her what is bothering her without any judgment, just showing that we are listening. Then we make a suggestion for a solution. Sometimes she likes the solution, sometimes she makes her own solutions, and sometimes we go through several potential solutions until we find the right one.

Finally, we make it a point to notice her attempts to problem-solve on her own and encourage it. Even when the attempts are annoying or destructive, we praise the attempt and then go back to talking about what is wrong and helping her think of solutions. Positive feedback goes a long way.

Nicole M.

> Bringing your child onto the problem-solving team means you don't have to have all the answers.

It may take more time for you to bring your child into the process, but what a pay-off down the line, when he becomes an active problem-solver in his own right. And bringing your child onto the problem-solving team means you don't have to have all the answers. This can be a relief to you—and empowering to your child.

 Often, the solution to a given problem is not our own, but our children's. My son came up with the list of things that need to be done before he goes to bed, and he's also the one who came up with the idea of giving him a timer with a sweep hand so he could see how much time was left to accomplish those tasks. We were thinking of approaches that were far more radical. However, my husband remembered that our son had to buy in, too, or it wouldn't work as well. So, we asked him. And we were impressed, and we tried it, and it helped a lot. Not perfect, but enough improvement so that we no longer reach our limits every night.

So we really have a team of disciplinarians that includes our children, and their ideas about what will work, and what will not. The bonus is that if they choose the consequence or solution, and it doesn't work out, they're far more accepting of trying our solution the next time. We all get to take a crack at a difficult problem.

I suspect we're teaching them all sorts of things about problem-solving that we're not focused on, but which we hope will serve them well later.

Heather P.

Sometimes all it takes is loosening up your thinking.

I was feeling as if I had too much to do the other day. I wanted to put laundry in, make a phone call—the usual stuff. I had just brought in the mail with my three-year-old and toddler. There was a pile of catalogs I wasn't planning to even look at. They were headed for the recycling bin. A light bulb went off. I asked Julia if she and Anna would like to tear the catalogs into tiny pieces. She looked at me as if I was crazy. "Really? We can do that?" They spent an hour making catalog bouquets. Meanwhile I did what I needed to do. I felt good watching them having so much fun.

Karen K.

Sometimes your role is simply to be the cheerleader!

When my three-year-old is playing with a friend and they are having trouble sharing or negotiating about something, I try to interject some confidence into the situation. The other day Julia and River were at the park together and from what his mom and I could gather from afar, they were fighting over who would take a particular stick home.

We observed until it was clear that they needed help. I said, "You two are having a challenging time with this stick. I bet you can come up with some ideas about how to solve the problem."

Within seconds they were firing off ideas. "We could break it in half. We could find another one, a big one, a medium one, and a small one. I can have this one, you can have that one."

They felt pleased with themselves for finding a solution, and for being able to bring home some nice sticks.

As Julia and her friends get older, I notice that they're able to solve more and more problems on their own, with fewer interjections from parents. We parents feel as if some of that hard work of helping our kids in social situations is paying off!

Karen K.

Sometimes it's just "No"

This book is full of examples of parents finding ways to compromise, negotiate, or otherwise find win-win solutions when facing conflicting needs with their children. It can be helpful to see other parents using creativity and empathy to find mutually agreeable solutions to the various differences or problems that arise.

But it is important to bear in mind that there is a place for a firm "no," the kind without negotiation or fun alternatives, and then helping your child move on.

"No" is not a bad word, even to empathetic and respectful parents. The balance of yes's and no's will shift as your baby grows into a child.

> There is a place for a firm "no," the kind without negotiation or fun alternatives.

 When Meara was a baby, she was all needs and I was all "yes" if at all possible. Now, as a four-year-old, she is mature enough to understand and tolerate more expectations of her—that she not only receives, but gives as well. And because I have said "yes" to her needs and desires when possible (versus saying "no" arbitrarily or frequently just to exert control as a parent), I believe that she feels a positive foundation of trust in our relationship. I think that this has contributed to her accepting limits and "no's" more flexibly and easily.

Maureen C.

Carefully chosen non-negotiable boundaries, where necessary, are good for parent and child alike. The previous chapter explored the value of clear rules and guidelines for your child to follow. Placing boundaries around your child's options helps keep your child from harming himself, others, or property. "No" can also help your child balance his needs with other people's needs, a valuable lesson.

As you decide how to respond to your child's behavior or requests, you will need to weigh things that he may not be fully ready to take into account. Only you can judge whether the situation calls for a firm "no" (with support for your child in moving on) or more give-and-take. It will depend in large part on how you judge the situation at hand, for all concerned.

Taking others' needs into account

Sometimes a simple "no," with an explanation, is in the best interest of others. Children are designed to think of their own self-interest first, and it is important for parents to respect that as developmentally appropriate, even as limits are set. In some cases by saying "no" you are helping your child avoid being inconsiderate to others and you are giving him an opportunity to see his desires in a larger context.

 My five-year-old daughter has asked for a puppy but I said no. It wouldn't be fair to bring an animal into our family right now when we wouldn't be able to give it the best conditions or meet its need for space and a bit of freedom.

By setting firm boundaries in situations such as this, I've given Accalia the chance to think about how her actions may affect other people or things and how we can't just consider ourselves in many decisions. Empathy is something that Accalia has started to naturally develop the older she becomes, but these examples of "no" also help her consciously consider the effects of a decision.

Amy N.

Honoring family priorities

As a family member, your child will sometimes need to accommodate family priorities.

Sometimes I need to get an errand done with her, and she says she does not want to or that she will be bored. I remind her that sometimes we have to do things for our family that we don't want to do, because these things have to be done.

Maureen C.

Knowing your own limits

Sometimes your personal needs and desires will conflict with your child's, and you will need to decide if a firm boundary would be best. You are in a relationship with your child, and as such, you need to make sure there is give and take on both sides. You will also want to make sure you are taking care of yourself for the long haul. Sometimes saying "no" is a way for you to honor your own limits (and we all have limits!), to conserve your energy, or to make it possible for you to keep the day going smoothly in other ways.

> Sometimes saying "no" is a way for you to honor your own limits.

 I may say "No" if I'm too tired to tell her a story when the lights go out. I may tell her that I can't play with her if I need to cook, make a phone call, or otherwise be engaged. I tell her what I have to do, and that I can play later. If she wants me to play tag or play with her at the playground, and I don't want to, I say "no" and encourage her to ask her friends or to do something else on the play structure.

Maureen C.

Saying "no" in order to take care of your own needs is not just for you; it provides many benefits to your child. It's a great thing to model for your child; you want her to be able to communicate her needs now and as an adult. It helps sustain you, lest you get burned out or resentful from too much giving. When you give yourself permission to say "no" when you need to, you make it much easier to say an enthusiastic "yes" when you are truly up for it.

We have a big mud pit in our back yard. Most days I am more than happy to allow the kids to get down and dirty: mud in their hair, mud all over everything—just plain mud fun!

But some days I am just not up for the aftermath, which is a bath and lots of cleanup. I am having terrible reflux with this pregnancy and leaning over the tub or shower and trying to get them clean is very hard for me.

So on my bad reflux days I declare a "no mud day." Sometimes the kids are sad and upset about it, but they accept it, and we do something else. In fact now before they go outside they ask if it is a "mud day" or a "no mud day."

Gracinha O.

Separating your child's needs from his wants

Sometimes a firm "no," rather than negotiation or compromise, is in the best interest of your child in ways he simply cannot see. As the parent, you may be able to discern your child's underlying need below the request he is making. His wants may not be in line with his true needs.

 When I can see that Clio (age three) is really tired and needs to nap, I have to say "no" to her many requests for things that will only help to distract her and keep her up longer (for example, snacks or starting a painting). In fact, when the requests start coming in abundance, then I know it's naptime.

This upsets her in the short term, but I know it's really what she needs in the long term. It's one of the fairly rare times when there's little room for negotiation.

Cheri R.

In some cases, your child may be relying on you to say "no," even if she is not conscious of it.

 I remember when I was eight and at my first overnight camp, the director offered me a chance to stay for another session at half price, since it wasn't full. With him standing there, I called my parents and asked. Part of me really wanted to stay, because we were having lots of fun, but I had been away from home a while and I think a bigger (but quieter) part of me wanted to go home. I protested loudly when my parents said "no," but once I saw them, I was relieved and happy to be back at home.

Amy M.

When there's no time

One of the classic times for a firm "no" is when you are on a schedule. You will want to make it as easy as possible for your child to be himself and still meet the schedule. But in the process, "no" may still come up a lot, because children do not tend to think of time in the same way we do. The more open your schedule is, the less you will need to invoke the time-crunch "no."

I say "no" a lot less frequently now that we're home schooling. "Yes, you can help me make the waffles this morning," as opposed to "No! We have to hurry!"

Missy C.

Testing limits

Sometimes your child may test limits. His behavior suggests he wants you to bend, but in reality, he's doing research: he wants to see where the limit is. Affirming limits can be reassuring to him. Although it may sound like fun to get everything you want, in practice such a thing is likely to be scary, because it suggests there is no caretaking adult making careful choices in the child's best interest. If you discern that your child is testing limits rather than expressing a need, a simple "no" can be just the thing.

Sometimes using a sense of humor when saying "no" to my four-year-old can help: "What? Another video! You're joking!" said in a silly voice, when I know that she knows she is trying to push the limit.

Maureen C.

When a simple "No" will do

Learning when to deny a child's request requires balance. You will get a feel for when a simple "no" will do, and when something more elaborate is called for.

I try to negotiate some things, but I also know that sometimes my child is just testing to see if there are limits. I think setting limits is good for kids. When my three-year-old asks for something she knows she's not going to get (stuff at the store, or whatever), a simple "no, honey" or "not today" is just fine with both of us.

The same is true around behavior boundaries. In public, a stern mommy look or quick "no" to get behavior back in line is just the response to testing that she's actually looking for.

I feel it is my job to provide structure and consistency, but that I do not always need to be clever and fun about it. It's a matter of balance.

Karen K.

You can't always make your child happy

And indeed, it's not your job to try.

Of course, you will do well to be as open as you can to your child's desires and emotions and to take them into consideration. But remember that gentle discipline is not fundamentally about making your child happy. Gentle discipline is not a ticket to a smooth and carefree family life, in which both parent and child co-exist in perfect harmony and contentment. On the contrary, being empathic to your child often means giving him permission to have strong emotions. Sometimes it means holding him while he cries. If your child is upset, it does not mean you have failed him. Life is like this sometimes.

> Gentle discipline is *not* a ticket to a smooth and carefree family life, in which both parent and child co-exist in perfect harmony and contentment.

I've had to realize that I am not always going to be able to make my child happy. Just because she is unhappy doesn't mean I'm punishing her. She may feel upset and angry, and that's okay.

Meghan S.

All of us are confronted at one time or another with the clash between reality and our desires. Parenting brings with it a range of emotions, including anger, disappointment, and sadness. It is not our children's job to spare us these emotions by behaving in just the right way. Similarly, it is not your job to spare your child the anger, disappointment, and sadness that come with his own clashes with reality—even when that reality is your own limitations and needs.

When your child is unhappy, it is important to validate his feelings and support him.

 Saying no when I need to has taught me better how to accept and tolerate (four-year-old) Meara's expression of intense negative feelings when she does not get what she wants. Her reaction to

---

Perseverance pays off!

It is so easy to be put off by negative behavior and miss an opportunity to really connect with your hurting child. Sometimes you may need to regroup and come back again.

It is the second week of school and my six-year-old daughter is showing resistance to getting ready to go to school. I am not sure why. I spend some time just sitting with her in my lap and trying to help her just be and connect with me, but she seems distant. She is not making eye contact and not really wanting to have a conversation. I ask her to get dressed, but she doesn't. I offer to help, but she resists that.

Time ticks on and we are now going to be late. I tell her if we do not leave this minute we will be late, but she is still not motivated. Usually these sorts of prompts

are all she needs. Something is wrong, only I am not sure what. I am not feeling connected to her or able to help her. After my, "You are now late," prompt, she sits on the floor of her room and starts to throw toys at the drawers. "Hey, no throwing toys!" I say. Intellectually I know that saying not to do something is not as effective as saying what you would like someone to do. Plus since I am having trouble connecting with her this morning, it is unlikely that she will want to do what I ask. I have forgotten all this in the moment.

She ignores me and throws another toy. Now that has pushed my anger button and before I stop to think about why, I yell very loudly, "Kia, no throwing toys!"

Then I leave the room, because when I am angry I am not parenting the way I would like. I need a few moments to collect myself. I feel frustrated and remorseful that I didn't handle the situation differently.

I can tell that by the change in sound

these no's ranges from acceptance to objections to screaming in protest. I try to acknowledge her feelings no matter
how she expresses them.

It helps for me to remember that I myself don't like
not getting what I want, but that I learned early on to
squelch or internalize the resulting bad feelings. Unlike
me, she expresses them, at her own developmental level.

Maureen C.

Be on the look-out for the temptation to make his feelings go
away, either by convincing him that you are right, by telling
him "Cheer up" or "Don't cry," by apologizing for his feelings,
or by automatically trying to fix the situation to restore harmony. Your child has a right to his feelings. Let your child know
that it's okay to strongly dislike what is happening to him, either

coming from her room she has withdrawn
to hide in her dress-up clothes box. Not
only have I not been able to help her, I
have caused her to withdraw and sulk.
Now I feel like a horrible mother.

But wait! I know I am not a horrible
mother, and that sort of judgmental self-
talk doesn't help me. What I need is a little
empathy for myself. I just blew it for a
moment, but why?

So first I focus on my feelings. I am
worried that she is not happy at a new
school and with a new teacher and I feel
anxious that we are late. So I tell myself I
am worried and anxious and it is difficult
to help my daughter under the pressure of
time. I realize that if I had taken the time
to explain this to her I probably would not
have felt so angry. I also acknowledge that
I was thinking that the toy throwing is
something she should not be doing. She is
too old for such silly behavior, but I realize
I am judging her rather than trying to
understand why she would be doing that.

I think to myself. "I really need to just

connect with her right now" and go find
her.

" Kia?" She is hiding. I get as close as
I can to her. "Um, just now when I raised
my voice really loud . . ." I think she is listening, but I can't see her face yet. "I am
sad that I was not able to understand what
you are needing this morning. Will you
come out and talk to me?" She does. "I
want to tell you that I am worried that you
are not happy at school and I am getting
anxious about being late."

Something changes. All of a sudden,
she starts to tell me how she is not happy
at school. I listen and then say, "Oh, you
are being asked to do lots of seat work.
Your hand is getting sore. You feel lots of
pressure to do the work." Now I understand! And understanding feels wonderful! I tell her that I will discuss this with
her teacher this morning. Then she gets
ready to go, much to my relief.

Katrina K.

that he wants eggs and you have none, or that he wants you to read a book and you have to make dinner first. Your child's sadness, frustration, or anger are feelings, not attacks on you or your choices.

If you find yourself trying to stop your child from feeling his sad or angry feelings, you may want to try telling yourself: "I don't have to do that. It is okay for my child feel his feelings."

 Sometimes, my respecting my own needs (while still trying to meet as much of his as possible) means my child is unhappy. (And vice versa!) It's an odd evolution. Now that he is seven, his needs aren't always the most primary ones, yet our ability to find ways to meet both of our needs at the same time has increased. Yet, doesn't he have a right to feel emotions other than happiness?

When I try to convince him to see things my way (e.g., the importance of my needs), often what I'm really doing is trying to change how he feels. When I step back, I realize this sends the message that he is responsible for my feelings and I'm responsible for his.

To teach my child to manage his emotions, I need to supportively help him understand his feelings instead of protecting him from them.

Lisa S.

Above all, you want to send a message that emotions are valid, safe, and that your child can move through them.

 Children are still inexperienced at dealing with emotions. Sometimes all I can do is be with my son while he feels sad, angry, or frustrated and try to help him learn how to deal with these things. Being three is difficult. He's not a baby and not quite big. He is navigating new territory and needs a lot of extra patience and understanding.

Laurie D.W.

It's not all or nothing!

This chapter has explored some positive, practical ways to maintain boundaries with children. In real life, the baby's diaper may need changing, you may need to make lunch, and you may just plain crave a moment on the couch with your feet up. Such is the nitty-gritty reality of a parenting day!

This is a good time to remember that gentle discipline is not all or nothing.

Gentle discipline is easiest when you are feeling grounded and relaxed. That's when you are most likely to have the presence of mind to be creative, compassionate, patient, resilient, and spontaneous. So if you are feeling discouraged, you need to be attentive to your own well-being (more on this in Chapter 8.), and cut yourself some slack in the meantime.

Remember that gentle discipline serves you as much as your child. It can take energy and presence of mind to use it, especially when you are still getting used to it. However, when you can find an empathic and respectful response, you save yourself the energy and headache of power struggles. You also get the satisfaction of solving the real problem, rather than just the behavioral symptoms.

Gentle discipline is not another thing you "should" be doing, but a tool you can use when you're up for it, to work for you as a parent, to make life easier and happier for both you and your child.

And above all, if you find yourself parenting in a less positive way for an hour, a day, a month, take it in stride. Parenting has its rhythms. Don't worry. You will have many opportunities for more positive responses!

Chapter 6

Your Bag of Tricks

The last chapter looked at some of the main tools for responding positively when you are faced with a difficulty. This chapter will look more closely at related issues such as finding the balance between consistency and flexibility, where comfort and play fit into conflicts, how to evaluate a new technique, and how to break a negative behavior spiral. It will offer you more tips and ideas for responding positively.

"No. I mean Yes!"

Receiving consistent messages from parents can help a child feel her world is predictable and therefore safe. But being empathic and respectful as a parent sometimes means you change your mind. Consistency for its own sake is meaningless and can box you and your child in. Parents need to find a comfortable balance between consistency and flexibility. Gentle discipline works best when it is real and responsive, not when it is ruled by some ideal of consistency or a fear that if you bend at all then all is lost.

Many parents find that being consistent involves:

- Getting beyond the automatic "no,"

- Making conscious choices in the first place as much as possible,

- Being open to observations about what is working and what is not, and

- Being prepared to make a course correction as needed.

Weaning ourselves from automatic No's

Sometimes, it's easier to say "no" than to think a situation through. Children have a way of coming up with ideas parents wouldn't have thought of, and it's easy to miss the opportunity to stop and consider what they are saying. Sometimes, parents are focused on another activity, and find it hard to shift their concentration to a child's request. Society seems to train parents to say "no" more often than not.

As you grow into parenting you may find that automatic no's are often arbitrary, and even counter-productive for all involved.

 When I first came to gentle discipline, I spent a lot of time going, "Wait, Mommy's crazy! Of course you can do that!" Until I stopped doing the knee-jerk "No!" to every silly harmless thing. I can see in the past year since I've changed this around, how much easier it is on all of us.

Betsy S.

When you are distracted, you may say "no" without thinking. Sometimes your child's reaction gives you pause to realize that saying "yes" would really work better.

 This morning my daughter (22 months) asked me to read her a story, but I was distracted by leaving for work and said "No, honey, mama has to go to work." She began to get upset. I hate leaving her when she is upset. So I told her, "Okay, honey, I'll read you one story and then mama has to go to work."

Then I heard this voice in my head, saying, "You're wimpy. You're changing your mind because she got upset. You are undermining your own authority!" But it just didn't feel right to leave her upset when I had enough time to spare a couple of minutes, and I was certain that she would then be fine with me going.

So I sat with her, read a short book, and she very happily kissed me goodbye and went to play with something else. I know I did the right thing by changing my mind.

Mariah W.

Anytime a child catches you making too hasty an answer, you have an opportunity to start over with more thought and care. It's like flexibility training for your brain.

 My mother once said she could always tell the difference between people who had children and people who didn't—the ones that didn't had very little flexibility and the ones that did knew how to compromise and bend better. I know that's absolutely true of me since I had my daughter.

Jessica K.

The key to consistency

Being consistent in parenting starts with making conscious choices in the first place as much as possible. Take the time to choose actions and words that you believe will be effective.

I try to say what I mean the first time as much as possible. I do this by trying not to say anything until I can calculate the consequences

> Take the time to choose actions and words that you believe will be effective.

for me of asking my child to do or not do something. I also say, "Let me think about that," more often. We try to say, "Yes," to as many things as possible. We've also started involving her in the solutions and negotiations. It helps when she gets to have an opinion first. My daughter says, "Mama, I've got a deal for you!" I see this as a great type of compromise. We're both looking for the win/win solution and it's nice to see her including my wants into hers.

Hannah S.

It's no mystery why this can be hard for parents a lot of the time. Many of us struggle with being distracted, being too busy, and moving too quickly. So if you find yourself getting into a muddle, take this to mean that you are probably overwhelmed at the moment. Slow down if you can. Is there some task or concern you are pursuing that you could eliminate or delay? Sometimes you may miss opportunities to take one thing at a time and go more at your child's pace.

The key to flexibility

Being flexible starts with keeping your eyes open to the evidence before you. Sometimes you need to adjust your own ideas and expectations in order to be flexible and responsive. It's a big part of being attached and in tune with your child. Exercise flexibility before saying anything definitive. Ask questions and get a sense of your child's side of the equation. It will help you to empathize with her point of view and it will give you valuable time to think about what to do.

Occasionally it really is best to switch gears.

 It's important to me to be sensitive to my children's needs, which are not always the same. Sometimes I can't really tell how they are feeling until they react to my first answer.

My five-year-old and four-year-old frequently ask if I will put them to bed instead of Daddy, but sometimes they are quite happy if he goes up instead of me. Sometimes they are still upset, in which case I will go up. I am sure my parents would criticize that. But it feels appropriate to me.

Sometimes I tell them they can't have a snack because it's going to be dinnertime soon. If they are very hungry, they ask again and then I usually find something to help them wait.

Katherine Q.

Remember to take in all the evidence before you change your mind. Just because your child objects, that certainly does not automatically mean that you have made the wrong choice.

 My husband and I took our kids to the park the other evening. After we had been there a little while, our son (three years old) threw a rock. Not at anyone, but it's behavior we don't allow. I told him if he threw a rock again, we'd have to leave. He threw another rock. When my husband went to pick him up to take him to the car, he put his arms up in the air and did not object at all. He was ready to go home and didn't know how to tell us that except to do something that wasn't allowed. In this case, our son was relying on us to be consistent so that we could meet his needs.

Brenda E.

What will I be teaching her if I change my mind?

Not being the parent who is "always right" can actually help you teach valuable lessons to your child.

 My five-year-old daughter sometimes calls me on it when I say "no" to something that really isn't that big a deal: "Mommy that is not a good reason."

She isn't just being bratty; sometimes she's right. If I am wrong, I will say so.

I want her to learn that everyone makes mistakes. Being stubborn just because, "I'm the mom and that's why, doesn't make sense. I want her to know how to stand up for herself and to see that it is okay to admit it when we are wrong.

She has a real knack for keeping me real and honest.

Mara A.

By contrast, when you stick to your first answer despite evidence that it's not for the best, you detach yourself from your child and your better judgment. What a recipe for pointless power struggles!

I see a big problem with frequently following through for the sake of following through. I've seen how it deteriorates into a power struggle in a matter of seconds.

Hannah S.

Finding the balance

As with everything else with parenting, there's no clear right or wrong line between flexibility and consistency. The more grounded and present you are, the more likely you are to strike a productive balance that works for your family.

"Is this for me?" Evaluating a new technique

Your child and you keep coming up against the same old problem and your same old responses aren't helping. You may brainstorm with a friend or co-parent, or you may turn to a book for new ideas. As you consider a new approach to a current problem, you may ask yourself such questions as:

- Is this technique age-appropriate?
- Does this technique fit with my child's developmental level and individual style?
- How does this technique affect my relationship with my child?
- Do I feel respectful of my child as I do it?
- Does this help solve the problem?
- Can I be consistent in applying this technique?

At its core, gentle discipline is about treating children as we wish to be treated. As you go along, you will most likely develop your own intuitive way of assessing new options.

If an option feels good and right, doesn't make me feel guilty or ashamed, doesn't make me feel unkind or thoughtless, then it is probably a good tool. That doesn't mean it will work, necessarily, but it is at least worth trying.

As my son has gotten older (he's now seven), I have found that discussing the discipline options with him is a good way to evaluate them.

Heather P.

Trial period. Sometimes trying something new involves an adjustment period during which it still feels awkward. If that happens, you may benefit from the input of someone who has found it useful. But if the new method doesn't begin to show signs of becoming a comfortable fit, it may be time to leave it behind.

Usually, if something isn't working, the first thing I check is not the approach itself, but my consistency in use. It may well be a perfectly fine approach, but if I'm not staying disciplined in my use of it, then it isn't going to work. My first step, then, is being consistent for three days, really paying close attention to that. If that doesn't do it, then yes, a change is needed. If it does begin to work better, then no change is required–except from me.

Heather P.

One size does not fit all! Remember, every child and every parent is different, so what works beautifully for one family may be wrong for yours. When parents compare notes about the latest technique touted in the media, you are likely to hear a range of reactions. Typically, one swears by it, another tells of how it went awry with his or her child, another found it useful to get through rough spots but prefers other methods generally, and yet another finds it philo-

A hug after hitting?

Your child hits her brother, and then she bursts into tears and wants a hug from you. When you are practicing gentle discipline, comforting can always be an option, because your intention is not to be your child's adversary, nor to make your child feel bad. Connection between parent and child is integral to gentle discipline.

> I have a "no exceptions" rule to being asked for a hug: I never want to turn down any of my children for wanting a hug. It doesn't matter what took place three seconds beforehand, whether they told me they hate me or they kicked the dog. When they ask for that hug, they are asking for a connection when they need it badly.
>
> *Jessica K.*

Comforting definitely seems to make the message sink in deeper, in my experience. When I lovingly correct my daughter (age two), empathize with her reaction, help her identify her feelings, and comfort her however she needs it (and often that involves nursing), she seems much more receptive to the discipline and less likely to repeat the offense. When I used to try and just ignore the reaction completely, my daughter definitely acted out more and got more upset.

Sonia M.

Should I force an apology?

It is hard to watch your child hurt someone else. If you are the target, you may be hurt and angry yourself. If your baby is the target, you may feel outraged and passionately protective. If another child is the target, you may feel embarrassed by your child's behavior and concerned for the hurt child. It can be tempting to make your child say he is sorry.

You do want your child to learn that hurting others is wrong. You want him to feel for the other person, and to experience a healthy remorse. You can nurture these reactions in your child, but you can never force him to learn or feel anything on command. Perhaps you have had occasion to hear a child bark out, "sorry," full of resentment at being forced. Or perhaps you have seen a child push another child, realize that an adult witnessed it, and quickly utter a nonchalant, "sorry," before moving on. These hollow apologies are not helpful to anyone.

To encourage empathy, you might say, "Look how Michael is crying. He was playing with that toy. He looks so disappointed to have it taken away." Be sure you're saying it gently, with compassion for both children. Avoid laying on the guilt. That can engender more resentment and shame, rather than creating an opening for compassion. (And remember to say you're sorry whenever you hurt your child, since modeling is such a powerful discipline method.)

If your child is reluctant to apologize, there are many ways he can show concern for the other person without saying "I'm sorry." Your child could give the other person a gentle touch, help him brush off, or bring him a cup of water. Your child could say, "Are you okay?" "I wish I didn't do that." Or "Next time I'll be more careful." He may want to talk about the problem that he was trying to solve by his actions, providing the opportunity to consider better options.

> We never insist that three-year-old Julia say she's sorry, but we do insist that she give thought to how she could correct a situation. For example, we might say: "Anna got hurt. How can we make her feel better? What could we do differently next time?"
>
> *Karen K.*

sophically problematic. Each of these parents is right, for his or her family.

Steer by your parenting goals. Parents are inundated with so many messages about what they should be doing as parents and how their children should be acting. To stay grounded in the face of your various parenting challenges, you need to have a clear idea of what you are trying to do. Only then can you find the best way to do it.

I get frustrated with the generally accepted notion that my job is to make my daughter into a good child. Most people I encounter are surprised and more than a little perplexed by the fact that I care very little about raising a child to fit into the mainstream mold of how a child should behave.

My focus is on building a framework for the type of internal discipline that will serve her well through her life. So I try not to worry too much about whether she has a tantrum at the mall or whines for a toy. I deal with those situations of course, one at a time as they occur. But I feel that every parenting problem is actually an opportunity for teaching and learning (not just on Bella's part, but most assuredly on mine as well).

At each uncomfortable crossroads we have reached on this parenting journey, I try to ask myself whether my reactions are empowering my daughter to develop a sense of internal discipline. Later in life, when the stakes are much higher, that is what will really matter.

My main goal is to lay the groundwork for a child who can think outside the box, who knows that not all situations have a cookie-cutter solution, and who expects to be respected and to have her voice heard. I actually want my children to question authority. Yes, even mine.

Jeanette L.

Beware of hype

 To me, parenting is all about keeping doors open and relationships open. So many parenting techniques close doors in exchange for short-term fixes. Gimmicks don't work for weight loss, parenting, love, or money. The real thing takes real work.

Karen K.

> Gimmicks don't work for weight loss, parenting, love, or money. The real thing takes real work.

Shaking loose from a negative spiral

Sometimes you may notice that your child is starting to succumb to a negative spiral, in which she is more and more likely to do things that are not working, and your attempts to reach her are having no effect. How can you hit the re-set button? It's good to have a few options handy.

Silliness can break the dismal mood.

Sometimes to break the ice and get everyone silly we read a hysterically disgusting little book called *Dirty Bertie.* My girls will laugh so hard and if it is a tough day where we haven't laughed enough, it turns the day around.

Or we just say, "Don't smile. Don't you dare crack a smile." This ends in a huge smile and a tickling session. We don't tickle my oldest. It is, for some reason, like torture to her. We have to respect her on that. Instead, she likes it when we wrestle.

Heather S.

Play can be the magic solution!

The last chapter talked about identifying your child's underlying need, and trying to find a win/win solution from there. Often play may be exactly the need that a child has that is interfering with your adult agenda. Being playful can help you meet both needs at once.

One of my favorite "reserve" games is "fire truck." My son (four years old) loves fire trucks and I've saved a critical appointment that I had forgotten about a few times with this one. I pretend to ring a bell. We pretend we are the fire-fighters and we jump into our "fire clothes" (anything we can find) and hurry out to our "fire truck" and get our seatbelts on as fast as we can. What usually takes 20 minutes takes about three. I have to save this game for special occa-

sions, though. I'm also careful about maintaining the spirit of the game by not trying to sneak in a few of my own tasks while we're racing.

Another game I often use is, "I bet you can't beat me." For example, "I bet you can't get your clothes on before I get all the dishes put away. Oh, darn! You are so quick! Well, I'll definitely beat you with getting my shoes on." Of course I don't. "How are you so fast? I never win!" He says, "I won!" and I say, "Yes you did, and actually so did I because we are on time! We both can win!" Then we both giggle.

Lisa S.

When it's time to get ready for bed and your child is tired, it may work to turn it into a game: offer to count for each task, and see how long it takes her to get underwear off, shirt off, pants off, or pajama top or bottoms on. Or ask that she do it with one foot up, one foot on top of the other, or

Surprise her with your own silliness.

 One of my main tactics is to get really silly. For example, instead of yelling I will start singing instructions operatically or tell them what I need to happen using a silly voice. It lightens the situation and many times, they will do the thing they were having a hard time with prior to that.

Stacey T.

LOUD silliness can sometimes change the mood.

 My children were cranky and fighting, and instead of trying to work it through directly with them I suggested we scream, "Oatmeal!"

other little challenges that make it fun and new.

Sometimes it is easier for someone outside of the situation to see the playful solution.

Scarlett is 18 months old. She throws an absolute fit every time I change her diaper. She screams, she thrashes, she twists and turns. It is so frustrating. We do this every day and it is always the same. (Although she lies very nicely when anyone but me is changing her!) Sometimes I get so caught up in my own frustration that I can't even think about how to get her to settle down.

The other day, while this whole scene was playing out, my two-and-a-half-year-old daughter came into the room. She started asking Scarlett, "What does the pig say?" and making the noise. Scarlett calmed down long enough for me to change her. What quick thinking on my older daughter's part!

Anna L.W.

Of course, when you consider stretching yourself into being playful in new ways, it is important to always honor your own feelings. Some people are naturally more playful than others, and sometimes you just might not have play in you. It's okay.

I think it is important to give myself permission to not be playful all the time. I feel this way for two reasons.

In my experience, when I try to be playful or use humor in a situation when I am not feeling at all humorous or playful, it backfires. At best, it feels very forced and my children see through it. At worst, it comes out as sarcasm or teasing.

The other is that I just don't think it is a bad thing for kids to see that people have different personalities, different needs, and different ways of approaching life.

Elsa B.

at the top of our lungs on the count of three. It got us all laughing hysterically, and my daughter even apologized to her brother after that. We have used it several times since. One morning, while arguing about a train game, we took a break to scream "1-2-3 Toot Toot!" so loud we couldn't help laughing. Got blood flowing back into our brains, too.

Hilary D.

Try running. Using the body's big muscles can be good for blood flow, too.

My mom used this strategy on my brother: As he was getting out of control (either mad or rowdy) she would say firmly, "I think you need to go run around the house five times!"

She would not quibble about whether he needed shoes or a jacket; he could put on whatever he chose, or not. (Once he took off all his clothes, to the horror of passing missionaries who decided our house was a lost cause!) If he got wet or cold, that could be dealt with when he came back, providing further diversion. It worked very well.

Eventually he started deciding for himself that it was the appropriate thing to do. At least once, when he had a friend over and they were getting on each other's nerves, he said, "I think we need to go run around the house five times!" They ran in opposite directions, making silly faces every time they met, until they were both laughing and panting and the original quarrel was forgotten.

Becca S.

Loud, running silliness may sometimes be required.

Whenever we need to break the mood all anyone has to say is, "Fart!" or "Run! I farted!" Silly, huh? That word can make any kid giggle.

Heather S.

Sometimes good old-fashioned positive energy is what is needed most.

To dispel a negative mood, it sometimes helps to find reasons to give my children praise, helping them feel better inside and allowing them to pull themselves up out of the nosedive their behavior has been in. Finding even the tiniest thing to give a compliment on can begin to turn that negative energy around.

Carissa D.

A change of scene can bring a change of attitude.

 Sometimes changing the environment helps reverse the negative energy. We might go outside to play, take a walk around the neighborhood, or do an energetic activity such as dancing.

Carissa D.

Sometimes all that is needed is more of your attention. It may be hard to stop what you are doing, but if your child stops what she is doing, it may be worth it.

A little quiet reconnection can be just the right medicine.

 When my daughter was a toddler, I used nursing as a soother besides nourishment. Temper tantrums didn't occur very often because I could say let's have some "booba" (what we call it) and talk about what had happened. While she nursed, I would talk to her about what was wrong. Nursing was and is still available any time–even if she's been in trouble. It's a constant source of not just nourishment but of comfort and mama.

Kati S.

Activities that are simple, intriguing, and physical can draw a child in long enough to help her pull herself together.

 When we start to notice her getting to the frustration stage where our words just don't penetrate, we act out the following motions:

• Raise your hands in the air

• Touch your toes

• Raise your hands up high again

•Tickle your armpits (this almost always gets her giggling)

•Take some deep breaths.

When we started this, it seemed very important that we do the actions along with her. As simple as this sounds, it has worked amazingly well. It provides enough of a break in her building emotions, and just a little bit of physical movement to work out some energy. Except for a handful of times, she's been able to calm herself enough that we can move forward and work through the issue that got her heated up in the first place. The few times it hasn't worked (when she told me "Mommy, I do not want to raise my hands in the air!") I've recognized that she really does need an emotional release, things have gone too far to cut off and I try to support her as best I can.

I even witnessed her doing the whole sequence herself at one point. She was trying to open the refrigerator door without asking for help. She started to become visibly and audibly frustrated. Just when I was expecting her to have a mini-meltdown, she stopped, raised her hands in the air, went through the whole sequence. Then she calmly stepped back to the refrigerator and opened the door.

Jeanette L.

Then again, sometimes you just have to go back to bed.

 One morning when my daughter was two-and-a-half, she woke up on the extreme wrong side of the bed. After about 15 minutes of conflict, I said, "That's it, we have ruined this morning. We have to start all over." She looked at me like I had sprouted a second head!

I took her into her bedroom, tucked us both into bed. We cuddled for about 15 minutes. Then we got up and started the day all over again. What a difference. She seemed like a brand new kid. We both just needed some serious re-grouping.

Eileen K.

 For a long time, Julia needed to get in her bed and have me read stories if life was getting out of control. I think she associated that place with the warm feeling of closeness she has at bedtime.

Karen K.

What works for your family?

In a nutshell

As you become familiar with gentle-discipline-in-action, you will gain many skills that will serve you throughout your parenting years. You will also find that, for all of the emotional and intellectual discoveries along the way, it doesn't have to be particularly complicated. You will develop a few key ideas to guide you.

What does it boil down to for you?

It all boils down to a few things for me–giving my children lots of devoted attention and loving consistency, listening to them, modeling the behaviors and values that I'd like to see them have, and being honest and straightforward with them about what I expect.

Karen K.

I wrote a gentle discipline "cheat sheet," a little synopsis of the things I try to do instead of yelling and punishing.

• Instead of focusing on what the child can't do, tell her what she can do.

• Before saying no, take a moment to think about why they can't do it, and whether there is a way to let them do it in a safe and appropriate way.

• Empathize with them when they are upset that it is hard when you can't do what you want to do.

• Try to offer alternatives instead of just taking away an item or stopping a behavior altogether.

• If you do say no, but then realize you acted too hastily, explain to the child that you have thought about it and realized that you were wrong.

• Make sure that your reaction is a "logical consequence" to the problem, i.e., if they hit with a stick, take the stick away.

• Explain why they can't do or have something.

Ginger F.

145

My entire mothering framework is based on probably two main things: Love and attachment. Spending time with my three-and-a-half-year-old daughter: meeting her age-appropriate need for nursing, snuggling, co-sleeping, being carried, togetherness, focused attention, and playing together.

Respect/validation. I treat my daughter and myself with respect, and model (and explain) respectful behavior toward all other human beings. My greatest priority is to show continuous respect and validation of Grace's feelings, emotions, opinions, and beliefs.

Kathy E.

Chapter 7

Care with Consequences

$\sim\sim\sim\sim\sim\sim\sim\sim\sim\sim\sim\sim$

P arents who practice gentle discipline vary widely in how they think about consequences. One principle that is common to many parents who make empathy and respect a priority is their recognition that negative responses to a child may cause some emotional or physical harm. So care is required. When considering a consequence to a child's behavior, it is worth taking a careful and open-hearted look at any potential costs or benefits to your child, to your relationship, and also to yourself, so that you are able to go forward with open eyes and clarity.

Let's explore the ups and downs of consequences, beginning with the consequences Mother Nature supplies.

Natural consequences

Children need to experiment with a range of behavior options, trying on different choices and experiencing their results. Some actions result quite naturally in unpleasant consequences without a parent's intervention. For instance, if you don't look where you're going, you might bump into a wall. If your child is developmentally ready to understand the cause and effect, then he may learn to make a better choice the next time. This is learning in its purest form. When you can do so safely, and when you feel it would be helpful to your individual child's learning process, you may choose to let your child experience the answer to "What if?"

Some questions to ask include:

- Will others be affected by this behavior?

- Is my child developmentally ready to learn from this experience?

- Will the consequence come soon enough so that he will see that his behavior caused it?

- Can my child try this safely?

 In my experience, it's better to say nothing and let him be independent and learn on his own that sand tastes yucky or that he's going to knock over a pile of books. If it's safe, I let him learn to look out for himself. If it's not safe, I get over there and help him out. That's when he needs me.

Anna W.

Safe experiences

When considering safety, you will need to draw the line between degrees of harm or risk you consider acceptable in the service of learning and what are unacceptable. You may find that a combination of your support and some allowance for bumps and bruises works in some situations.

Lately, my 11-month-old son has started climbing up on the couch and getting off again. I believe it's important for him to be allowed to be on the couch so he can figure out the best way to get up and down on his own.

It amazes me how smart he is sometimes, really. His latest "strategy" is to push the cushions off the couch and roll off (head first) into the pillows. Sometimes he tries to turn around, but mostly he goes head first and then flips. Yes, sometimes he bumps his head, and cries for a short time, but I feel strongly that this is all part of the learning process. It would be a waste of time (and a struggle) for me to constantly tell him "No!" and pull him away.

April Mae T.

When a negative consequence is too severe for your child to experience first hand, you can sometimes model it for her. Children with cautious temperaments often learn about natural consequences quite well from observation, and do not need to experience any negativity themselves in order to adjust their own behavior.

I have taught my daughter that touching an electrical outlet hurts. I touch it with my own finger and pretend to get hurt. I say "Ouch! Hurts mommy! Hurts baby too. No touching outlets." Now when we are out and she even spots an uncovered outlet, she points it out to me and says, "Ouch!" and I say "Yes, that's right."

I have also taught her that it hurts to touch a hot stove. I allowed her to touch quickly with one finger. Now when she's in the kitchen she looks at the stove and says "...'ot? 'ot?" And I can tell her yes or no. She understands the difference between hot and cold. It takes a bit more energy to model, but it's a lot easier than saying "No!" or "Don't!" all the time.

Cheryl L.

Gentle guidance

In some cases, you can gently guide your child in seeing the natural consequences of his choices and considering alternatives.

My daughter hates having her hair brushed, and I didn't want to make it a power struggle, so I asked her periodically, "Can I brush your hair now? If we do it, it won't be all knotty and painful." She just kept up with the "No thanks." This went on for almost three days, and she had dreadlocks starting to form. I said, "Let me show you," and took her to the mirror to show her the dreadlocks. I showed her how I would have to pull the strands apart one by one and it wouldn't be as easy as putting a brush through her hair every day.

She sat and watched television while I brushed and worked on her hair. It took half an hour. I believe this was a natural consequence. She saw the result for herself.

Now, she brings the brush to me every morning, living in fear of another long session.

Unfortunately, natural consequences for her are often consequences for me also because she is young and still requires my help. I find I am often living out the consequences of her actions with her, but I consider it a learning process for her.

Janine G.

Every child learns differently

What will your child learn? Good question!

Each child has his own threshold for physical comfort and a unique learning style. Some children are less sensitive to the negative consequences of their behavior and therefore do not learn from natural consequences in the way we might have expected. A child who does not mind minor bumps and bruises may not be as quick to learn caution with his body.

When you're expecting natural consequences to shape your child's behavior, you are likely to learn a lot about your child's individual perceptions and reactions.

I have often heard the advice that on cold days, if a child does not want to wear a coat, parents should offer two choices: "Wear your coat or carry it."

I followed this classic advice for about a year, with my four-year-old son obediently carrying a coat to preschool that he never chose to wear. All the time I was thinking that I was teaching him to be prepared for changes in weather.

One day, after about a year, we were walking into a store while light snow drifted down—I in my winter coat and he in his t-shirt. It finally dawned on me that he just doesn't get as cold as I do!

So now, if I want the comfort of knowing that a coat is available for him, I toss it in the car. But I don't think he has ever needed a coat on days that he thought he didn't and I thought he did. I do ask him to step outside to make his decision, and when it truly is cold for him, he grabs his coat.

Lisa S.

Parent-imposed consequences

Sometimes the natural consequences of your child's problematic behavior are either not safe, not visible to her, or not sufficiently unpleasant to naturally motivate her to change her behavior. In such instances, you may choose to intervene with a "logical" consequence. In some cases, you may do so simply to solve the problem-at-hand. At other times, you may be more overtly trying to motivate your child's behavioral choices in the future.

Explore the potential costs of logical consequences

There are many ways to parent with empathy and respect, and no one can tell you how or if logical consequences should fit in to your particular family. As with everything else about parenting, it's highly individual. Indeed your own feelings may change as time goes on.

If you use some logical consequences, you will want to proceed with care and with your eyes open, tuning in to how your choices are affecting your child and whether you feel the results are positive and effective.

Gentle discipline encourages us to consider both natural and logical consequences with care and thoughtfulness. Almost any parenting technique has the potential to be harsh. It

> Gentle discipline encourages us to consider both natural and logical consequences with care and thoughtfulness.

depends, in large part, on the reactions of the individual child. Parents who use gentle discipline ask questions like these.

"How does this consequence fit with my goals?" Most of the time, the goal of using logical consequences is simple: to stop a child's problematic behavior. One of the big arguments made in favor of harsh consequences is: "They work!" Well, do they?

Sometimes, having a strong and consistent reaction on your part distracts you from noticing that the behavior you are trying to stop may be continuing or even getting worse. As the child's behavior continues, your response may be either repeating or perhaps gradually getting harsher. Remember to keep your eyes open to the outcome of your use of consequences and make adjustments accordingly.

Aside from short-term behavior management, what about your long-term goals? Relying on logical consequences places a great deal of focus on what the parent can do to respond to a particular behavior; it is a reaction to misbehavior rather than a means of getting at the root cause. It can be a relief if you find a way to reduce a negative behavior. But if you don't address the underlying problem that gave rise to the behavior in the first place, you may simply find yourself chasing after new manifestations! A child who is punished for hitting still needs to find a positive outlet for his anger, or he may express it in other problematic ways. Your child was trying to meet a need by acting the way he did; how can he better meet that need in the future?

 When I think about how my goals influence my approach to discipline, I sometimes go through a thought exercise. I imagine myself transported to a foreign place. I am starving and no one around me seems to hear me or acknowledge my attempts to communicate. I try yelling and tugging on people. Then I see a basket of fruit, and I take some.

If someone were to come to me, and yell at me, lecture me, and make me feel ashamed for my behaviors (yelling, tugging on people, and taking things that weren't mine), would this teach me anything? Probably not.

I think my reaction would be very different if someone came to me and said, "You are really hungry and need food! Yelling and taking someone else's things are not okay. Here is how you can get food when you are hungry. You can communicate this way, and you can ask this way." I would be much more likely to change my behavior the next time this happened.

Lisa S.

It's worth bearing in mind that long-term, the most effective discipline leads to children developing self-discipline. You ultimately want your child to do the right thing because it's the right thing, not simply because she fears your reaction to the alternative. Using natural or logical consequences doesn't replace teaching your child about positive problem-solving, taking initiative, and thinking for herself.

"How does my child feel?" You may intend to help instill regret in your child, or to make your child see clearly that what he did was wrong. But logical consequences have the potential to engender emotional fall-out you did not intend. Your child may feel fear (of your reaction, or of the consequence itself), resentment (at you for choosing to do something he doesn't like), shame and low self-esteem, or hurt feelings (as if you have withdrawn your love for him).

Tune into your child's internal reactions, and explore how you feel about this dimension of the consequence. Rather than turning a blind eye, as some discipline methods suggest, take your child's emotions into account when choosing your approaches to solving problems.

"How does this affect my relationship with my child?" Negative experiences supplied by Mother Nature are one thing. Those supplied by mother or father are another matter entirely. When you impose a logical consequence, you are placing yourself as the middleman in the cause and effect scenario. This adds another layer for your child to process, because now the parent-child relationship is brought in. You are, to some extent, putting yourself in opposition to your child. Your relationship becomes an instrument of behavior modification. You may be teaching your child to fear your disapproval and a future action from you if he does the same thing again. The effect of this within your relationship is worth taking into account.

Notice whether or not you feel emotionally distant from your child during the consequence-oriented interaction. How

> The most effective discipline leads to children developing self-discipline.

do the feelings on both sides affect your ability to be a resource for your child in making better choices?

Overall, you want to present yourself to your child as an ally, empathic to his feelings, and responsive to his needs—even when your needs are conflicting. If your goal is to enlist your child's cooperation in changing his behavior, find ways to be as aligned with him emotionally as possible. By earning your child's trust, you are much more likely to reach him with your point of view than if you approach him in opposition.

"How can other people enlist my cooperation?" Another way to decide whether a consequence is gentle or harsh is to think about how you prefer to be treated. Consider how you would feel if a friend or family member imposed a similar consequence on you because of your behavior.

 My husband hates it when I don't move the toaster out from under the cabinet when I use it (he says it's a fire hazard). What if he were to scream at me when I forget, or to hit my hand to "teach" me? Since this is a safety issue, would that be acceptable?

Frankly, if he did react that way, I wouldn't be with him. I choose to be with people who respect me and treat me with love.

I do my best to move that darn toaster out every time, because I know from the way he handles it that it is about my safety and not some control issue. My reactions are not clouded by his response as they would be if he were to hit me for it. Then, I would be reacting to the fact that he hit me.

Patty C.

Of course, as parents we have different responsibilities to our children than we do to each other, so our interactions with our children are different than our interactions with other adults. With this in mind, you may also want to consider imagining yourself as your child's age and temperament. Would it make sense to you if you were the child experiencing the consequence? Putting yourself in your child's shoes can be a good test for whether a particular response would be appropriate.

"Is my child learning from this?" Consequences will fit into each child's learning process differently. Clearly, not all children react the same way, even in the face of unpleasant consequences. Some are sensitive to even the suggestion of unpleasantness and never make the same mistake twice, while others seem oblivious to even severe consequences.

What conditions help you learn? It's worth remembering that many of us learn best when we are feeling good, not bad. And most of us are most resilient and ready to try new options when we are feeling competent and connected.

And what helps your child learn? What kind of responses on your part bring out your child's resourcefulness, openness to seeing the effects of his or her actions, and ability to consider new options? The answer may differ depending on your child's age, temperament, and the particular issue at hand.

And don't forget to ask: "What is my child learning from this?" You don't want the unpleasant consequence to become a big distraction from learning about the problem at hand. And you want to beware of lessons you never intended to impart.

> If your child is not ready to learn something, it is unlikely that he will learn it until his readiness changes.

 In the face of harsh consequences, a child might become resentful ("This is unfair. I can't trust adults."), vengeful ("They're winning now, but I'll get even."), rebellious ("I'll just do the opposite to prove I don't have to do it their way."), sneaky ("I won't get caught next time"), or shamed ("I'm a bad person"). Whew!

Miranda J.

Bear in mind that you don't have to force your child to learn. The spirit of learning is self-motivating. Indeed, you can't control another person's learning. If your child is not ready to learn something, it is unlikely that he will learn it until his readiness changes. Gentle teaching can help your child embrace a new understanding or behavior as soon as he is able.

 I don't think all learning must occur through suffering (negative consequences). I think that our culture "rushes" and forces learning–pushing children to be independent, responsible, generous–when those are skills that can be learned without being forced if they aren't rushed.

Lisa S.

155

Is there another side to rewards?

Gentle discipline is in many ways about providing positive learning experiences for our children. And yet some apparently positive behaviors—such as bribes, rewards, and praise—can have negative side effects.

Bribes

Bribes are treats offered to encourage a behavior to happen, for example, "Be good in the store and I'll buy you some candy." Some parents feel that these encouragements are helpful, either on a regular basis, or to get through a particularly tough situation.

It is worth noting that bribes have some aspects in common with threatened punishments, in fact they can be punishments in sheep's clothing: "If you are disruptive in the store, no candy for you." A bribe can also be a distraction from solving the underlying problem, having the intent to merely make the child's behavior conform to our wishes. And, if made into a habit, bribes can encourage a child to ask "What's in it for me?" before behaving well.

Rewards

Rewards are treats offered after a child has done something the parent approves of. Some feel that since they are offered after the fact, they are entirely different from bribes. Others feel that they are still manipulative. Indeed, some feel that the "gold star" approach to working with children's behavior is degrading for the child.

Praise

Praise can be used as a verbal reward for a child doing what his parent wanted him to do. The parent rewards his or her child with approval or a compliment. Some caution is warranted here, though, because you want your child to feel your love and acceptance unconditionally. If over-used, praise can unintentionally communicate that you approve of your child only when he is acting as you desire.

If you get in the habit of saying "good boy" for setting the table, the implication may be that he would be a "bad boy" if he didn't. "I'm proud of you for sharing toys," might sometimes sound to your child like, "I would be ashamed of you if you were having trouble with sharing."

One way to share your good feelings without inadvertently judging your child is to describe what he is doing, his own satisfaction, and the effects of his choices. "I see you are setting the table so carefully. You like to make sure we will have what we need to enjoy the meal." Or: "When you get the table ready like that it gives me a chance to make sure the meal is yummy and ready soon." Or: "Oh, look at how pleased Marianne is that you gave her a turn on the tricycle!" These messages encourage your child to develop his own motivations for positive behavior.

What to do?

Some parents feel that used with care, bribes, rewards, and praise have their place. Others try to avoid them. Think, observe, and do what feels right and comfortable to you. For more food for thought, *Punished by Rewards*, by Alfie Kohn, explores these issues in detail.

Choose consequences with care

Some parents decide not to impose any consequences on their child's behavior. They may look to natural consequences and modeling to shape their child's behavior to a great degree. When their needs and desires are different from their children's they may try to develop a habit of looking for a third option that both parent and child prefer. Some parents prefer to avoid using their power over their children at all, while not succumbing to martyrdom.

Other parents feel that imposing consequences is part of their job in both shaping their child's behavior and solving the problem at hand. So much depends on the parents' and children's personalities.

If you decide to use consequences to some degree, the most helpful consequences are ones that:

- Are age-appropriate,

- Address the problem at hand,

- Take the child's needs into account,

- Involve a minimum of coercion on the parent's part,

- Are as gentle as possible to address the problem,

- Are predictable, and

- Don't express your emotional baggage.

Make it age-appropriate. Trying to make a toddler—or even most six-year-olds—clean up a big mess all alone is not realistic. Calibrate your consequence to what your child is capable of understanding and doing, and how much help she needs.

Address the problem at hand. You may decide to take action to solve an immediate problem that your child does not appear ready to solve on her own.

 If my two-year-old was throwing toys in a manner that might break them, I might say, "Stop throwing that because it could break." If he continued throwing toys, I might put them away for a while. If he was throwing toys that wouldn't break but might break something else, I might say, "If you don't want to stop throwing the toys, we will have to go to the play-room where nothing can be broken."

Maya S.

Some consequences are much more a matter of practical problem-solving than teaching.

 My two-year-old daughter likes to play with a cup in the bathtub. Sometimes she dumps water outside of the tub. We tell her to keep the water in the tub. We play with her and show her how to play with the cup while keeping the water in the tub. We try to distract her with another tub toy (but the cup is her favorite). If she does it again, we tell her if she dumps the water outside the tub then we will take the cup away. If she does it again, we take the cup away.

She generally accepts this easily. She doesn't cry or scream. I think she understands that she wasn't able to control herself from dumping water outside the tub, so we have to help her control herself.

Amelia B.

Consequences that are related to the problem at hand, and that ideally do something to address or solve it, are sometimes referred to as "logical consequences."

 I might tell my four-year-old: "If we get the bath done quickly, we'll have time to play cha-rades before bed." Or, "Yes, I already made the cookies by myself. You took too long getting in the bath and I couldn't wait any more."

Ann Marie H.

Try to avoid consequences that are arbitrary and unrelated to your child's actions. If a child marks on the wall and is told he can't watch his favorite television show, the two unconnected events may engender confusion and resentment, without help-ing him come to terms with his creative impulses and the prob-lem of wall defacement. Having him help clean up the wall is a consequence that is more likely to help him think about his actions.

Take your child's needs into account. Make sure the consequence reflects your child's personality. A child who never wants to be alone would suffer a great deal from isolation. A child who yearns to understand things, as most do, usually prefers a clear explanation of what happened, why the consequence is being imposed, and what happens next. A very sensitive child may take your disapproval too much to heart.

Make sure you remember to ask yourself: Why did my child behave in this way? What need was she trying to meet? How can she fulfill that need better right now, as well as in the future? If your child grabbed a toy, she may have felt desire for the toy and jealousy of the friend. She may need your help in working with her desires and her friends more gently in the future. If your child was getting out of control due to hunger, food should be the next order of business, and the consequence may need to wait for another occasion.

Use a minimum of coercion. Choose a consequence that is in your power to make happen, or that you believe your child will participate in willingly. The more the consequence requires you to force your child to do something, the more you are setting yourself up for a whole new battle. The resulting drama (Will he sit on the chair for five minutes?) can easily distract from the original problem (Knocking over his sister's block tower), and can be defeating for both parties.

Be as gentle as possible. Empathy and respect are important, even when imposing consequences.

Most importantly, consequences that hurt a child's body or self-esteem are quite costly to both parent and child. If you have decided not to be physically harsh with your child, make sure you are just as sensitive to emotional harshness. Sometimes a parent can shame, berate, or become emotionally cold to his or her child without fully realizing the toll it can take on the child.

The consequence does not always have to be unpleasant to help change behavior and solve the problem. Indeed, with a verbal child you can ask him to help you figure out what should happen next.

I enlist my toddler in remedying the mess he's created, giving him as much responsibility in the process as he can possibly handle. I find this attitude is immensely more effective in quelling an undesirable behavior than if I were to create a consequence that doesn't relate to the problem. I try not to become adversarial and chastising in my actions or my tone of voice. Instead, I try to be matter-of-fact. "Well, looks like there's a mess to be cleaned up. Let's get on that."

Amber S.

Make consequences predictable. Predictability makes life more manageable. If your child knows what to expect, he is more in control of the outcomes of his behavior. A child is unlikely to learn anything about a particular behavior if it sometimes gets overlooked, sometimes gets a lecture, and sometimes gets a severe punishment.

Giving your child reminders can help too, so that he or she is not caught unaware. This is particularly important for very young children, who have short attention spans and little impulse control.

 When our two-year-old son is doing something inappropriate, we always remind him what the consequences will be if he does it, so we're not just surprising him. For example, we might say, "If you hit the furniture with your bat, I will have to take it away." He knows in advance what we expect of him and what the consequences will be if he doesn't obey. It not only helps him to behave properly; it also avoids temper tantrums on his part and anger on my part.

Beth C.

Having a consequence in mind, and a system for working with it, may help you stay calm and constructive in a difficult situation.

 My daughter is a toddler (29 months) who is exploring her limits and wants things her way. I am pretty flexible about that. But when it is something that needs to happen, and I have given her a choice about fun ways she can do something, but she still refuses, I use counting. I'll tell her, "I'll count to five and then I will help you put your shorts back on." Or, "I'll help you close the refrigerator door."

When I don't do that, I feel that I completely lose control of the situation. Having counting as a backup helps me avoid getting mad or forcing her to do it.

Ljubica P.

Keep your emotions separate. The most effective and helpful consequences are the ones that come without extra emotional baggage. You may feel angry or frustrated, and you can talk about your feelings. (For more on healthy outlets for your frustrations, see Chapter 8.) But ideally, the consequence itself should be administered in a spirit of trying to help your child or otherwise address the problem. When you can be quite matter-of-fact about the consequence happening, you help your child see that you are not out to get him, and indeed you are trying to work with a tough situation as best you can.

Your consequence is unlikely to help anyone if it comes laden with yelling, resentment, or humiliating messages. If you are not careful, a blast of anger may become an unintended additional punishment. Your feelings are your feelings, and although they do need an outlet, they should not be things you hurt your child with in the name of teaching him a lesson.

Take your time. Spontaneous consequences in the heat of the moment may be more lashing out than true discipline.

 Small infractions I can handle, we have pretty clear guidelines there. But I try to talk to my husband before I hand out discipline if I'm really mad. He does the same. I explain to Murphee what she did was wrong, and get her to tell me why it was wrong. Then I tell her I'm too angry right now to decide what will happen next, I need a time-out. I either wait for my husband to come home, or call him on the phone. It really helps to know we have a united front! It also helps me to remember it's not just "me being the bad guy."

Loree S.N.

Reinventing time-out

One of the most interesting things about consequences in gentle discipline is how differently each family works out the details of what they do and why. Any technique that is tried by gentle discipline parents is likely to take on different interpretations and forms in each family. Parents may use it in the classic way, soundly reject it, or find a creative adjustment that makes it work for them.

"Time-out" is a great example of this. In traditional "time-out," the child is asked to sit somewhere for a specified period of time (and that amount of time varies with the child's age). The intent is to impress upon the child that what they were just doing is unacceptable. Also, a child who is about to do something problematic may be told that doing so will result in a time-out, in the hopes of making the child think twice.

Some parents have found that a sparing use of the classic time-out can work for them.

 Personally, for hurting people or animals, I found time-outs useful. We used the classic sit-in-that-chair-until-the-timer-goes-off approach, though I did allow a small toy if desired.

Yes, I considered it to be a punishment, and I was okay with that. For me, this was a good solution for many reasons. It got the child away from whoever was being hurt. It gave the child a chance to collect himself. It got the child away from me (if I was being hit) before I lashed out to protect myself. It gave me a chance to work with the "victim" without interruption. And it was easy to do consistently; both my husband and I could use it exactly the same way.

Rebecca W.

 I have definitely adapted some of the approaches to meet my children's personalities. For example, my older son is sensitive and even a head shake from us was sufficient. It is much harder to get my younger son, Brendan, to realize that he needs to try something different. Brendan does respond to time-outs. In almost every case, asking if he knows that a time-out is the consequence for whatever action is enough to make him remember the rule, and apply it. But the time-out cannot be more than a few seconds long, even though he is nearly three years old.

Heather P.

Other parents try classic time-out and find that the fit isn't good for them or their children.

 Putting a child in a spot and setting a timer never felt right to me. In fact, the first time I tried it (after my daughter was about three years old), she looked at me as though to say, "Mom, what the heck is this? It doesn't make any sense!"

Alyson L.

A parent's perception of time-out may depend a great deal on the child.

 Time-outs typically work with Keithen (almost five years old) because the time on his own gives him space to vent his anger and then to calm himself.

Time-outs aren't effective with Kaylee (almost three years old). If she is sent to her room, she will come running and screaming out of it right behind me. She needs someone to talk to her and validate her feelings and help talk her down.

Carissa D.

Time-out does not have to be a chilly exile. We all need a break sometimes! Many parents use time-out, not as an end in itself, but as a temporary removal from the situation, a chance to rediscover better options.

Some parents give their children a lot of say in how it gets implemented. The more power you give your child in any discipline process, the more likely he will be able to make it work positively for himself.

 What I do with my girls during a situation where they really need to either calm down or take a break is to tell them "You need to calm down now, find a place to do it." Or "You need a break. Please find a place for a break."

Sometimes they will go to their rooms, sometimes go sit on the stairs, sometimes they will plop their little bum down right where they stand. Their "break" is as long as they need, and I tell them that when they go to wherever they want to go. That way it's completely up to them if they need to be in isolation or just a few feet away from the group. It also teaches them to listen to themselves and recognize their emotions.

One day my youngest (four years old) hit her sister, so she went and took her "break" and after about 10 minutes she was still sitting there. So I went over and asked her if she was ready to rejoin the group. Usually her "breaks" are 30 seconds to a minute. She actually replied "No, I think I might hit her again if I play with her now. I'm going to sit more." I did a double take!

It was so wonderful to see how honest she was and how she really can recognize when she's still feeling nasty! After about five more minutes she came back and said, "I think I'm okay now," and went off to play! That situation really reassured me that this type of "break," "calm down time," "time out," or whatever you want to call it, works–at least for her!

Andra F.

A break in the action can open up lines of communication, making new options possible.

I take my two-year-old into a quiet place and hold him on my lap for a couple of minutes and we talk about how he can make better choices. He says that he's sorry and we hug and kiss. It works really well.

Beth C.

My husband and I have found that when we get down on the floor and lie down with her (or wherever she happens to be) we can talk, she can be a bit more open, and we have a much better resolution. This doesn't always work. Sometimes I am too mad, or the other child needs attention, or whatever. However, when I can make the effort, it usually works. My husband and Murphee sometimes get off on a tangent and just talk. It works well for both of them. Time-out is just a break from the action, a time to get yourself together before getting back in the game.

Loree S.N.

If your child is out of control, you may need to let him know that you can be with him when he is ready.

 I tell three-year-old Maddy that I think she needs to take a break and I will sit in the room with her if she can control her behavior or try to control her behavior (by doing deep breathing or trying to talk to me instead of covering her ears and screaming). If she starts screaming instead, I tell her that I need to be in my room and when she can stop screaming, then I will be happy to have her come to me. I leave all bedroom doors open and she can see me from her room.

Jessica K.

Some older children may do well processing their feelings and options on paper.

 With my daughter, I used a combination of time-out and a "think sheet" with her from the time she was a little over three on up to about eight or nine.

I would remove her from the situation, direct her to her table and chairs, and ask her to respond to a think sheet when she was emotionally under control. At earlier ages (probably between the ages of three and six), she used pictures to communicate. As she began to write, she could use words or both pictures and words. Here are some things I asked her about:

1. What happened from her perspective?

2. Who was affected by her behavior?

3. How could she do things differently?

4. How could others do things differently?

5. How did she feel?

When she was finished, we would talk about the think sheet. She is an artistic, verbal child and this worked very well for her. Filling out the think sheet fulfilled a need for her to express herself creatively and have someone problem-solve with her in the process.

Donna F.

Time-out can grow and change with the child

 My daughter is almost eight years old and my son is four-and-a-half. When they were very tiny, I would hold them in my arms and talk about getting along.

When they were older, I would help them leave a bad situation and I would sit with them and find something for them to do.

At a somewhat older age, I would take them away to play with something else and leave them saying, "Please join the rest of us when you feel like you can get along."

Now, I can say, "I can see that you are having a hard time getting along. I think you need some time by yourself. Why don't you go outside or up to your room?" They'll stop the activity that was causing trouble.

It isn't punitive; it's just good advice. If the obnoxious behavior continues, and it rarely does, I will help them find something better to do.

Liz B.

As you explore how you feel about consequences and where they fit into your family, remember that there are no clear-cut answers. Your values, your knowledge of your child, and lots of trial and error will help guide you.

Part Two

Gentle Discipline for Parents

In practicing gentle discipline, you are likely to find that you need to focus not just on what your child is doing and feeling, but on your own thoughts, emotions, needs, and behaviors as well. As parents wishing to parent with empathy and respect, we need to tune into our feelings, take care of ourselves, and focus our personal growth around empathy and respect. All of the principles we've applied to gently disciplining our children are gifts we need to bring to ourselves as well.

Chapter 8

Set Yourself Up for Success

$\curvearrowright\curvearrowright\curvearrowright\curvearrowright\curvearrowright\curvearrowright\curvearrowright\curvearrowright\curvearrowright\curvearrowright\curvearrowright\curvearrowright$

It's funny, you know. I spent most of my sons' toddlerhood looking for books that would tell me how to respectfully manage my children's behavior in very practical, "how-to" terms. There is a serious lack of such books and now I know why. It's because what generally needs managing is one's own reactions and approaches to the behavior. Once we manage ourselves rather than our children, the rest usually sorts itself out.

Amber S.

Empathic and respectful parenting takes a lot more than good ideas; it takes a parent who is ready to take on the challenges of the day. As you may have had occasion to notice, it's one thing to parent when you are feeling good. It's a whole different ball game if you're feeling stressed out, overwhelmed, depleted, irritable, or angry. It's also much easier to parent when you have positive perceptions of your child and yourself, compared to when you are laboring under negative or cynical ideas about children and parenting.

There are several key ways to set yourself up for success, and this chapter will explore them each in turn. You can:

- Make sure your own needs are being met.

- Be familiar with your "triggers," the things that set you off, and work with them directly.

- Find healthy outlets for your anger.

- Do a mental inventory and replace negative messages with ones that serve you better.

Positive parenting starts with well-being

Parenting can be incredibly demanding work, requiring reserves of patience, creativity, and empathy. Do you have what you need to face the day?

Sometimes it may seem easiest to put all of your focus on your child and neglect your own needs. Yet this may put both you and your child at risk. Know your own needs and be proactive about meeting them as best you can.

Do you feel connected?

Feeling connected to loved ones is no less important for parents than children. Make sure you are doing what you can to feel connected to your co-parent if you have one, your friends, and your child. True connection means not just living in the same home, but making a real heart connection that can help sustain you.

Sometimes one-on-one time with other adults can recharge

your batteries. Strengthen and fortify your support system, the people you can call on when you need a sympathetic ear, or to take your child when you desperately need a break. A strong support system can help you be an effective parent. (Chapter 11 will explore building a support system.)

Good health is essential

Make sure you're getting plenty of exercise, fresh air, and sunshine. Frequent healthy snacks will keep your energy up just as they do for your child. Don't forget to drink plenty of water. Make a point to tune into your body frequently during the day so that you can take action as needed.

 Sometimes if I wait too long between meals, I don't realize that I'm hungry, especially if I am involved in something interesting. Then all of a sudden I go into a tense panicky mode; I feel as if there's a big dark empty space inside me, I'm in danger, nobody loves or understands me, and sensory input becomes uncomfortable. Sometimes I still don't "feel hungry," yet eating or drinking something helps a lot, very quickly. But if I let it go on too long, I start to feel very uncertain about whether I want to eat or not and I get panicky about that or even nauseated.

Becca S.

It may be tempting to stay up late after your child goes to bed so you can finally do all the tasks you have been unable to do during the day, but be aware that you may be paying for it the next morning. Some people can get by with very little sleep—others need a great deal to be at their best. Getting the rest you need at night—and perhaps grabbing some "down time" during the day—can be a huge factor in how resilient you are.

A big one for me is sleep. I have really noticed how getting enough sleep allows me to be much more patient during the day. I didn't even realize how much being tired was affecting me until I actually started to get some good sleep. Oh, and water. It is unbelievable how crabby being dehydrated can make me.

Ginger F.

For me, keeping my cool is all about remembering to take care of myself. It's the only way I can be the parent I want to be for my son.

Because I'm so anxious, I can get very preoccupied or easily irritable if things aren't going perfectly. It helps immensely for me to get enough sleep, eat regular meals and snacks (this is huge for me), and take time for myself every day. I need some time each day to breathe deep, reflect, read something other than parenting books, or do something else relaxing. If I just take that moment, things go pretty well even in the face of crayons on the wall, water all over the bathroom floor, and other routine annoyances.

Mary Beth K.

Take some time this week to notice how such physical needs as sleep and food can affect your own ability to cope. This can help you appreciate better how these well-being issues can affect your child, too.

Take time for yourself

It can be hard to find enough "me time," particularly when children are young. Most parents need to feel engaged in creative and meaningful activities that refresh them in addition to the important work of being parents. What relaxes you? Is it scrap booking, knitting, biking, a job you love, a book group, or something else? Taking some time to remind yourself that you exist separately from your children may help you appreciate your time with them much more.

My advice would be to take excellent care of yourself. As busy parents, it's hard to take care of ourselves but it is vital. Do what feeds your soul as much as possible. A massage, a mother's helper, a mom's support group, good nutrition, whatever. For me, yoga is relaxing.

Jane D.

You may be able to do some activities with your child nearby—some will require that you find someone else to be with your child. If you are with your child all day, can someone take your child for part of the evening so you can have some time off? If your child is still breastfeeding frequently, you may need to keep the time modest or arrange to be accessible to your child for short breaks as needed. Even a small block of time that you know you can count on can make a difference. Is there a way for you to join a gym, or go for a run? Could you trade-off child care with a compatible parent friend? Can you afford a modest amount of paid child care each week? Some parents find that letting their children watch a child-friendly video can provide a sanity-saving break.

When you do have a bit of free time, resist the temptation to give it all to doing chores or paying bills. Set a timer if you have to, but make the commitment to give some time to yourself on a daily or weekly basis.

 My one-year-old daughter has an illness that requires treatments at least once a month. They last all day long and have to be done at a children's hospital two hours from our home. Those days leave me wiped out to the core! I've learned that I need something restorative to look forward to after those exhausting trips: a run or a massage or a pedicure scheduled for the next day; dinner being brought over by a supportive friend; or a long hot bath and a glass of wine.

Karen K.

Pace yourself

Look closely at the things you take on during a given day or week. What are your top priorities?

Give yourself a boost

What makes you feel better, keeps you on track? What activities make you happy? Try to remember ones that you haven't been doing since becoming a parent.

Are there three things you can do for yourself this week that could make a positive difference in your sense of well-being? List them. Commit to them. Do them.

> For me being able to keep my cool is an every day all day kind of thing. I need to take care of myself all the time, so that when I am dealing with my son I don't feel tired, hungry, stressed, or have to use the bathroom.
>
> For me it meant changing my lifestyle. I don't drink caffeine anymore, I exercise regularly (especially yoga), I eat well, I make sure I get enough sleep (when I can), and so on. I also go to therapy to deal with my abusive past. I've learned that I get stressed and am tempted to yell or hit when I feel like I don't ever get my own needs met. I start to feel resentful. So I try to meet my own needs, and it really helps.
>
> *Jennifer M.*

Take care of yourself so you can take care of your child. Taking advantage of even the smallest opportunities for self-care can help get you through.

Are these the things that get the most of your time and attention, or does the week get frittered away with less important tasks? Are there tasks you can take off your list, or at least reserve for after the most important ones are completed? Trying to do everything can drive you crazy. Take the time to identify your needs, set your priorities, and streamline accordingly.

Slow down when you can.

For me, the main thing is to just slow down. Sometimes I get aggravated because I want to just hurry up and get the kitchen cleaned so I can go put the laundry away before my husband gets home. I stop and remind myself that playing with my child is far more important than washing the dishes. I have chosen to be a stay-at-home mom so I can raise and nurture my child, not so that there is somebody at home to put the laundry away. So, often it takes three times as long to do something as it would if I were just doing it without him around, but I have made peace with that and it's okay.

Jennifer K.

Build breaks into your day so that you can breathe and regroup.

It helps me to keep the kettle going on the stove—a tip gleaned from watching my mother raise us (12 children). If I have a cup of tea, I need to pause and sip, pause and inhale.

Bonnie S.

On rough days, I'll call my husband at work to find out when he's coming home that night. If it's just a couple of hours, I can usually refocus and hold on. If not, I try to visit a neighbor or go for a walk.

Jennifer V.

You and your child may both need a rest.

I have found a way to avoid getting to the end of my rope and to avoid the temptation of putting my child in time-out. I have scheduled a "family quiet time" in the middle of the day. I make sure there is plenty of time for a walk to the park or something else fun and then my son (who doesn't nap) has a one-hour rest. This way he doesn't melt down as easily and I don't reach the end of my rope. That one hour allows me to recharge. My son is a loving sweet child, but he literally does not stop talking. It's amazing how long he can go without a moment of silence.

Lindsay B.

Take your own stress seriously

Stress can make us particularly reactive as parents. Although reducing stress can sometimes be a complicated endeavor, taking it seriously as a parenting issue is a great starting place.

 The more stressed or out of control I am feeling about things, the more likely I am to bark orders and expect immediate responses. It's like I'm at my breaking point and I want to feel in control of something. Unfortunately, the behavior resulting from my orders makes things more stressful for me, for my daughter, and for my husband. It's a vicious cycle.

Kirsty C.

I've found that my worst situations are the days that other things, besides my child and discipline, have me stressed out. It's the outside stress and responsibilities that get in the way of me being the kind of parent I want to be, and I lose my patience quite easily.

Beth C.

Is there something deeper going on?

It is worth noting that underlying problems like depression (including postpartum depression), bipolar disorder, or other mood disorders can wreak havoc on your ability to parent. Chronic fatigue and other medical issues can also make it hard to meet daily challenges head on. If you suspect that you may have a physical or mental health problem, seek out the professional help you need to get yourself back on track.

When it got to the point that I was relieved that I wanted to lock my son in the closet rather than smack him for being a chatter box, I finally got some professional help. I found out I have a mood disorder, bipolar II. I take medication and I feel 100% better. I am not constantly, every day, all day, violently aggravated by the kids. My brain feels as if it has slowed down enough that I can see what's happening and respond, if not calmly, let's just say very firmly. I am in control most of the time.

Medication in conjunction with therapy can work wonders.

Miranda J.

Well-being issues don't have quick fixes

Sometimes, you may be able to identify a trigger or an unmet need that is bringing you down—but there may be nothing much you can do about it for the time being. When you're in the middle of a move, when you are sick, when a relationship with a loved one is in a rough patch—in short when life is getting the better of you, chances are parenting just got a whole lot more challenging. And if pregnancy or premenstrual hormones enter the picture, stand back!

 I'm two months into this pregnancy now. The mood swings make it a challenge to keep from swinging from "Earth Mama" to "Mommie Dearest." Trying to maintain consistency in my interactions with my daughter is so hard. I find myself snapping at her for little things that, in the grand scheme of life, don't really matter. Sometimes I feel abundantly patient. Sometimes my patience evaporates in a second.

Sarah M.

When you know that you are feeling low, this very self-awareness can help you cut yourself some slack (and your child, too). This is not the time to judge yourself as a parent—or to have overly high expectations of your child's behavior. Sometimes you just have to get through the best you can and know that brighter skies await you both.

I'm pregnant, my husband has been working all the time, we have been traveling, and now my daughter and I are both sick. I haven't been able to refill my reservoirs of patience and be the parent I like to be. Just being able to go for a run today helped a huge amount. It seems as if the whole family is depleted right now, and we all need more while being able to give less.

Karen K.

Janet didn't get that casserole in the oven in time and well, it was the END of the World!

Know your triggers

As your offspring emerges from gurgling baby perfection to the independent exploration of todderhood, she may eventually develop a way of pushing your buttons. We all have our sensitive areas that can make us snap—all of us, even your ideal mama friend who always seems so patient and calm.

For some parents it's situational, like loud noises or feeling hot, or the irritations may be more interpersonal.

 I have two major triggers: 1) When I don't feel that I'm being listened to (and not just by my daughter, but if I'm feeling that way in general), and 2) If I'm not able to complete a task because I keep getting interrupted. I try to remind myself that if I don't get the grocery list completed or dinner cooked, it's not the end of the world. But I am still learning how to cope with my triggers effectively.

Jessica K.

Consider taking some time this week to notice when you find yourself losing your temper. What are the things that set you off? Too many errands, time pressure, feeling unappreciated, your co-parent working late? These are your personal land mines, to be avoided or defused whenever possible.

You may find some surprises lurking in your gut reactions. The parent-child relationship is emotionally loaded. Perhaps seeing your child asserting her independence may trigger a fear that your parenting authority is at stake. Or certain behaviors may re-stimulate painful feelings from your own childhood, particularly behaviors for which you yourself may have been punished or shamed as a child.

 My main issue, personally, is compliance—the issue that caused my parents the most angst. I was not a compliant child. I still carry their outrage, frustration, and fury over my own non-compliance, and it comes out on my kids. I've learned, and am still learning, to finely filter when compliance is actually required, and when I'm just reacting.

It usually comes up when time is limited, I'm already in a hurry, and I'm not in a patient mood. Then I crave a quick reaction from my kids, not for their sake, but for my own. Then I find myself frustrated, yelling, unable to think on the fly.

Heather P.

Sometimes realizing that something is a trigger for you can help you react less strongly when it does come up ("Ah-ha, there's that trigger again. This is about me, not her. I do not have to take this out on my child.").

In fact, upon examination, you may find that you can eliminate one or two of these trouble spots. For example, you may be able to ease up a bit on your preference for order if you realize it helps you enjoy your child more. Or perhaps you could eliminate it by a structural solution such as getting more help around the house or even hiring a cleaning service if possible. Making a conscious choice to make such changes can eventually start a new mental habit, particularly if you are kind to yourself in the process.

For the triggers that are hard to get rid of, set yourself and your child up to run into these as rarely as possible. For example, if a hot car makes you cranky, can you limit your summer outings to ones where you can park in the shade? Can you make sure to bring a bottle of ice water for yourself? Can you do the grocery shopping at night? Sometimes changing how you do things can help you get around a trigger.

I now start laundry at night because I find that I can fold it early in the day when the kids are fresh, but not in the late afternoon when they're fried.

Karen K.

If a specific behavior drives you batty, it may be well worth it to put a lot of your positive energy into helping your child work with you on it. For instance, if you have a hard time with loud noises, you may want to make a priority of working with your child on "inside voices," find a place where she can bang her drum without bothering you, or give her time outside where she can bellow to her heart's content.

Find healthy outlets for your anger

Other parents get angry at their children, too. All of them. The question is how do you express that anger so you can feel better and move on? If you try to stifle negative feelings, you are likely to increase your stress level and run yourself down. You may also be setting yourself up for a big explosion when you just can't take it any more.

Expressing your emotions helps you cope. It also helps you be real—to yourself and your child.

I remember someone saying to me once when I was first struggling with the real stuff that came out of me when my son started heading into discipline territory. She said, "Do you want to be a perfect mom or a real mom?"

She went on to illustrate how wacky and weird it is to grow up with fakeness or passive-aggression from family members who smile while wanting to throw something through a window.

So, I've accepted (not fully, I guess, but I'm working on it), that I'm a real mom. When I lose it, I apologize. When I'm angry, I say, "I'm angry." I'm trying to be as honest as possible with myself and my son on this journey of motherhood.

Beth D.

Notice your emotions. Label them at least to yourself. ("I'm feeling so angry right now.") Validate them, just as you might with your child. ("It's natural to feel angry when I'm in a hurry and my child is resisting getting ready to go.") Feelings aren't right or wrong. Someone else may react differently to a similar situation, but your feelings are still okay and they are natural.

 I thought the greatest challenge we would confront when taking a gentle approach to disciplining our son would be to find effective alternatives to spanking. I never anticipated that the real challenge would be for me to get my own anger under control.

Monica D.

You may find it helps to take a moment to get in touch with the underlying emotion, too, the sadness, disappointment, or fear that gave rise to the anger. Are you afraid you will be late? That your child will never learn to work with a schedule? That others will think you are not an effective parent if you can't get out the door in a timely fashion? Are you disappointed because you thought your child was going to be able to rise to the occasion better than she is? Are you hurt to see that your child is not sympathetic to your need to go now? Getting in touch with your vulnerability may have the added benefit of helping you see that your reaction may have more to do with your own hopes and needs and less to do with your child's behavior *per se*.

When you are in touch with your own emotions, it makes it possible for you to empathize with your child's emotions, too.

Do you want to be a perfect mom or a real mom?

Own your emotions

Make sure that you are expressing your emotions, not making them your children's problem.

 I need to be careful. Saying that I am angry or tense will often generate a change in her behavior. I want to make sure that that change is for the right reasons. She sometimes seems very concerned with making sure I am no longer tense or angry (as if this is entirely in her control). She will ask me "Are you happy now?" or "Are you still angry?" She will do things, like smile or hug me to "make" me happy. I don't want her to feel responsible for my emotions or for my happiness. That is not the message I am trying to send.

Rebecca K.

How you talk to others about your child's behavior and your reactions is very important.

 I have been learning to speak in terms of myself. "The kids this-or-that, and I went crazy today." Instead of saying (and believing) that the kids "made me crazy." This realization, sadly, came to me many months ago after I saw the sadness in my first daughter's eyes to hear me blame her for my own misbehavior during a rant to a friend over the phone.

Pei L.

How can you let it out?

Gentle discipline does not require that you are always calm— just that you are real, and as empathic and respectful as you can be in any given moment. Feigning calmness when you are feeling angry is not helpful to anyone; you end up with a bottled up emotion and your child is likely to get a mixed message about what is really going on with you. As situations arise, practice finding ways to let the anger out in respectful ways so that the air is cleared and you can both move on together.

I think the trick is not to try to stay calm all the time or expect myself to be patient when something comes flying at my head, but instead to figure out what to do when I am angry. I look for ways to express myself and my anger without hurting my child.

I also pay attention to my own feelings when I am irritated about something. Should I have blown off that little bit of anger about the dumped out laundry basket or 19th nursing or loud noises, instead of ignoring myself and trying to be calm until one little thing causes me to explode?

I think that the way I can protect my children from my anger is by getting in touch with it, really paying attention to myself, not by focusing on being calm.

Mallory P.

What are your options for truly releasing your frustration or anger so it doesn't stay inside waiting to burst out—but it also doesn't hurt your child? You may need to experiment until you find something that works for you and your child.

I've found that one thing that can help refocus me is finding a physical way to diffuse that negative energy. Clapping my hands hard and fast gives me a way to release the frustration that is building up inside me and can sometimes work to capture my child's attention.

Carissa D.

After really bad days, I used to greet my husband at the door, hand our son to him, and get into the car and drive. Sometimes I'd even scream, which was a great release.

Trying to remember to breathe really helps sometimes.

When my son is out of sight, sometimes I throw things. I just have to remember to close the door when I throw my slipper across the room. Just the act of it does help release something in me. Someone once explained to me that that's why exercise is such a good release of anger, because it's physical. You can pound your feet into the sidewalk.

Beth D.

It's okay to really sound angry. The idea is to get the anger out, without taking it out on your child.

 There are plenty of things I can yell that won't hurt my children. I once yelled at my child the following unhelpful things: "Don't dump that on the floor! Can't you stop making a mess for two minutes? Stop throwing things at my head, do you want me to be hurt?"

What if I had yelled, "I hate scrubbing the carpet!" Or "When things are thrown at my head, I feel angry and scared that I might get hurt!"

With the second way, I don't feel I am attacking my child even if it is loud, and I even feel like helping her. I don't think expressing strong feelings loudly is a problem. I also think that when I let myself have these feelings (and even express them through screaming) I really am calmer and more patient.

Mallory P.

Try new things, and notice how they work for you and your child. Be creative. Sometimes you may need to feel your way through an option, noticing how you feel and how your child feels.

Your child will benefit

Expressing our emotions helps normalize emotions for children. We help them see that strong emotions come up for everyone, there are helpful ways to get the emotion out, and then we move on. Our children need to learn these skills from us so that they can manage their own emotions in healthy and productive ways.

 I tell my two-year-old when I'm getting "grouchy" and feeling "angry" (and show him the American Sign Language signs for them). Not only has it helped him express himself when he's feeling it, but the other day I was getting irritable and he said, "Mom, you grouchy?" and signed the sign for it. I told him that I was feeling grouchy and he came over, patted me on the arm, and said, "It okay, Mommy. It happens."

Betsy S.

I remind my daughter (three years old) that I love her all the time, even when I seem angry, and that sometimes people aren't as nice as they should be when they're tired or frustrated.

I firmly believe that expressing anger (in a non-physical way) is much better than letting it simmer under the surface. I need to be able to model anger for my daughter in a positive way. And if she learns from this that people get angry, they act a certain way, and then they get over it and are nice again, then she will learn that anger is just one

The better you understand yourself, the better you can parent

The more that I think about gentle discipline (and any thoughtful positive discipline approach), the more I see that the way it begins is with a deeper understanding of ourselves. It is not just "something to do," it is a way to live both with our children and with all of the people we love and come into contact with.

Jessica K.

How has your knowledge of yourself expanded as a result of your parenting? How has knowing yourself better allowed you to bring more empathy and respect to your parenting?

You may enjoy comparing notes with a friend. Sometimes a book can get your wheels turning. Try *Giving the Love That Heals: A Guide for Parents* by Harville Hendrix.

What I like about this book is that it helps me deal with MY issues, and how

they prevent me from being the parent I want to be. This book is helpful at getting me to identify why certain behaviors set me off.

Mariah W.

Sometimes it may seem like gentle discipline would be so much easier if you never got angry or encountered other nuisance emotions! But remember that gentle discipline is all about being honest about what is really going on with you and your child. Make yourself at home in gentle discipline, finding a way to truly honor your own emotions, style, and preferences in your parenting. You won't be like your neighbor. You don't have to adopt artificial ways of talking or approaching problems. We are all strongest as parents when we are most authentically ourselves.

Get to know your emotional style, your strengths and weaknesses, your personality, and how all that leads to your most natural parenting style—and work from there, bringing out the best in yourself.

of those things that's part of life and isn't something to fear.

Beth F.

When your child understands your emotions, she will be better able to understand your actions and reactions.

 When I am feeling tense (often because of a combination of work and household pressures and my daughter demanding instant gratification), I tell my daughter how I feel, and flutter my hand on

I would describe myself as most certainly anxious and nervous. Tons of nervous energy indeed. I tend toward the side of control freak and would even throw some good old obsessive compulsive behavior in there for good measure.

Before I became a parent, I thought plenty about my personality and how it would affect my son. It sounds simplistic, but making the decision to hang loose on things has helped me let go and be a better parent. Having a philosophy in place keeps me honest and even when I'm not 100% successful at it, I can always reel myself back in. (See me grabbing *Kids, Parents and Power Struggles*, by Mary Sheedy Kurcinka, back off the shelf, again!)

It's not always easy though. My need to "keep order and get things done" can really get in the way of what's truly important to me. I've spent my share of time beating myself up for not just relaxing and going with the flow of things and yes, for getting upset with my son for being completely developmentally on target.

Mary Beth K.

Remember, your child needs you, a living, breathing, human parent, not some ethereal ideal or perfect robot. If you are able to work on your own weaknesses with a spirit of self-love, you will be giving an enormous gift to your child.

I think there's an awful lot of pressure on moms to be perfect. I'm arriving at a place in my life where I think my goal as a mom—well for my whole self in all my roles really—is to keep growing and learning but also to accept myself as I am, complete with my limitations and my preferences and quirks that might be unaccepted by society/the neighborhood/the parenting books.

I feel better when I'm just living than when I'm trying so hard to be some way I think I should be but I'm not and analyzing each interaction with my kids to death (and then a little more). I think we grow best when we first understand and have compassion for ourselves.

Michelle N.

my heart to show her. She has come to understand that if I tell her I am feeling tense and need a couple of minutes to calm down or finish a task, that I will meet her needs shortly. Sometimes she accepts that, waits quietly, and is rewarded with my full, happy, grateful attention 10 minutes later.

Rebecca K.

Delete negative messages

One of the biggest ways we can set ourselves up is by getting rid of messages that undermine our commitment to gentle discipline.

Cover your ears!

There are so many negative messages out there about children, egging parents on to do battle with our children—even our babies. You may hear these messages come up in your own head. Or a well-meaning friend or relative may blurt these out. Be on the lookout for these distortions, and don't be swayed by any messages that undermine your attempts to be empathic and respectful to your child.

"Nip it in the bud!" If you don't eradicate a behavior immediately, this voice warns you, your child will still be doing it (hitting, not sharing, or whining) in college. The truth is that there is plenty of time to work with your child to learn appropriate behaviors, and the best time is when she becomes developmentally ready.

"She's manipulating you!" Sure, some older children do learn to manipulate, but it seems that even babies can't show any needs or opinions these days without being accused of manipulation. Trust that your child is not your adversary, even when things are hard. The more you show respect to your child, the less she will need to adopt coping mechanisms such as manipulation later on.

Do a mental inventory

As an exercise, ask yourself:

- Do you ever find yourself treating your child in ways you always promised yourself you wouldn't?

- Do you ever open your mouth and someone else's words come out, like your own parent's or those of another authority figure from your childhood?

- Do you ever feel as though you are torn between what your heart is telling you to do and what you think others think you "should" be doing?

Make a habit of noticing any instance in which you uncover a "disconnect" between your developing parenting beliefs and your actions. These "ah-ha" moments are incredibly valuable.

Be on the lookout for these concepts that don't fit. Bring them to the light of day. See what ideas about your child, yourself, and parenting in general need to be updated in your mental outlook. In this way, you make room for a deeper understanding of your children and the kind of parent you want to be.

"Who's in control here?" This voice threatens that there has to be a boss, and if it isn't you, it's your child. This is baloney. Children can be demanding, that's their job, but it doesn't mean they really want to be the boss. Nor do they need to be bossed. When you work together with your child, you can own your authority without controlling—or being controlled by—anyone.

"Naughty child!" When you label normal childhood behaviors as naughtiness, misbehavior, defiance, or disobedience it can be harder to find positive responses. Your child's behavior may not be what you want it to be, but your child is still the beautiful and lovable child she always was. There's no need to judge her harshly. Help her find her way to better options.

These negative messages may infiltrate your parenting when you are most in need of more positive ideas, especially when you are stressed out, frustrated, or overwhelmed. Any time you can talk back to these unhelpful voices, you clear the way for a more empathic response to your child. How freeing that can be!

When you're trying to counteract such negative messages, you may need to do a mental house cleaning. Perhaps you've been through the process before.

 I remembered that I had discarded many of the beliefs I inherited about babies when I first became a mother. I no longer believe that picking up my child whenever he cries will spoil him or that attached children will not develop independence. When my son was three, I realized that my discipline approach was also based on many inherited beliefs I no longer agreed with. I realized I needed to do the same thing with notions of discipline that I had done with baby care.

Lisa S.

Examining your goals can bring clarity about what you're trying to do with discipline, helping you develop positive thinking that is aligned with your deeper beliefs.

 I looked at the long-term goals of my parenting. I want my child to grow up to be independent, secure, kind, respectful of others, responsible, and have good judgment, among other things.

If these are my goals, I thought, then why was I spending so much time trying to get immediate results and approval from others? Should my success as a parent be measured by others, by how quiet, compliant, polite, and socially acceptable my child was? I realized that it should be measured by me, by the strength of my connection with my child, and by the long-term results.

Lisa S.

Once you notice the negative messages, you can talk back to them.

 I know when I am at my wit's end with my two-year-old, it is largely because of that horrible expression: "Who is the parent here?" And the only answer is: "I am! And he should be doing what I say." Agh!

I hate it.

It doesn't help me remain calm. It doesn't help me problem solve. It doesn't help me be playful and fun. It makes me short-tempered, it sets up unrealistic expectations for everyone, and it makes me doubt my commitment to gentle and positive discipline.

Some of the alternative answers I've been giving myself are: "I am. That's why I need to be the example of patience." "Yes, I'm the adult, and that means I do have better control of my emotions." I'm trying to give myself answers where "being the parent" means that I have to take the high road, as it were.

Betsy S.

Having realistic expectations about parenting can be a big part of keeping negative and simplistic messages at bay.

 Compromise is work. People often walk into marriage knowing that they are going to have to work at it and make difficult decisions and compromises. While actually making the compromises necessary to make a marriage work is more difficult than most people expect, at least they expect it. With kids, many people feel (subconsciously) like "Finally! A relationship I don't have to compromise in! Finally, what I say goes!" People don't always expect that they are going to have to compromise and they can't just issue commands.

Jessica S.

The more you define your own values and practices as a parent, the quieter the extraneous voices will be.

 There are times when I feel that I'm literally holding back the voices from my past that want to lash out at my children. It's the times when I realize I haven't even thought about holding those voices back that I know I'm parenting in the moment and in a mindful way.

Amy N.

Put it all together

There are many ways to fortify yourself for the parenting challenges ahead. You can be diligent about meeting your own needs, so that you have deeper reserves of patience, creativity, and good cheer to draw from throughout the day. You can get to know your personal triggers, and find ways to manage them so they don't manage you. You can put some time and effort into cultivating respectful ways to get your anger out so that anger is a safe emotion to have around the house. You can be vigilant about negative messages that would like to creep in and undermine your attempts to bring respect and empathy into your parenting.

Above all, remember that you are doing the best you can. Let every step toward gentler parenting remind you that you are becoming the parent you would like to be.

Chapter 9

Get Yourself Back on Track

~~~~~~~~~~~~~~~~~~~~~~~~~~~

W hen you're run down, overwhelmed, distracted, or starting to lose your temper, you're in danger of parenting in
ways you would probably prefer not to. It happens to all of us.
This chapter explores:

- How your own state of mind can set the tone with your
child;

- How you might keep your cool when you're starting to lose
it;

- Whether you might benefit from putting yourself in time-
out; and

- How you always have the opportunity to start over.

Parents set the tone

You may notice that your child's behavior tends to actually be better, the better you feel. When you feel good, you are likely to have more positive perceptions of your child and the world in general, and a lot more resiliency when you do face challenging situations. Not only that, you may tend to be more active and timely in meeting your child's needs, steering you clear of a lot of unnecessary behavior problems.

Next time your child's behavior takes a nosedive, check in with your own state of mind—you may be surprised at what you find.

 When my daughter is "acting up," I have finally learned to do a self-check. Since I started doing this, things are going more smoothly for me as a mother:

- What attitudes am I sending out?

- Am I thinking that my daughter is in my way or a nuisance rather than a contribution to the family?

- Am I angry with my husband or myself?

- Am I behaving in an overly distracted way (such as spending too much time on the computer, procrastinating, or getting sidetracked) which tunes me out from my daughter's signals?

- Am I being unfocused, indecisive, wishy-washy, or asking my daughter too many questions?

- Am I being impatient with myself?

- Am I trying to accomplish too many things around the house and not taking time to smell the flowers, smile, laugh, and dance?

- Have I kept us in the house all day?

- Am I not taking responsibility for my own happiness?

I can promise you that when my daughter is "acting up," the answer to one of these above questions is "Yes!" Notice that none of my questions have anything to do with what my daughter is doing/saying/being.

Amy R.

Take the cranky parent challenge!

Take a day or a week to notice what is going on with you when your child is pushing your buttons. As you go, ask yourself:

- Is there a pattern? What situations or states of mind on your part seem to result in problems between you and your child?

- What actions can you take in the moment to get yourself back into a more positive mode? Does it help to take deep breaths? To stop and get down to your child's level?

- What can you do in advance to set yourself up in advance for more well-being and therefore more centered parenting? Get to bed earlier? Go for a run three times a week? Limit activities and obligations that overwhelm you?

You may also want to compare notes with a friend or your co-parent. Both the similarities and the differences may provide food for thought.

Tricks for keeping your cool

Each parent struggles with staying calm at one time or another—sometimes many times a day. Here are some tricks that have worked for other parents. What works for you?

Stop the action

When you're charging ahead, you have no time to choose your course. A short break can make a big difference.

When I am feeling completely at the end of my rope I make myself take a deep cleansing breath before I say one word. Not the kind of breath you take before "yelling" under your breath, but the kind that gives you little pleasant tingles down your spine. Then I have had a second, at least, to formulate an effective sentence.

Lindsay B.

Two things help me a lot. One is to literally stop and do nothing at all for a few moments, or as neutrally as possible stop someone from getting hurt and then do nothing. Stopping for even a few seconds, deciding not to act right then, really does seem to interrupt the impulse to do things the way my parents did. Then I can think about the situation and decide how to handle it best.

The other is "Parenting Cards" that I got from the Natural Child Project [**www.naturalchild.org**]. I try to keep them where I'll be likely to see them, and when I'm getting frustrated or overwhelmed or angry I can pick up a card and think about what it says. Sometimes it's not a helpful card, so I choose another. It's just one way of stopping and interrupting my own behavior I guess, but it works.

Of course I don't remember to do these things every single time, but I am getting better at remembering. That's my goal. Not to be perfect, but to be getting a little better as a parent every day.

Michelle N.

 Sometimes, when I feel the anger rise up, I stop and think about why my children are annoying me. Usually it's because I have goal ABC and they have goal XYZ. I stop and decide if I can just put ABC on hold for a few minutes and then get back to it later. Sometimes I need to just stop and focus on my kids. And when I am not focusing so much on fighting them, I can enjoy them and the anxiety goes away.

Pamela G.

Use your imagination

You may be able to "trick" yourself into good parental behavior for a critical few minutes until you feel more in control.

 I sometimes pretend that people are around— I'm much more patient in public, trying to look like the model mama!

Betsy S.

 I think it's funny how I never yell at other people's kids, yet they probably annoy me even quicker than my own kids do! So sometimes I ask myself: How I would respond to someone else's child in the same situation?

Krista M.

When I'm having a really, really difficult time I ask myself, "What would a good mom do? If I was a good mom right now, what would I need to do?" That has helped me get through some really tough spots. I can, at the minimum, "pretend" to be a good mom in that moment, even if I do not feel like one.

The first time I thought of that, it was a turning point for me as a mother. It made me look inside as well as outside and just enhanced the feeling that I have choices to make as a parent even during my toughest times.

Elizabeth B.

Get in touch with your tenderness for your child

Identify some sense-based experience of your child that helps you feel his vulnerability—and reach out for it when you need it. Is it looking at those round cheeks, the shortness of his shins, or how small and dimpled his hands are? Is it listening to the high note in his voice, or feeling his tender skin?

I touch my boys' skin, really feel them, when I'm feeling anxious or stressed. They feel so small and fragile and perfect and innocent. It puts my impatience into perspective.

My older son (three years old) often offers to give me some of his "balance," which I think is funny, but I let him because it helps me regain what is important.

With my younger son (20 months), touching his skin just helps me be more aware. His skin is so soft and smooth and warm and alive. If I grab his sleeve it doesn't re-center me the same way as if I grab his hand or touch his chubby cheeks. There's something about that physical connection.

Physical touch from me helps my boys, too, when they see me trying not to burst into anger. It helps them feel connected to me, not a target. It also helps them when they are losing it themselves.

Anna W.

A hug can bring you back to your child when you need it.

 The hardest for me is when I get hurt by one of my boys. My anger seems immediate. Sometimes I pull them into a hug just to feel how small they are and feel their little heartbeat, and it helps me react in a physical way that dissipates the anger.

Anna W.

Maybe it's a mental image of your child that speaks straight to your heart.

 Many people recommend taking deep breaths and counting to ten. That alone wasn't enough for me. I discovered that it helped if I used visualization at the same time. I carried a joyful image of my child in my mind's eye that I could call up while I took those deep breaths. With my son, I used to picture him smiling and laughing as he rode on the carousel at the Children's Museum.

Carissa D.

Change the scene

When you're starting to feel negative try changing the physical space you're in.

 I live in a really small house where my kids are practically in my lap every second of the day. Going outside gives me a little space to breathe and center myself. It gives the kids some time to be wild where they won't break anything or hurt themselves/each other.

Lauren K.

 The other night I felt ready to explode. I put my boys in the bath because it always calms them down and I got in with them. It calmed us all down.

Erin B.

Change your self-talk

Identify a key question or a helpful mantra that helps you switch gears mentally.

 To help myself avoid yelling, I am learning to practice positive self-talk. For example, say I tell my child for the hundredth time not to pick up the cat by its tail and he doesn't listen. Meanwhile, the baby is crying in my arms to nurse and my oldest child is asking me for a snack. Now normally in my head I'm thinking, "Why don't you ever listen to me–I just can't deal with this," and then I yell.

So instead of saying all those negative things I'm training myself to say things like this: "I can handle this calmly. I know why he isn't listening to me. He's three and he doesn't understand it hurts the cat. I can take care of everyone in turn. I can remain calm."

Lauren K.

 For me it boils down to "people before things." When I look into my son's excited little face, the value of whatever he has just torn up, thrown in the toilet, or dismantled seems vastly diminished. Part of it is just accepting that when I was childless, my possessions seemed valuable because I couldn't conceive of how valuable a child's health and happiness are. It's a values shift–of the very best kind.

Deirdre C.

 Something that my husband and I say if one of us is reaching the end of patience over something is, "It's not about us. It's about our daughter." That helps us to analyze the situation and see what we can do to help our daughter learn from the incident, and not treat it personally.

It goes like this:

I take a deep breath and remind myself, "It's not about me. It's not about how I feel about my magazine/laundry basket/book/wall/scratched bathtub. It's about our daughter." Then I do some more deep breathing.

I try to put myself in her place. Why did she do XYZ?

I try to let go of my own feelings about it. I try to think how she might learn and move on from this or what I might do to help her.

Nicola C.

 I meditate on short phrases by reciting them in my mind. I use a short prayer most frequently because of my beliefs but I've also found the alphabet in French can do the trick.

Bonnie S.

 For me the urge to hit is usually precipitated by thoughts of "He's gonna get it" or "He's driving me crazy, I can't take this."

I try to change the way I think. I say to myself: "He needs me to teach him what to do. I can do XYZ." It really helps focus my thoughts on how to help him, not control him.

I tap into a different way of looking at my child in that moment. Instead of the behavior that's annoying, I focus on how much I love and cherish my little one and let it be the dominating feeling for a moment to put my own behavior and thoughts into perspective. By focusing on how much I treasure him, even at his worst, I can regain my objective in the big picture, how I want to better him, not tear him down physically.

Anna W.

 I have worked on self talk. This always helps at least a bit. It is hard to yell when I am telling myself, "I love me, I love her, I want to find balance."

Teri J.

 My husband and I see "love" as an entity. We think, "What would love do now?" It is amazing how differently we react.

Janine G.

Jump ahead

Imagine a peaceful resolution.

 Parenting is stretching the limits of my patience. Most of the time I can now visualize the resolution of conflicts with my son when they begin. So, if I have a technique to share, it's to try visualizing a happy ending before things escalate. I remind myself, "This too, shall pass," and it will all be over quicker than I think.

Melinda R.

 Sometimes it helps to imagine what the two of us might be doing after the conflict gets resolved.

Carissa D.

Call someone

> It takes
> significant self-
> control to walk
> away when your
> impulses are to
> lash out.

As parents we all need a trusted person we can reach out to when we're at the end of our tether, someone to "talk us off the roof." Is there someone you could call?

 The number one thing that has helped me is to have a great friend to talk to when I'm totally overwhelmed about things. She's my cousin. It's so helpful to have someone to vent to, someone who understands.

Jen W.

 I call a friend and cry. Not often, but when it gets this bad, a friend will usually come over or invite us over. Just not being alone helps hugely.

Jennifer V.

You can offer the same support to your friend, when he or she is in a bad space.

Change your delivery

Sometimes getting down at your child's level so that you can peer face to face might help you snap out of an impending tirade. Opening your hands to your child in a gesture of giving can change your energy. Notice your voice; can you make it sound like you're talking to a friend? What shifts in posture or delivery help you rediscover your compassion?

 If I feel as if I'm going to start yelling, I try to breathe and talk to them in a very calm and loving voice. I find that when I use a soft voice that I'm paying attention to, it somehow helps calm me.

Allison G.

Take time for yourself

It's easy for parents to get into an "all or nothing" mind frame, and lose perspective on what matters most. Sometimes ordering a pizza or popping in a video, even if this is not how you wanted the day to go, can be worth it to help you avoid losing your temper.

 Seriously, sometimes I just pour myself a glass of wine and relax, put the television on for my daughter, and ignore the annoying things so long as they are not harmful to anyone or anything. Of course, I only do this when it's at least close to happy hour time (not the middle of the day) and I usually don't even finish the glass of wine. The time to relax helps immensely.

Jennifer V.

Time-out for parents

Taking a "time-out" to regroup can be a great option to keep in mind, especially when your child is not upset. This tool may be particularly handy for times when you can feel the anger surging and you sense that you could very easily lose your temper and create a whole new problem.

First, of course, you'd need to stop the problem if it is ongoing (such as eggs being dropped on the floor or a baby getting hurt).

Then let your child know that you are upset, that you need a little "time-out" to calm down, and you will come back shortly to talk about the problem. Assure him that you love him.

Once alone you can cry, scream into a pillow, take deep breaths, or do whatever helps you move through the emotion.

Once you are feeling more yourself, you can return to your child and solve the problem at hand.

It takes significant self-control to walk away when your impulses are to lash out. Sometimes you may feel rooted to the spot and unable to take yourself out of the situation. With practice it gets easier, because you can remember having succeeded before, and how much better you felt at not having lashed out.

 Sometimes it seems like nothing is working to get through to my child and even though I am trying hard to resist the urge to yell or to spank, I feel as though I am about to boil over. When I feel that I must have a few minutes to myself in order to keep my own cool (or to regain it), I sometimes tell my children that Mommy needs a time-out.

Because I am just as stubborn as my children are, this is an amazingly difficult step to take, but I've found that walking away can often make a huge difference. I had to allow myself to accept that walking away didn't mean giving in. Taking those few minutes apart gives both of us time to calm down, refocus, and be ready to talk about what is wrong.

Carissa D.

When your child is upset, too

If your child is upset, too, it can be a very difficult time for him to watch you walk away. You must weigh the costs and benefits of the options as you see them—to temporarily break off contact with your upset child vs. to stick around when you sense you are at risk for losing control. These are not easy choices. Some parents feel at times that a "parent time-out" is still in the child's best interest. The parent may put the child in a safe place and close the door for a moment, or the parent may close him or herself into the bathroom for a moment.

 Sometimes walking away can be hard because a screaming little person follows me! I make sure he or she is somewhere safe and then lock myself into the bedroom or bathroom.

Carissa D.

Help your child understand

During a quiet moment, you can prepare your child in advance for the idea of a parent "time-out" by explaining the purpose of it, and how you love him always but sometimes need to calm down. You can let him know the behavior that you are trying to avoid, such as yelling or hitting, and how a time-out may help you treat him the way you want to: calmly and with love.

You can play-act it a few times with your child so he can see what it feels like to have you announce that you need a time-out, walk away, close the bathroom door, and come out calmer—perhaps ending it with a hug. You can switch roles and have him say he needs a time-out, and you can be the one waiting.

Some families get into a routine where the child becomes accustomed to seeing mommy or daddy take a brief time-out, and the child may follow suit when he is about to lose control. Parents are modeling all the time!

Does it help?

If you do try using a "parent time-out," keep your eyes open to how well it works for both parents and children. Some families get into a groove with it and everyone benefits.

 The other day, my frustration was starting to show in my voice. My four-year-old looked at me and said "Mommy, do you need a time-out?" It let me know that I was getting annoyed and that the solution was obvious to him! He has also said "I need a time-out" and taken himself off to his room rather than get angry at his baby sister, who annoys him a lot right now. I was very proud of his response and told him so.

Rebecca W.

Some families find that the child becomes too distressed, and that somehow the parent must find a way to remain in the room. Other families find that the "parent time-out" only raises the stress level of everyone involved!

 I've tried "giving myself a time-out." The kids follow me and even if I lock the door they scream at it and practically try to kick it down! This stresses me out more than anything!

Brianna D.

"Parent time-out" is not for everyone. You will need to work out how you feel about it and how well it fits your family, just like with any parenting technique.

You can always start over

If you find yourself getting off track for days at a time, remember: You can still start over. What helps you get re-centered as a parent? If you can think of one or two key things to start with, concentrate on those for a while until you start to feel as if things are going better.

 I get out of control sometimes, and sometimes I don't even realize for a couple of days how bad things have gotten. There are three things that I try first:

1) If I am still relatively sane, the next day I try to remind myself to not tell him what to do too much. Before I say anything to him, I ask myself if what he's doing is going to hurt anyone or anything, and if it's not, I bite my tongue. He then seems more willing to listen when I do tell him to do something because I am saving it for important stuff.

2) If I am still sane but can't remember what I'm trying to accomplish in the whole parenting thing, or need to vent, I journal. Sometimes on paper, often typing, because I can type faster than I write. Usually it starts off "That stupid kid! He did this and this and this," and gradually gets more constructive.

3) I take a "mental health day." I spend time with friends in adult-only situations, and/or do something totally indulgent and non-kid related. (I don't go shopping because there are kids at the mall!) And I do it guilt-free. Because I need that down time to help me be a better mother.

I keep repeating these; interspersed with talking to like-minded friends and calls to my own mother, until things are better and we are all treating each other like human beings again.

Erin D.

Sooner or later all parents have their slumps, their bad days, their moments of lost temper. Being committed to gentle discipline means seizing opportunities when you have just enough presence of mind to pull yourself back, regroup, and start over. Any success, small or large, is to be celebrated. As parents, we're growing up, too. When we can manage to bring more positive energy to our children and our various challenges throughout the day, our children are in an optimal position to make better choices, too.

Chapter 10

Learn from Your Mistakes

 I believe one of the best things I can do for my children is to remember that like them, I am also still a work in progress. I need to give myself the room to learn and grow.

Mary Beth K.

 I am the best mother of all when my daughters are sleeping, as I never get impatient with them when they are in that state.

Martha B.

Disciplining our children would be so much easier for us parents if we had it all figured out in advance and never had to worry about such things as bad days. Unfortunately life is not that simple, and at one time or another you are likely to find yourself encountering dilemmas that lead you to expand your knowledge about parenting and about yourself, to seek new skills, and to plumb your reserves for patience, empathy, and the fortitude to start over fresh. This is the real work of gentle discipline. On the upside, the parenting years can be a time of accelerated personal growth, a time to learn a great deal about yourself, another person, and relationships in general.

This chapter explores three aspects of this parental learning process:

- Recognizing that parenting is a learning process, and so embracing your own learning as you go;

- Identifying and reducing negative habits that interfere with your being the parent you want to be; and

- Working with your mistakes so that you can learn what you need to and move forward.

Any time you seek to work on a less-than-ideal part of yourself it is of great importance that you begin with a sense of compassion for yourself. The more positive energy you can bring to your "growth edges" the more you nurture your own growth as a parent. In essence, we parents need to bring gentle discipline to ourselves.

Parenting is a learning experience

If you are lucky, the need to actively practice discipline as a parent presents itself a bit at a time, allowing you to take baby steps and grow alongside your toddler. Sometimes new challenges may surprise you and you may be temporarily lost until you get your bearings once again.

Much as you might like to get it all right the first time (wouldn't we all!), chances are you are learning and growing as a parent with each day you spend with your child. Sometimes your own growth as a parent may be in step with your child's. Sometimes, your child may march ahead and you will be scrambling to keep up.

 Life in our family was so peaceful and wonderful, and we were such good parents—the models of gentle and attached parenting—until our daughter turned three.

Suddenly, we were replaced by our parents (or pod people, maybe). It's been a struggle almost every day for nearly a year now. I have read, then read some more, and then gone looking for more information. After I've read it all, and think I have a pretty good handle on it, I start to sound like my mother again. It's scary to notice myself doing or saying something that I know I shouldn't, but can't quite seem to stop.

It has been a struggle for me to do something other than what I was taught as a child by my own parents.

Michelle N.

After working with gentle discipline for a while, you will probably acquire an idea of the way you would prefer to approach your child. But when the going gets tough, a great deal of gentle discipline in action involves facing your own emotional reactions and finding constructive ways to interact with your child. You may find that your own reactivity can be a force to reckon with.

I feel terrible about yelling at my daughters. I just had a big scene with my four-year-old daughter about picking up toys. This is a common issue for us. Logically, I know what to do to make it go smoothly: Make it a game, or turn it into some happy time spent together. But sometimes I'm just too impatient and I just want the girls to clean up after themselves, darn it. It starts to go bad when my little daughter gets distracted. I remind her. She whines and stomps. I lose it and start shouting at her the same way my dad shouted at me when I was little.

Krista M.

Sooner or later, parenting will probably confront you with weaknesses or personal challenges that you may have been able to ignore for most of your pre-child years.

One thing for certain is that my son keeps me on course in my own life and growth. How well I do with him is a mirror of how well I am doing with myself.

Ann M.

Compassion will help you move forward

Remember that gentle discipline works best when you treat yourself with gentleness, too. When love is the priority in family life, you always have new opportunities for healing and nurturing exchanges. When things get off track, treating yourself and your child with compassion presents an open invitation for everyone to start over. This is good for your hearts. Parents need compassionate treatment as much as children, because we have a difficult and important job. Being compassionate to yourself as a parent makes room for you to be human, to make mistakes, and to grow up alongside your child.

 The personal work is the most difficult part about gentle discipline. I was just saying to someone yesterday that I wish I had been able to work out all of my emotional problems and learn more productive behaviors before my son was ever even a glint in my eye.

It's pretty darned hard to come face to face with your issues and shortcomings over and over again, every single day. And even harder to face failure on the occasions that they prevail. But it's all so worth it if it means that my son can grow up and not have to find himself in the same predicament.

Amber S.

Care for your "inner child"

If you sometimes see yourself having your own "temper tantrums" (as most parents do at one time or another) there's a good reason for that. Some psychological theories suggest that in all parent-child interactions, there's a second, invisible "child" participating to a greater or lesser degree, and that's the little child inside of the parent. This is the child you once were, way back when, and the little vulnerable part of yourself that endures.

Most adults have some emotional wounds from their own childhoods that still need to heal—sensitive spots that can be re-awakened by becoming a parent. These wounds can be particularly raw for those who were spanked, shamed, or otherwise treated harshly at some point in their lives.

Some feelings and situations may be particularly powerful triggers for the "inner child" who desperately needs to feel safe, even if that means striking out. If such feelings are triggered, it can be incredibly hard to act like a mature, skilled, and compassionate adult. This kind of reaction may be at the root of many difficulties in translating the theory of gentle discipline into practice.

This psychological experience makes the practice of gentle discipline that much more meaningful if you stick to it. If you can find a way to treat yourself with love no matter how lost and confused you feel, you can nurture the "scared child" feelings still harbored in your adult body. Being gentle to your son or daughter can also help you heal your own wounds from your past.

Some people find that it helps to write in a journal or work with a counselor to identify such feelings and find ways to deal with them.

Gently review any negative habits

It's easy to come up with a list of things you'd like to avoid in your parenting. Here are some common behaviors that many parents try to avoid:

- Nagging: Repeatedly demanding that "x" get done, even when it's having no effect.

- Berating: Focusing on the behavior or mistake repeatedly without adding new insight.

- Commanding: Trying to make someone do what you want right now, like a drill sergeant.

- Dominating: Imposing your will on another person because you can. Endeavoring to win power struggles for the sake of winning.

- Yelling: Trying to control by sheer loudness of voice.

- Hurting: From roughly pulling an arm to get the child to come, to spanking.

- Shaming: Using words to blame or embarrass your child.

- Punishing your child when it might be more helpful to find positive alternatives.

Some of these, if not all of them, are so prevalent in our society that it is easy to fall into the mindset that parenting has to be this way. There is even a widespread perception that children make parents behave this way, that this list is what discipline is all about, and what a "misbehaving" child deserves. Chances are that some of these actions may find their way into your parenting repertoire, whether they are welcome or not. This is not how parenting has to be.

Most parents who practice gentle discipline have some "growth edge," some aspect of their parenting that they wish to work on. This is a big part of the journey of parenting for thoughtful parents. You want your child to trust that you have her interests at heart. You want to show empathy for her feelings. You want to use your own power kindly, proceeding with an eye to both her needs and yours. Sometimes, your own reactions or old habits may get in the way.

In allowing yourself to be vulnerable with your children, you allow them to be safely vulnerable with you. You nurture the bond between you and the goodwill that will allow you to move forward together.

Notice your negatives

Take some time to notice whether any negative habits have become a part of your parenting. Just notice, initially, and try not to judge. Remember this is not about being a good parent or a bad parent—this is about feeling your way through your choices, and supporting yourself in becoming the kind of parent you wish to be.

Once you have one or more negative habit you'd like to examine, ask yourself:

- Do I consciously choose this behavior, or is it reflexive?

- How do I feel about doing it?

- Are there costs to my child and/or to our relationship?

- When do I tend to use these options?

- How does my child feel about this behavior on my part?

- How does this behavior affect my relationship with my child?

- What alternatives might I try to address the problem without relying on these negative habits?

If any of the listed behaviors have become habits, you may need to wake yourself up to their forgotten costs. Observe or imagine the effect on your child. Depending on the exact behavior, your child may feel humiliated, her feelings discounted, or her plans railroaded. In general, you probably want to avoid parenting tools that are likely to generate resentment or damage the connection between yourself and your child, while doing nothing to set her up for better options in the future.

Upon examining your own feelings, you may find that you yourself feel uncomfortable in remembering these incidents. This discomfort is a sign that it is not a good fit for you, and that you, too, will benefit from finding an alternative.

Such negative parenting tools are clearly undesirable if more positive alternatives are available. This is not to say that these behaviors never take place in the homes of parents who practice gentle discipline. They do. Sooner or later, every parent will find him or herself using one or more of these behaviors (and being tempted many more times). One of the big differences, though, is that a parent who is committed to gentle discipline is likely to perceive these for the most part as mistakes,

Make a "Goodies" list

Record your successes. Setbacks and negative interactions are so much easier to notice and dwell on than the glimmers of hope and the leaps forward. How discouraging—and needlessly so. Do something really challenging and keep a list of parenting successes.

Designate a note pad and keep it handy. When you notice that you or your co-parent are handling a parenting challenge well, write it down.

- When have you and your child faced a difficulty and worked things out well?

- What are some of your great moments as a parent?

- When have you seen your child try out new positive options?

- What behavior problems have gone away?

These past successes can buoy you when you get discouraged with yourself as a parent or with your child. These successes can help you stick with gentle discipline when the going gets tough. Recording both parents' successes can help you celebrate together. Whatever you can do to really take note and remember the successes will help you keep going.

One day, Sam, who is almost three years old, started to get frustrated playing with another (older) girl. She was staying very close to him (which makes him anxious) and doing more than he wanted with his drawings and toys. I could tell he was getting angry, and he started to pitch his body back and whine.

Then, he stopped and looked at me and said, "I need a break."

So, we went out of the room and we

habits that can be hard to break, or things done in desperation, but not discipline *per se*.

I don't consider spanking a positive parenting tool. I consider it an outward cry for help from the parent's child within. Some parents are doing ten times better than how they were treated, but are still not at the point where they can control themselves and overcome their inner demons. I honestly believe that spanking is the last resort of a parent who has run out of resources and support and good information. As a famous horse trainer once said, "Violence begins where knowledge ends."

It's not something to vilify yourself about. I think it's a symptom of inner conflict a lack of support and resources needed to think of options that are more effective.

Mariah W.

talked about asking people to move back or not touch. He kept saying "I taking a break. I taking a break." Then he said, "I ready to play now." He went back in and did great.

I had only suggested he "take a break" a few times before—starting about three months earlier. It happens mostly when we host playgroup and he gets overwhelmed about sharing his toys or kids using them "the wrong way!" We have just moved into a quiet room and sung a few songs, then talked about "the problem" and some "solutions." It really seemed to help him calm down and re-group. I'm proud that he was able to initiate it himself this time. He did and it really helped.

Betsy S.

The rewards are worth the time and care you put into your parenting.

The high points of gentle discipline have been when I can see (especially in my daughter since she is older) when the children choose not to do something they shouldn't, due to the guidance they have gotten before they were faced with the choice. While it does take more time than more automatic, authoritarian methods, in the end gentle discipline is easier, because it teaches rather than punishes.

Heather H

I am encouraged by the sense of mutual respect that my children and I have for each other. I am so pleased to see consideration, listening, loving gestures, and the ability to forgive and forget. At the end of the worst of days, we can climb into bed together, read some stories, apologize, and talk about how we can change things tomorrow. We work as a team. I love that.

Amy E.

The plus and minus of YELLING!

Some parental behaviors may take on different meanings depending on how and when you use them. You will need to assess the behavior's effects on your child physically or emotionally. As you examine your habits, look at them carefully and honestly.

Yelling is an example of this. Some parents feel that yelling is at the top of their list of things to eliminate, some wish to reduce it, and others feel they are using it in a workable fashion. If you find that yelling has made its way into your parenting repertoire, you may want to examine how and when you are yelling, and what it means to you.

There are different forms of yelling, each with its own meaning and repercussions. For the purposes of this discussion, let's define yelling as "using a very loud voice."

Do you yell to control your child?

A habit of yelling to get your child to do what you want is probably not productive. When you yell, you may have the illusion that you can make your child do something by mere will and force of voice.

I must remind myself frequently when dealing with children: You can't drive a car with the horn, and you can't control a toddler with your voice—no matter how loud. I know, because I tried to get my two-year-old daughter out of trouble so many times when I was nursing her twin baby brothers by talking to her, then yelling.

Brooke S.

If you find yourself frequently yelling at your child about something, take this as a wake up call that you need to revisit your options for proactively and positively responding to the challenge before you.

Yelling can also be a measure of your stress level—and can be a red flag that you need some self-care before you can expect yourself to parent with more composure.

I used to yell at my husband when we first got married until he put his foot down that under no circumstances was that acceptable behavior and he would have to reassess his marital situation if I continued to yell at him. That pulled me up short. While it took a long time of adjusting (and failing) and trying again, I broke the habit of yelling at him. He was extremely patient but firm in communicating that he would not be treated in that manner and to please accord him the respect he deserved.

I try. Oh, do I try with my two-and-a-half-year-old daughter. But I still find myself yelling at her sometimes, in part probably because she can't really defend herself as eloquently as my husband. She does, however, speak from much closer to the heart by crying and saying over and over, "But I love you, mommy! I love you! No shouting!" It makes me feel so disappointed in myself.

Doni P.

Do you yell to communicate?

Some parents feel it is helpful to use a loud and firm voice to communicate how dangerous or unacceptable a particularly problematic behavior is. Keeping yelling to a minimum can help make this kind of yelling more useful as a communication method.

Do you yell to express your emotions?

Yelling can also be a way of expressing your understandable frustration, getting it out, and moving on, so as to avoid lingering bad feelings or bigger explosions down the line.

Some parents feel they are "yellers" by nature, that it is their emotional style. Parents do need to accommodate their unique personalities in their parenting one way or another.

Some parents have found ways to yell out their frustration without directing it at their children (see Chapter 9).

I have been talking about yelling and being loud with my girls lately. I yell out of frustration. I feel this "build-up" inside, like a pressure cooker. Just yelling ("AAAAACCCCKKKKK!") makes me feel better. If I do this early enough, I can explain that I am very frustrated, and that I need a time-out, and I will deal with the situation in a few minutes.

I think my two-year-old respects that I need some time, but doesn't really understand what that means. But my five-year-old moves out of the room quickly (and usually gets her sister to come and play in the other room). We can talk calmly in just a couple of minutes. I'll either call them

out, or go back and see them. More often than not, one or both girls will ask, "You aren't mad at me, right?" or something to that effect. Sometimes they even ask me almost right away, "Feel better?" My answer is almost always, "Yes," and I can usually smile.

When I yell, it's only occasionally because of something related to my daughters. The rest of the time, I yell because of some other frustration. Both of my children pretty much know that's how I release steam, and I truly believe I'm a better parent for it. I don't have a huge resentment build-up, I don't have this need to be perfect all the time (which is a huge burden off me), and I'm very careful to explain things to my girls rather than just yelling at them.

Loree S.N.

How do you feel about your yelling?

It is important to weigh the benefits with the cost to your child of hearing a loud and upsetting expression in the short term. Each parent will have to come to his or her own conclusion based on his or her particular family situation. Some parents feel that a certain amount of yelling is okay. If you do, you may want to make sure you are open to your child following your lead—yelling when she is upset, too.

If you wish to reduce your yelling, acknowledge the reasons for your yelling and try to find specific and practical alternatives for the situations that act as triggers. It takes time to cultivate more gentle options.

Perhaps you may feel that a few of these less gentle methods are okay—in moderation—as part of your parenting, since none of us is perfect. There are no easy answers here—and no two parents come to the same conclusions or have the same style. Only you can define exactly which options need to go.

Make changes

If you decide to make some improvements, even if you are trying to change a deeply ingrained habit, take heart. It's never too late to change. If you have done something in the past that you regret, you can put it behind you and work on new ways of parenting. Granted, it can be quite hard to give up the emotional release that negative options can give you when you are seeing red, and parenting can be intensely frustrating at times. It's easy to slide back into old habits. It's also easy to have great intentions for making changes but never get around to it in the hustle and bustle of family life.

You will need commitment and a plan. Some tactics that might help:

- Place a lot of your effort in prevention, so you will have fewer times when you'll need to keep your reactions positive during tense situations.

- Work hard to increase your positive tool kit when you are not facing a big challenge; lulls are the best times to try new things, and the practice will serve you well when things do get hard.

- If your habit is hard to break, you may have to make new skill development your top parenting priority for a while, so that you have some time and energy to devote to it.

- Immerse yourself in resources and information that encourage you on your way (resources are listed in Chapter 11).

- Get the support you need from people who know how hard this is and who believe in you as a parent; you may set up regular check-ins with a key support person.

- Take care of yourself so you have more patience and energy to help you get through the tight spots.

- Think of it in positive terms; do it because you believe in yourself and your child and because you want better options for both of you. Guilt and shame are poor motivators and tend to be counter-productive.

- Be patient with the process. You may take some steps backward, but each step forward makes the next step forward that much easier.

- Keep your eyes open to the pay-offs. You may find yourself on a roll.

 Day three with no time-outs! Wow, my three-year-old is actually getting more and more cooperative just through me talking things over with her. She had some crying fits today when I was firm, but then I found strength in myself to try to change the subject with some humor. I also offered to rock her and give her sympathy even though she still didn't get what she wanted.

Life is so much better around here with my attitude adjustment. My husband started barking at her and threatening time-outs and I gently said, "Honey we are on a roll." So he got down to her level, touched her arm, made eye contact, and gave her two choices and she responded. I think it surprised him that she cooperated instead of continuing to resist. I hope that that will inspire him to try to be more patient in the future.

Darshani S.

In some cases, you may find yourself falling back on negative habits while you are cultivating more sustaining options. Changing your behavior will take a lot of time and perseverance. Sometimes it's one step forward and one step back. That's how it goes. The important thing is that you are doing what you can to bring as much empathy and respect to your parenting as you can today. Yesterday is gone. Tomorrow is a new day. You are engaged in a meaningful process of personal growth, and you deserve to pat yourself on the back. It isn't easy!

Identify ideas, resources, or people that motivate and inspire—rather than shame and discourage you.

I strive to remember that if I "give up" and yell, I'm giving up on myself, on my own potential to grow and change, to rise to the occasion, to learn from my child as he learns from me. This helps me to see things through his eyes, and live in the moment as he does.

Deirdre C.

When you do create options that truly work for you, it can be very rewarding to see the ripple effects.

 I have noticed a big difference in how my daughter interacts with her little brother since I stopped yelling. She stopped yelling, and she will often guide him through things. She seems so much more loving toward him since I started being more gentle, and started using natural (or sometimes logical) consequences.

Patty C.

 I have a son who is checking his limits. It started after he turned three years old. I find that when I fight back, yell, or threaten it only seems to encourage him to up the ante. It is easy to react in a negative way without thinking. Conversely, it takes a lot from me to put all my energy into gentle methods. But the cooperation and the pleasant feeling that prevails at home makes it very much worth the effort. I feel good because I know that I am modeling appropriate behavior to my children when I encounter disagreement.

Rekha T.

Make the best of your mistakes

Everyone makes mistakes. Everyone has bad days. You get to start over, right now. Once you have admitted a mistake or identified a negative habit, make the best of the situation and move on.

- Give compassion to yourself,

- Examine the incident,

- Feel your feelings,

- Learn what you can,

- Clean up your mistake,

- Apologize, and

- Forgive yourself.

Give compassion to yourself

Be compassionate with yourself, no matter what has just transpired, because:

Being harsh with yourself will not improve your parenting. Berating yourself, calling yourself names, hating yourself, and/or feeling the urge to punish yourself are dead ends. They lower your self-esteem and raise your stress level without inspiring new options. If you wouldn't talk to your child that way, why say it to yourself?

When you notice these things happening, make a point of refuting the negative messages inherent in these harsh attempts at self-discipline. Instead, treat yourself to empathic, respectful, gentle self-discipline.

Harshness breeds harshness. The flipside is also true—compassion breeds compassion. Gentle discipline starts with how you treat yourself.

 Compassion for my child also includes the child and adult within me. Being able to forgive myself fosters my ability to forgive my child. I have to be able to say that it's okay that I messed up; that I'll react differently next time.

I believe that if I can't be compassionate with myself, then it limits my ability to be compassionate with my child and allow for her mistakes and learning process.

Elizabeth B.

You deserve compassion even after a mistake. Your child will sometimes suffer from your mistakes. You're human, and you're doing your best. Non-judgmental awareness of where you still need to grow can help you to feel whole and to persevere in finding more positive ways of meeting your needs in the future.

There is no perfect parent who always gets it right, never loses his or her temper, and always has a cheerful creative solution to the problem at hand. Lucky children have parents who care enough about them to be willing to change and grow as parents, looking at their own weaknesses, mistakes, and uncertainties, and trying to work with them in positive ways.

The more you are able to be compassionate and respectful to yourself, the more you fuel your own growth and deepen your ability to treat others with empathy and respect. Try to keep your sense of humor about it all. The rest of us are in the same boat.

> **Lucky children have parents who care enough about them to be willing to change and grow as parents.**

 Tough days happen in every life work. The difference is that if you were in an office you might get a special recognition award at the next department meeting for dealing with such a difficult "client."

Betsy S.

Examine the incident

Look carefully, without judgment, with open eyes and an open heart. What were the different things going on that led up to the incident? What need were you trying to meet? What were your options as you understood them then?

Feel your feelings

What feelings led up to the incident? How are you feeling now? And how is your child feeling? Offer compassion to both yourself and your child for any suffering on both sides.

Notice any guilt or shame that you feel, but don't let yourself get stuck in those emotions. At some level, you were undoubtedly struggling. Acknowledge that you were doing your best with a difficult situation, and possibly powerful emotions. Give yourself permission to be human.

Learn what you can

What can you learn from this incident? Could a situation such as this be avoided in the future, by addressing a root problem? What other options might you consider in the future if a similar situation were to arise? Make a plan, something specific you can do to make a similar mistake less likely.

The best possible outcome from a mistake is learning. Take something positive from each experience.

Clean up your mistake

Is there an action you can take now to improve the situation? If you have threatened a punishment that you now regret, you can explain to your child that you have changed your mind. If you have taken something away from her roughly, you can give it back and talk about it. If you have been nagging, you can sit down with her and work on finding a better alternative together. If you have been yelling, you can take a deep breath and find a different voice. If your child is able to talk, she may be able to help you identify a way to make amends.

> The best possible outcome from a mistake is learning.

Apologize

Don't be afraid to apologize to your child. You may find that it is deeply meaningful to both of you.

The times when I do lose it and yell at Gabriel, I make sure to apologize when I've calmed down. We talk about it together. I want him to know that everyone makes mistakes, and I want to be an example of what to do when mistakes happen.

Beth C.

I remind myself that there's no such thing as spoiling a baby or a child who has too much self-esteem. I have to take every opportunity to build, not tear down. If I catch myself yelling or scolding or doing something less loving than I would like, I step back, take a minute, regroup, and apologize to my child. I let her know that it's okay to do something wrong. I let her know that I value her enough to admit to her when I have lost my cool.

Sharon G.

While you never want to take it for granted, the generous forgiveness of a child can touch your heart. Children are shining examples of unconditional love.

 We had been at odds with each other all morning, and I said, "I'm sorry I've been so grumpy with you this morning. Mama shouldn't be so grumpy." And my three-and-a-half-year-old son replied, "Thank you for sayin' dat, mama."

Jennifer P.

Sometimes an apology helps you see that you're doing better than you think.

 Last week, we had a bedtime battle and I lost my temper. I told my daughter (three) that I wasn't getting back up for anything (I was trying to lie with her until she fell asleep the way we do every night. But she was overtired and feeling ornery). I insisted that she needed to lie still and go to sleep and she needed to do it immediately! (Apparently I was overtired and feeling ornery, too.)

Anyway, the next day we were playing house, and she (the imaginary mama) said these exact words back to me (the imaginary child). I looked right into her eyes and said, "That's how I sounded last night, huh?" and she said "Yep."

So I started apologizing, and explaining I was tired and grumpy. She took my hands in hers and interrupted to say, "It's all right, Mom. Even when you are angry, you are always in my heart."

I think that the foundation of attachment, security, and self worth that our kids get from gentle discipline helps them understand and forgive us when we slip up.

Rebecca K.

Forgive yourself

It can be hard to accept that you have hurt your child or otherwise let her down. But you must acknowledge that it has happened and it is now in the past. You can't change it. What your child needs from you now is to make a fresh start. There's no need for negativity from a mistake to cast a shadow on the hours and days to come. Forgiving yourself is an essential step in healing and putting the mistake behind you.

Self-forgiveness is an art, and one few of us have been taught or even seen modeled for us by others. Parenting is a great time to learn. Part of it seems to be gaining a balanced perspective on the situation.

Remember, if your child were to make a mistake, you'd hope that she could find a way to forgive herself, and let go of the negative feelings attached to the mistake. Forgiving yourself is a great thing to model for your child.

Be in it for the long haul

Making the commitment to parent with empathy and respect is a meaningful self-growth path with rewards that extend way beyond parenting.

 I don't see how you could truly discipline your children gently and not have it extend into other areas of your life. You can't spend every day trying to model respect and empathy and all the other ideals gentle discipline promotes, and then go to the store and be rude to the checkout clerk.

Learning about gentle discipline for children has also helped my close relationships with adults. I pay attention more. I am more considerate of other people's feelings. I am more accepting of others. It really has been a very liberating experience. I no longer feel the need to micromanage every little thing. I have grown as a person, and not just as a parent. But it was becoming a parent that made it possible for me to grow like this.

Jennifer K.

> Forgiving yourself is a great thing to model for your child.

Examples of Self-Forgiveness

Anyone who cares deeply about the quality of his or her parenting has had to come to terms with the painful reality of mistakes. Each parent has his or her own way of finding perspective, forgiving him or herself, and moving on. What helps you?

I describe the behavior: "I yelled, I lectured. I know that is not the best way to discipline. I will keep trying to do better. As I practice it, I will get better at it." Short and sweet, but with repetition and consistency, is a better way to teach (which is what discipline means).

Daryl S.

I remind myself that I've only been a parent as long as my oldest child has been alive.

Heather H.

If I've acted less than respectful to Accalia, the first thing I do is apologize and make it right with her. Then I just have to tell myself that I'm immediately wiping the slate clean and starting over.

Amy N.

I've come to the point where I realize that if I don't forgive myself, then I won't be able to move on and to improve. There's no place in the present for guilt from the past.

Rachel J.

My lowest point happened about a year ago when my daughter was two. She is quite spirited and she had been whining and crying for an entire day and then most of the night. The next morning, she woke up and immediately started whining and I completely lost it. I screamed at her in a way that I have never screamed at anyone. Luckily, my husband was home and he quietly walked over, picked her up, and gave me a sympathetic (not patronizing) glance. It was exactly what I needed. I cried for days after that, I couldn't believe I had lost control like that.

I managed to forgive myself by remembering that I am not a perfect parent or person and she would not suffer irreparable damage because I had lost control. My mantra during the bad days is, "Tomorrow will be better."

Jessica K.

I tell myself and my children that I am human just as they are. I admit to my mistakes and do what I can to fix them. I feel that there are learning and growing opportunities in all mistakes. That's what I tell my kids.

Amy E.

Every bit of education I have imparted to my daughter has come back three-fold for me. I have become much less judgmental and much more empathic toward other people. I feel as if I am evolving as a person and I am enjoying it.

Jessica K.

 For my family, one of the most beautiful and unexpected benefits of our gentler approach to discipline is the realization that the roles of teacher and student are fluid and can be exchanged between parent and child. As I struggle to learn as well as to teach during this phase of my relationship with my son, I often worry that I'm not very good at either. But sometimes, when the practice of gentle discipline really seems to be working, I am heartened by the conviction that we are shaping each other in positive ways.

Monica D.

As you go along, you may get into a rhythm with gentle discipline. Other times, you may find you've drifted away and need to reconnect with it.

 I still have room to grow. I get distracted by daily life, lose the pattern, and have to start over. I end up yelling because I forgot to establish a pattern or rule. Or I let something slide a few times because I am busy or tired, without explaining that the situation was different in some way. I take forever to gain new habits, and take a long time to prune out old ones.

But all of this is part of growing. It comes in cycles, in seasons. You don't just decide to change and then you are perfect forever after. It is similar to weeding a garden. Each year there are going to be weeds. But the longer you tend the same garden, the more you know where the weeds are likely to pop up, and the sooner you'll know to look for them so they can be uprooted.

Heather P.

Making the commitment to bring as much empathy and respect as you can into your parenting is a beautiful gift to your whole family.

Through a child's eyes

Sometimes the most powerful insight into your own parenting behavior may come when you are able to see your actions from the outside. Your discipline is an important behavior you are modeling for your child.

I started over-using commands about a year ago, after a particularly frustrating bout of not being able to get my first daughter into her car seat. The word "need" spewed from my mouth all the time, even when the situation wasn't urgent or dangerous. "I need you to get ready right now!" "I need you to get into your car seat, right now!" "I need you to be quiet while your sister's asleep." "I need you to get out of this room, right now!"

This phase started when my daughter had just turned two. She was not quite articulate yet. About six months later, I started hearing my demanding language coming back from her. "I need to be picked up, right now!" "I need you to come in here, right now!" You get the picture. She even managed to mimic my tone of voice and physical stance.

Pei L.

I knew I needed to stop yelling so much. But it really came to life when my daughter started yelling at my son or the dogs when she was mad at them. Talk about an eye opener! We've talked about it and agreed that we aren't going to yell anymore.

Now if I start yelling and don't catch myself (I usually do) my daughter will say, "Mommy, use your inside voice!"

Jen W.

I struck my older son once, on the leg, after he bit me on the arm. He taught me how powerfully I'd laid the groundwork for a non-violent approach to discipline. He followed me around the house for three full hours, saying in various tones of offended and hurt feelings: "You hit me, mommy! We don't hit! Hitting isn't nice. You hit me." He made sure that lesson stayed with me, forever. Despite my apology, the shock of having been hit by someone did not abate for him immediately. That, for me, was the point when my determination to use gentle discipline methods solidified.

Heather P.

I tended to resort to punitive methods when I was too busy dealing with a toddler, a baby, and a business.

One day, while I was working, my daughter was playing with her doll. She spanked the doll and said, "You are bad. Bad. Bad. Bad." I just started crying, apologized to my little girl, and told her together we would figure out this discipline stuff.

My husband finally has agreed to use gentle discipline. He used to always flick the kids with his finger for doing bad things. I finally had to ask him to cut it out because Ani was flicking Cameron and me all the time if she got annoyed at us. I explained to him what was going on and he stopped. A week or so later, Ani stopped flicking.

Heather H.

Being a really great mommy is really hard work. I congratulate all parents who take the first step and admit that there are things they would like to change.

Rebecca W.

You can do it!

With gentle discipline, you may need to put extra time in up front—slowing down to listen to your child, problem-solving when you could just lay down the law, and digging deep into your stores of compassion.

But as you go along, you are reducing power struggles, setting your child up for self-discipline down the line, and keeping communication lines clear between you and your child. All of this saves time and energy in the long run.

Parenting is a challenge. Remember that other moms and dads are joining you in your important commitment to make a priority of empathy and respect. Hang in there!

Surround yourself with encouraging voices.

 It's rough sometimes. Don't let the rough spots keep you from seeing the big picture: you are raising a wonderful little person, you are challenging yourself in ways that you never imagined, and you are both learning, learning, learning. The rewards are infinite.

It still just sucks sometimes because it's hard and much of it feels like guesswork.

Betsy S.

 First, take a big deep breath and remember that you are a good mommy. Repeat it until you believe it. Feel better now? Good.

Rebecca W.

At the end of the day

Each new day is a new opportunity to grow with and love your child. Taking the insights you can from your day can be a great way to bring it to closure, the good and the bad, and let it go.

 At night, before going to sleep, I lie in bed and replay the day in my head. I think about what went well, what was lousy, how I felt about it, and what I want to change or do differently. That helps me to plan the next day. To really think about it and put extra effort into behaving the way I want to behave really helps.

It's like trying to lose weight. You can't just tell yourself that you want to do it. You have to have a plan for how you are going to do it. Then you need to follow through on it. I know it's not the same thing as working through discipline issues, but the mental part of it is very important, in my opinion.

Michelle F.

Remember to begin and end each day with an unambiguous message of love.

 Every night (before we lie down) or morning (when I wake up with my kids), I make it a point to hug my kids and say aloud (while they hear it) that I am so lucky to have them for my kids. This is as much for me as it is for them to hear. This gives me a soft feeling in my heart to start the day or end the day even though the day may have had a few rough spots.

Rekha T.

Chapter 11

Your Parenting Village

M ost of us live in communities, so our parenting occurs within a larger social context where we have contact with many other people. Many of us have people around us who provide encouragement, modeling, and ideas. There may also be those who disagree about approaches to discipline. If a child is in someone else's care some of the time, parents take a special interest in that person's discipline style and its influence on their child.

Let's look at how other parents have built support for themselves and bridged differences when it comes to discipline in their parenting villages.

You deserve support

Most parents who practice gentle discipline need other parents to support them. It's all too easy to find yourself confronted with negative messages about children and parenting. To succeed in gentle discipline it may be well worth your time to seek out and surround yourself with friends who share similar values, and to create a personal library of resources you trust. Such support acts as an antidote against the negative messages about children and discipline that come from other sources.

Role models and sources of support

Role models

One of the best forms of support someone can offer you is modeling. There's nothing quite like seeing other parents putting empathy and respect into action. We all need ideas and inspiration to expand upon our own gentle discipline practices.

Who inspires you? For many, it's a special friend or relative.

 My friends who come by this approach naturally amaze me. I love listening to them interact with their children because I can learn so much from them. I feel that gentle discipline has been something I have had to teach myself. I think it's odd that something that seems so logical doesn't come naturally to many people, myself included.

Carissa D.

 I have a friend who is one of the gentlest people I have met. I have never heard her raise her voice to her child. She may talk to him with intensity, but always in a gentle manner. She has been an expert at redirecting his behavior, even when he was going through an extremely aggressive stage. Sometimes when I'm having a difficult time keeping my cool, I think of her and what she would do. It helps me regain some calmness and tune in to my child.

Another friend also has that innate gentleness. We

have been friends since high school, but we live across the country from each other. I often call her and ask what she does. When we visit, I gather ideas that I use all year until we see each other again.

Elizabeth B.

 My sister-in-law was one of my early role models in this approach. I remember watching her with awe, as she used reminders, rules, and logical consequences to obtain impressive responses from her five children.

Another friend had told me to seriously consider natural and logical consequences as an approach. She had been a kindergarten teacher, as well, and a good one.

Between the two of them, I picked up a few general ideas (e.g., apologize when you make a mistake; explain what you want for behavior, not just what you don't want), and absorbed the general attitude.

Heather P.

La Leche League

If you are looking to extend your support network, a great place to start is your local La Leche League group. Many mothers attend their first La Leche League meeting for breastfeeding support, and find great role models for gentle discipline while they're there. Loving guidance is one of the basic philosophical principles of La Leche League: "From infancy on, children need loving guidance which reflects acceptance of their capabilities and sensitivity to their feelings."

Friendships made through La Leche League can serve you well throughout your parenting years.

 I often watch other mothers at LLL meetings. After nearly three years of meetings and conferences, I continue to learn something every time. I may be a Leader, but I am not a mother of twins, or a mother of three, or someone else's mother. I am only the mother of Ashley. Every other mother can be a source of ideas for parenting situations.

Sarah M.

The women at my LLL meetings inspire me. I love to watch their examples. I enjoyed talking to some mothers with older children who had gone through the same discipline issues that I was going through with my son. They gave me some suggestions and some encouragement.

Beth C.

I really haven't read many discipline books. I think my greatest resources have been the other mothers I've met through LLL. Watching other mothers parent in the way I wish to is a great inspiration, and it makes me realize it can actually be done.

Amy N.

Get help when you are at low points

Sooner or later, most parents experience a low point.

My low point was probably when my third child was around one year old. Juggling three was a lot for me. It was then that I thought gentle parenting was made for people with one child (or whose children were born at least 10 years apart). I felt as if I didn't know where to turn. I didn't want to yell, scream, or spank, but also couldn't find my gentleness when it came down to it. Many times, I just walked away.

Amy E.

Keeping your parenting low points to yourself can be isolating and dangerous. Remember to reach out to other trusted parents who can help you sort through troubling incidents, offering insight, sharing personal stories, brainstorming other options, and conveying compassion for you and your child. By showing that you are human, you are likely to be privileged with glimpses of the human side of your friends, too.

What helped me a lot was to find a good "mama tribe" of other parents who believe in gentle parenting, too. Then I could see real life people acting out the things that I had read. I have to be able to take the portable phone to the bathroom, lock myself in for five minutes, and cry to my friends. They build me back up and send me on my way. They hold me accountable for being the kind of parent I profess to be.

I also receive a lot of support at the Gentle Discipline message board at MotheringDotCommune (**www.mothering.com**).

Amy E.

To find a La Leche League Group near you:

- Try the index of La Leche League Groups from around the world at (**www.lalecheleague.org**);

- Call 1-800-LALECHE (in the US) for English or Spanish or 847-519-7730; in Canada 1-800-665-4324 or 514-LALECHE for a French-speaking Leader;

- Look in your local telephone directory under "La Leche League," "breastfeeding," or "lactation;" or

- Call your pediatrician, health clinic, or local library.

You can also get together with a great number and variety of parents at regional La Leche League conferences. Indeed, you are likely to find a session or two devoted to gentle discipline, as well as sessions for fathers. Information about these conferences is available from your local Group or on the LLLI Web site.

More sources of support

Some mothers set about forming their own support group.

 It is not always easy to find a group such as this; we did not form overnight. I have met local mothers through online message boards. I've also met them at LLL Meetings, doctors' offices, and even our weekly farmers' market. Some friends come alone; others bring one or two additional links to our circular chain.

The support we gain from each other is priceless. I feel a strong connection to earlier days when women would gather together daily and help each other with life's responsibilities. We comfort each other, praise each other, and offer support when someone needs to be buoyed up.

I often joke that my friends help me be a better mother. It is a great and humbling truth.

Stacie B.

Many alternative parenting communities make a priority of empathy and respect.

 The families I've gotten to know through the educational and life philosophy of "unschooling" have been superb examples of how it's

Read all about it

It can be inspiring and intellectually stimulating to soak up resources that help deepen your understanding of parenting with empathy and respect. Reading an assortment of writing on gentle discipline can help you think through various ideas from many different angles, through many different examples, continually reinforcing the gentle orientation, and helping you put old models of parenting behind you.

Fabulous magazines

- *Mothering Magazine:* The Magazine for Natural Family Living, (based in US)

- *Natural Parenting:* Real Alternatives for Today's Parents, (based in Australia)

- *The Mother Magazine* (based in UK)

Terrific Web sites:

- The Natural Child Project: "Resources for Caring Parents," put together by parenting author Jan Hunt at www.naturalchild.org

- Parent Leadership Institute: "Fostering Healthy Parent-Child Relationships That Will Last a Lifetime" at www.parentleaders.org

- Attachment Parenting International: "Peaceful Parenting for a Peaceful World," at www.attachmentparenting.org

- The Web site for *Mothering Magazine*, "The magazine of Natural Family Living" at www.mothering.com

Enriching books

- *Kids Are Worth It: Giving Your Child the Gift of Inner Discipline*, by Barbara Coloroso

- *Kids Parents and Power Struggles: Winning for a Lifetime*, by Mary Sheedy Kurcinka

- *Becoming the Parent You Wish To Be: A Source Book of Strategies for the First Five Years*, by Laura Davis and Janice Keyser

- *How to Talk So Kids Will Listen, and Listen So Kids Will Talk*, by Adele Faber and Elaine Mazlish

- *Playful Parenting*, by Lawrence J. Cohen

- *Non-Violent Communication: A Language of Life*, by Marshall Rosenberg

- *The Natural Child: Parenting from the Heart*, by Jan Hunt

There are many more resources to inspire and help you as you make empathy and respect priorities in your parenting. Many parents find their own favorite articles, Web sites, and books that they refer to often as their children grow.

possible to live in harmony and with respect for each other without needing to adopt a punitive lifestyle.

Amy N.

Attachment Parenting International (API) is an international organization, with a Web site full of great discipline-related resources (**www.attachmentparenting.org**), a quarterly newsletter that often covers discipline ideas. Some areas even have API support groups that meet on a regular basis.

Online communities

There are several message boards for connecting with other parents who discipline with empathy and respect. It can be great to post a conundrum at bedtime and receive several replies by morning. You can find current ones by doing a search with "gentle discipline board." Two boards that are very active as this goes to press are:

- The Gentle Discipline discussion board, offered on the Web site of *Mothering Magazine*, at **www.mothering.com**.

- For Christian mothers in particular there is a wonderful resource at **www.gentlemothering.com/forum**.

Many email lists exist to focus on disciplining with empathy and respect. One that is currently active and strong is "Positive Parenting," available through **yahoo.com**. Email lists fluctuate considerably over time. If you do a search, you are likely to find many options.

Responding to criticism about your discipline

Some parents who practice gentle discipline encounter opposition from friends, family, or even strangers. Has anyone conveyed to you that you are going about discipline all wrong? That your child's (developmentally appropriate) behavior is your fault? Or has anyone stepped in to discipline your child in a way you felt was inappropriate?

When facing criticism about your discipline choices, you have many options for responding, depending on your relationship to the person, your situation, and your goals. The following suggestions have been adapted, with permission, from material written by Kelly Bonyata for her Web site, **Kellymom.com**.

Share your perspective

If you sense that the other person is open to your perspective, it can be helpful to find a diplomatic way to share it. Many people are only familiar with parenting methods which assume parents should control their children. You can share with them the idea that children do not need to be treated harshly in order to learn to make better choices. You can share the perspective that parents and children can have a relationship based on trust, that children are not usually misbehaving intentionally, but need help in meeting their needs in positive ways. You can reassure the other person that you want to use gentle discipline in a way that includes having boundaries for your child's behavior.

You can emphasize that these are your personal beliefs and that you respect the other person's need to hold his or her beliefs. You may wish to share what has led you to perceive parenting the way you do. Have you always seen things this way? Getting into a debate may be counter-productive. Is there a way to connect in a human way across your differences? Where is the common ground?

Learn more about the other person's perspective

What concerns this person about your approach? How did this person come to have that concern? Is there something this person could be misunderstanding either about your ideas, what you are doing, or your child? Has the person had bad experiences with other families practicing gentle discipline? Has this person felt personally affected by your child's behavior in some way? Is there a philosophical difference that would be fruitful to respectfully explore together?

Share your feelings

It may hurt to have someone cast aspersions on your heartfelt parenting practices. Criticism or interference can erode the good feelings in a relationship, which is a shame for everyone involved. Regardless of the issue in contention, if you are feeling hurt the other person may benefit from knowing that.

You may want to offer him or her empathy, too. If the other person is your parent, for example, imagine how hard it could be to watch your own grandchild being cared for in a way that you think is problematic. Your parent may be feeling anxious, fearful, and powerless. Your parent may also worry that you are critical of the parenting you received, since you are doing things so differently. Acknowledge that your parent needed to make his or her own best choices based on what he or she knew at the time. As a parent yourself, you know that that's the best any of us can do. Let your parent know how much you appreciate having him or her in your life, and what a gift he or she is in your child's life.

Assert your parenting boundary

No one loves your child more than you do. As the parent, you have the privilege and the responsibility to make careful choices on behalf of your child, from nutrition to discipline. You can let the other person know that you want to feel that he or she respects that you are in the best position to make these choices for your child.

Your child may be hurt or confused by hearing negative comments about his behavior or your parenting. You can let the other person know that it is not okay to criticize you or your child in front of him and that it is time to stop. Some firm but respectful phrases to close conversations include:

- "I'm parenting the way that feels right to me, and I need you to respect that."

- "These are tough choices and very personal ones. I'm doing what I feel is best for my family."

- "I respect your opinion and value your advice, but I have thought this out carefully and done a lot of research, and my mind is made up. I will be happy to respect your opinion, but you have to respect my decision—and it is my decision."

- "This is what works for our family. Unless it becomes a problem, we're not going to change things."

> Acknowledge that your parent needed to make his or her own best choices based on what he or she knew at the time.

If necessary you may need to say, "How I discipline my child is my choice and I will not discuss it any more." It's okay to make your discipline choices off-limits as topics of conversation.

Avoid the issue

When touchy discipline issues come up, you may find it helps to politely change the subject. You can go into another room to gently discipline your child if necessary. You may also need to limit your contact with some people who are determined to interfere or criticize. You do not have to defend your choices. You are the parent.

Partners in Discipline

You may not have had your discipline plan all figured out back when you were choosing your mate. Or maybe your ideas are changing now that you have a real live child in front of you. You two may find yourselves confronting important parenting questions when your child is beginning to test limits.

It can be very helpful to have a teammate in gentle discipline right in your house. If you have a co-parent who supports you in gentle discipline, you can grow together, share your challenges and inspirations, and support each other in doing your best. What better resource than another person who knows you and your child so well?

 My husband and I are my son's main disciplinarians. Luckily, we agree completely on how to raise him and discipline him. Of course, each of us has our stressed-out days when we need to be reminded of our son's abilities and feelings, so it's nice to have each other to be accountable to.

When I'm having hard days and I yell at my son, my husband will remind me how Gabriel is feeling or what he's thinking. I do the same for him. I wouldn't be as patient as I am without a supportive, committed husband.

Beth C.

My husband and I are on the same page as far as parenting goes. We work together as a team very well. His strengths are my weaknesses and vice versa.

Amy E.

Parents growing together

Each parenting team will have a distinct evolution into disciplining in a way that works for them. If you have a co-parent, where were you two with discipline in the beginning, and how far have you come?

 Logan and I had no blueprint for how to be parents. Our respected and respective parents and siblings parented quite differently, and the culturally normal way of parenting seemed to be based on a lack of respect for the child. We're also quite different from each other, with perhaps the biggest difference being the way we relate to people. Yet here we are, understanding each other's slight flicker of an eyebrow.

I guess the biggest help in finding our way has been not having a television. I have had to verbally process every thought and concept, every conflict and joy. My husband has patiently endured evening after evening of my talk about parenting theories. Yes, I've read the parenting books. But it has been the experimenting with the techniques, and the discussing the results with my husband, that has allowed us to actually learn what works for us.

There was a moment when I stopped thinking that Logan was someone I had to "train" to be a good father while I "trained" myself to be a good mother. I think it was the same moment that he turned my analysis back onto me, and pointed out that what I was doing wasn't in the best interests of our son. It was a moment of realization that we could all learn together. We have consistently found that modeling is the key to solving behavioral problems, and when Logan pointed out what I was doing, it was the start of some real growing up on my part.

The beauty of having my husband on my side was to have a reminding voice when things were starting to go awry: "Heidi, get up. This isn't getting the day off to a good start." It wasn't an admonishment but an encouragement to take control of the kind of day I would have. In return, it meant I could point out what Logan was doing that wasn't helpful.

"You're raising your voice, Logan," was a meaningful observation, non-threatening because "raising my voice" was initially discussed as a flaw in my own behavior, and constructive because we had already discussed techniques to use instead. For example, stopping to wonder if we were just expecting too much from a three-year-old, and stopping to see things from our son's point of view. I feel we're learning real life skills about treating each person with respect, being clear in our communication, and taking responsibility for our own happiness—skills I imagined I already had.

Finding families with a similar philosophy has also helped us to see things in the same way. Logan has attended men's sessions at La Leche League conferences, comes to LLL family events, and loves to listen to LLL meetings when they're at our place. "You women talk about such interesting things! Guys just talk about sports, politics, and what's on television."

We have also attended Playcentre since our son turned two. Playcentre is an early childhood education service run as a family cooperative in which parents are the teachers and their (parenting) education is considered as important as the children's. Logan has spent time with the other families on camping weekends, working bees, and so on. Logan doesn't talk much, but he really respects children and actually puts in the time playing with them.

Heidi O.

Bridging differences between parents

Whether it is a matter of details or the big picture, sooner or later most parenting partnerships need to bridge some differences when it comes to discipline.

 If we're having a conflict about how one of us handled a situation, then we talk about it later and try to talk it through, coming up with different things we could try. We also discuss it on a theoretical level—whether it really fits with how we think our child should be treated. We also consider her personality and whether a potential solution fits with her level of sensitivity, stubbornness, and other characteristics.

Elizabeth B.

If you are facing a difference around your parenting ideas, it is of utmost importance that you approach your co-parent with respect and openness. The person you are parenting with is going to have to find an approach and a set of ideas that feel right to him or her. Listen to him or her with a goal of understanding what his or her needs, feelings, fears, and hopes are.

Whenever possible, strive to find room for compromise. Is

The pressure to spank

Some parents who have decided that spanking is not going to be part of their parenting tool kit find they are up against a lot of opposition. The pressure to spank may come from family, friends, or perhaps their religious community.

You may find it helpful to point out that some experts take a strong stand against physical punishment:

> Corporal punishment is of limited effectiveness and has potentially deleterious side effects. The American Academy of Pediatrics recommends that parents be encouraged and assisted in the development of methods other than spanking for managing undesired behavior.
>
> *The American Academy of Pediatrics*

I might say something such as, "You know, the latest research shows that spanking is the least effective method of discipline. I could show you the data from the American Academy of Pediatrics."

Anna B.

Bolster your own understanding of the reasons to avoid spanking, as well as the research that backs this up. Many of the natural parenting Web sites contain detailed arguments against spanking. A great place to start is to search for "spanking" at Jan Hunt's The Natural Child Project (www.naturalchild.org).

Sometimes a personal exploration of your respective experiences around spanking can get the discussion into a personal mode and out of a win/lose debate mode.

If you are part of a Christian church that advocates spanking, there are resources to back up your desire to parent gently. As a starting point, try:

• *Biblical Parenting*, by Pastor Crystal Lutton, which offers the biblically researched, gentle, and practical method she calls "Grace-Based Discipline."

• Gentle Christian Mothers is a Web site "born out of a desire to help unite mothers who believe that God has given mamas a mothering instinct and whose hearts' desire is to nurture our children gently" (www.gentlemothering.com).

this an area in which you and your co-parent can agree to disagree? Although on the most important things you will want to have a united front, your child can also benefit from the observation that different people have different styles and ideas.

The Art of Conversion Sometimes one parent believes in a much harsher approach to child rearing, and it does not seem that you can both simply follow your own separate paths. A common area of disagreement is spanking. Passions may be high on both sides. Sometimes a heart-to-heart discussion can provide a breakthrough. Probing your own childhood experiences and personal histories may help get to the heart of the matter. Some people who received harsh discipline as children say, "I'm fine, look how I turned out." Digging a little deeper may reveal that there was more to it than that, as one mother describes.

 My husband thought that the whole gentle discipline thing was a bunch of baloney. But then I asked him how he really felt about his childhood; the way he was treated, the amount of respect (or lack thereof) he felt his parents had for him, and the messages that they sent him. The more he thought about it, the less satisfied he was with the answers.

Molly D.

Give some thought as to how you came to feel as you do about discipline. When you examine what attracts you to gentle discipline, you may realize that you have had different experiences from your co-parent, and these experiences may have made all the difference. Perhaps you have been exposed to a great deal more gentle discipline role models, and it has given you confidence that gentle discipline is a viable and wonderful approach. Perhaps you have read up on it and compared notes with friends. Perhaps you are the primary caregiver for your child, and so you have had more hours and days to soul-search on this topic. Knowing how you came to be where you are can give you insight into why your co-parent may not be seeing things the same way.

If your co-parent is not able to put in the same kind of time as you are in considering discipline, you may have the advantages of a great deal of insight that he or she is unaware of.

 I said to my husband: "I have spent the last three-and-a-half years researching discipline. I have read books, attended lectures, and surfed the Web for hours upon hours. I have arrived at my discipline method after this research. How much time have you put into thinking about your discipline method? I bet it hasn't been five minutes." He couldn't argue with that one. It gave him a whole new attitude toward what I am doing and why I'm doing it.

Jessica K.

Sometimes a busy co-parent is more likely to attend a lecture than read a book, and you might want to keep an eye out for the speaking schedule of inspirational speakers such as Barbara Coloroso or others whose books you have read and loved. You may consider making a gentle discipline "cheat sheet" for your co-parent, and post it on the fridge or email it to him or her.

Stopgaps Patience, love, and acceptance are key to supporting someone in considering gentle discipline. In the meantime, you may need to focus on the aspects of parenting and your relationship that are in your control.

If I can't bring him around, I can still do what I have to do. My husband's relationship with my daughter is separate and unique from mine. I can't control him. I can only control what I do. What is important is not that he does things exactly the way I would do them, but that we share the same values and goals for disciplining our daughter. His methods will differ from mine and I need to remind myself that it's okay.

Jessica K.

If you two are unable to resolve the issue at this time, is it possible to devise a plan you both are comfortable with for now?

Before our son was born, my husband and I disagreed about spanking. We made a deal though. First: We would not even talk about spanking, swatting, or hitting until our son was three years old. Second: He would use gentle discipline as I suggested it as long as it was working.

He had to trust that I was doing the research and that I knew what I was doing. He does very well, yells sometimes, but nothing physical at all. He was worried about Konur being a spoiled brat without being spanked, and that is very far from the case.

Lori H.T.

I was very worried that my husband and I would have opposite approaches to discipline. To head it off, I got him to agree to talk to me about it before spanking, hitting, slapping, or otherwise physically punishing our daughter. Our daughter is 16 months old and he hasn't done any of these things so far. Whew!

If he ever did, my plan is to

1) Brainstorm several alternative techniques that should help the situation;

2) Discuss our concerns about the problem and the solutions I've suggested;

3) Reach some kind of agreement about which of the techniques we will use in that specific situation, and what we will do if that one fails; and

4) Write down our plan and put it up somewhere where we can refer to it.

I think my husband will never be convinced that spanking isn't necessary unless I am able to show consistently that there are alternatives. However, he agrees that spanking or whatever isn't a quick fix, either. I completely trust him to follow through with his agreement.

Jen M.

It is hard to compromise when it comes to protecting your child and providing the best. It can take a great deal of time and loving communication to work your way through these difficult issues with a co-parent. The stronger your relationship, the better able you will both be to keep defenses down and trust each other to find the answers together.

With luck, perseverance in working together, and time, you may find that your co-parent will decide to make empathy and respect high priorities in his or her parenting, and to steer clear of more harsh methods. The mother in the last example now comments, several months later:

 My differences with my husband have not been a problem so far. As our daughter grows, I think he is realizing that spanking is not necessary. I have never been concerned that he will hit her. Sometimes being a parent is very different than we thought it would be; stuff that seemed so reasonable before we had kids now seems hopelessly naïve.

Jen M.

Finding your stride. As you grow together, you can stretch each other's ideas and skills. You can lovingly help each other to be the best parents you can be.

Friends as resources

Other parents can be great resources for us and spending time with such families provides wonderful playmates for our children. While the children play it can be helpful to compare notes on parenting, from sleep challenges to birthday parties. If you have one or more friends who practice gentle discipline, you can grow together right alongside your children.

Bridging differences between friends

Spending so much time around other parents and children can be challenging at times, too. No two people think of parenting in exactly the same way, and children have a way of drawing parents into tricky situations. How you handle these may depend to a great degree on your personal style as well as how close you feel to your friend.

Even with a trusted friend, it can be scary to bring up parenting differences, but the pay-off can be well worth it.

> No two people think of parenting in exactly the same way, and children have a way of drawing parents into tricky situations.

My two-year-old son had a conflict with my friend's smaller three-year-old boy on a slide, and I was worried about the other boy's safety. I intervened to remove my child from the slide. Afterward, I wondered if my friend might have disapproved of my actions, since she is a big proponent of letting children work things out.

I worried about it, role-playing the scene and imaginary subsequent conversations in my mind. It seems such a minor incident to have left me doubting myself and feeling defensive about my philosophy. Yet, I think it has been typical of my state-of-mind as I've been deciding how I will parent.

The next time I spoke to my friend, I summoned enough courage to bring the subject up. I explained that I was worried about her son's safety and I didn't know what else to do. To my surprise, she said that she was glad I had done something, and that she had been worried about her son, too. So all my worry about differing philosophies was unnecessary. Broaching the subject has given me the confidence to discuss other parenting issues with her without feeling defensive.

With many of my friends and family, though, I'm biding my time until the children are older, hoping that we can avoid too many conflicts in the intervening years. I keep my visits brief, don't complain about my life (to minimize unwanted advice), and avoid high-conflict situations.

Heidi O.

If you are tempted to analyze—or advise—another parent, remember to keep a humble perspective. It's always easy to witness other people's parenting and come up with a cause-and-effect analysis. If only the parent would do things differently, it seems, the child would behave better. But if you have ever been on the receiving end of that kind of well-meaning input, you probably know how much more complicated your situation is, and how many more factors you are taking into account when parenting the way you do.

 I think it's quite impossible to know the inner workings of another family. You get social glimpses of them, maybe many times, but still there are many complexities behind closed doors that you cannot know. Therefore, I would be slow to credit obnoxious behavior with "gentle discipline" choices.

Alecia I.

The more understanding you can be about others' choices, the more relaxed you can be when differences arise.

 Some of my half-siblings are far more strict with discipline, and far more hair-trigger (leaping to handle the slightest distress) with reassurance than I am. However, their children are even more sensitive than mine are in some ways, and far more stubborn in others. They do what works for their kids.

We have similar basic philosophies, but because of the differences in our children, what works for us would not work for them. At times, that has caused some friction, but we try to keep out of that space as much as possible.

I get some odd looks sometimes, and probably give a few odd looks, myself (not intentionally). But since we're not vastly separated in styles, as long as we don't try to apply what works for us to the other person's child, we're fine.

Heather P.

The ups and downs of extended family

Perhaps your own parents practiced their own form of gentle discipline when you were growing up.

 My mom inspires me. While our parenting styles are not necessarily similar, there are only a few times I remember feeling hurt from her actions. What I remember more is the amazing amount of patience and calmness that she possessed.

Amy N.

Perhaps your parents did things differently but are able to appreciate the value in what you do.

My parents support our way of parenting. They didn't always understand it or believe that it was the right thing to do but they stood by and watched. They've learned over time that what we are doing is better than teaching our children to fear us.

Amy E.

You and your child's other parent both bring with you myriad relatives who each have distinct ideas about child rearing. Some members of your extended family may be a source of support, in offering ideas, role modeling, and perhaps by helping take care of your child sometimes. The relationships your child can make with his grandparents, aunts, uncles, and cousins can enrich his life.

Bridging differences with extended family

One of the trickiest situations can be if one of your child's grandparents criticizes your discipline, or steps in to discipline your child in a way you are not comfortable with. Generally speaking, if you are there, it seems unnecessary for anyone else to step in, but the temptation appears to be strong in some cases.

Sometimes an indirect approach can allow you to broach topics that might be touchy if done more directly.

 I have problems with my family and my in-laws. Both sets of parents were stricter. My mom is more open to learning about gentle discipline, though, as long as I am careful to make it seem as if I'm discussing something "in general" rather than in reference to her behavior or parenting. I tend to discuss child development and gentle discipline a lot anyway, so it's easy to work a specific topic into the conversation when needed.

Sonia M.

Sometimes a direct approach is required, and you need to decide how gentle or strong your message needs to be, depending on the situation. Don't forget you can draw from your gentle discipline skills in this circumstance, showing respect and empathy for the person.

It's getting harder now that my son is getting older because when we go to see extended family, they are a little harsher than either my husband or I would be. I've calmly reminded my dad a few times that he doesn't have to yell or be harsh when he tells our son, "No." I also tell him that it's a reminder to say, "No, don't touch," not a punishment. It's difficult and sometimes I don't feel comfortable leaving my son with them because I know their tempers. However, I keep telling them and reminding them how we discipline our son.

Beth C.

Sometimes it's a matter of gentle (and repetitive) teaching—of how we think, and how we do things with our children.

When my father would discipline our child, I would talk about differences in parenting style as they happened. It wouldn't do any good to sit down and have a long discussion about discipline with my father unless it were to come out of my having responded to him in one of these situations. If I were to bring up a theoretical topic, he would be more likely to presume I'm "just a new parent" and don't know what I'm doing, or "I'll thank him later," or whatever.

I try to remember he loves my children and wants what is best for them, too. My father was quick to come around when my first daughter was small. He was aghast at the thought of not raising her the way we had been raised, but his yelling came to a complete halt when I showed him one day that he was frightening my sweet daughter.

I keep at it. I talk about it in front of our children so they see Mama and Daddy going to bat for them. I wouldn't make a huge point of it at all, just say something such as, "Oh, we don't say 'bad' because our child is not a bad person. She is a normal toddler and I am sure she will learn that books are for reading, not throwing." In saying it like that, I've hit on two important points: that "bad" is not a helpful word, and that my child will learn. I believe it's good for both my child and my father to hear.

Penelope G.

The more important the issue, the stronger your stance is likely to be. Your child is relying on you.

We've had to become more assertive to say, "Hey, that's not your place, not your right. Please talk to us about this issue, but don't try to control our children."

Rachel J.

If you ever need to leave your child with someone else who has a different approach to discipline, you may need to be very specific about the things that are important to you.

 Sometimes I feel as if I am being such a stickler when I ask whoever is playing with or watching my daughter to do or not do certain things. But I simply don't want her treated in some ways, such as:

- Saying "no" repeatedly without either explaining why or stating the same concept in a different way, such as, "Please don't do that."

- Using scare techniques to get my daughter to do something, such as, "Daddy's going to be home soon." I hate this because she shouldn't be afraid of any third person simply because someone told her not to put her feet on the table.

- Letting my child do whatever she wants without either redirecting or stopping the negative behavior. Someone actually let my daughter write on my walls with a crayon because "she wanted to." I was so frustrated! I didn't think it was cute and I certainly didn't want to reinforce that behavior with my daughter.

- Pushing food into my daughter's mouth or coaxing her to eat more. This is one of my biggest pet peeves. I feel like a tape recording saying, "She'll eat if she's hungry," over and over again.

- Television. For the most part, our families are good about not turning it on. But when they do let my daughter watch "Mister Rogers' Neighborhood" or something, they always tell me "how much she liked it." She's only 19 months old! She likes watching ants crawl on the sidewalk too, a more worthwhile activity in my opinion, than sitting in front of the television. I have disconnected the cable a few times to discourage television use in my absence.

Ljubica P.

You can be firm and clear as needed.

My mother-in-law tells a story of a friend of hers who spanked her granddaughter against the mom's wishes, and how the child was miraculously cured of the naughty behavior.

It was a great opening for our discussion. I said, "If one swat took care of the issue, then I am sure there were about 100 ways to have handled it in a nonviolent manner."

I also told her that if anyone laid a hand on my child or used discipline as an excuse for violence against him, they would not be permitted to see my child unsupervised again. I also told her that if that caused my son to fear that person, he would not be forced to spend time with him or her simply because they were related.

I can discuss it with her, and in the end, I get to decide. I never have to leave him with someone else when I don't feel comfortable about it. I don't think I have to offer a reason if it comes to that. He is my child. I decide.

Anna B.

This, too, shall pass

Many of us find that differences of opinion about discipline tend to become less intense as our children grow a little older. There may be a variety of reasons for the change. One is that differences in parenting don't come into view as often. Children spend more time at school or in other organized activities. They are also able to play with friends with less parental supervision.

Another possibility is that parenting answers may start to seem less cut-and-dried once children grow older and new challenges arise. All of us gain a little more humility. Or maybe parents just feel more confident that things are going reasonably well and so are less defensive about their parenting beliefs. Even family members tend to worry less once your children get a little older and seem to be developing normally. Whatever the cause, it can be comforting to contemplate a future with less conflict with your friends and family members, particularly when you're going through a tough time with your own child.

 When Adam was two years old, I used to remind myself constantly that he was a "strong, active child." In practical terms, this meant that we needed to stay very close to him all the time to keep him from hurting people. If he could throw an object, he often did, and he had uncanny aim. He was tall for his age, so he tended to knock other toddlers over at the playground. Our extended families didn't comment much, but they occasionally looked a little doubtful about our gentle parenting of this small boy who seemed larger than life.

At 15, Adam is still larger than life—over six feet tall. He is funny, friendly and a joy to be around. Friends and family often tell us what a thoughtful and gentle soul he is. They no longer seem slightly afraid he might break something or hurt someone. Neither are we.

He still has good aim. When we play catch, I need to remind him to throw the ball a little more gently to his dear old mom. He's still boisterous. The younger children at our church love to play with him. He makes a great "uncle" for them and for his actual four-year-old niece.

But he also has some skills that two-year-olds don't have—impulse control and an understanding of other people's reactions to play that results in pain. Seeing his almost-grown self is well worth all the time we spent finding soft things that were okay for him to throw, and apologizing to parents of other toddlers who had gotten hurt.

Nancy L.

Witnessing bad scenes in public

When you and your child are out in public, you are likely to witness harsh treatment of children from time to time. A parent may swat a child's behind or may call him names. Or a child may have a temper tantrum and the parent may threaten him. You may want to discuss these incidents with your child so that he can process his feelings and understand better the meaning of what happened. He may need your reassurance that you feel all children deserve better, and that you never wish to treat him that way.

Don't lose sight of the humanity in the parent you are witnessing. We parents have more in common with each other than differences. At some point, you are likely to do things you regret, too. If you are grumpy or lose your temper in public, chances are your embarrassment only adds to your stress level. If you see a parent acting badly, consider offering your support rather than your criticism.

 We can offer to hold the baby, or empathize. It can mean so much to hear, "I remember how tough that stage could be. You're not alone. Is there anything I can carry for you?"

Penelope G.

> **We parents have more in common with each other than differences.**

 Whenever I see a mama struggling with the very difficult job of parenting, I try to think of ways to support her in her struggle.

It's easy to criticize, but we all know it's difficult to discipline.

Empathy and outreach to other mothers is very important to me. I hope when someone sees me at not-my-very-best they understand that some days are like that.

Pamela G.

You are not alone!

No matter what challenges you are facing as a parent, there are other parents who have faced something related. Reach out to other parents to receive their support, hear their stories, and brainstorm your options. Find people locally or online who share your values and who can be there for you. Whatever you do, never doubt for a moment that you are the expert on your own child. You have what it takes to make the best choices for your family. You deserve support in developing and staying true to your vision for family life.

Part Three

Examples,
Examples, and Even
More Examples

Gentle Discipline Approaches to 10 Classic Concerns

Chapter 12

$\sim\sim\sim\sim\sim\sim\sim\sim\sim\sim\sim\sim\sim$

In this chapter, you will find ten of the most common discipline concerns and examples of how various parents who practice gentle discipline have worked with them. These are intended as a springboard for your own brainstorming. As always, use what you can and leave the rest.

- Whining

- Rudeness

- Running away in public places

- Car seat avoidance

- Cleaning up

- Bedtime

- Roughness with pets

- Getting out of the house

- Temper tantrums

- Hitting and other aggressive behavior

Whining

 I clearly remember as a child being told in a critical voice not to whine. I remember being unaware that I was whining. I was filled with emotions, and not focusing on how they came out. I remember how hard it was to focus on not whining, and how it almost felt as though I had to hide how I really felt inside. It felt as though I was being asked to switch moods instantly, something I find very hard to do even as an adult.

Mariah W.

 I have a two-year-old, a three-year-old, and a newborn. I have a hard time handling the negative emotions all my kids have, but especially the three-year-old. When she is having a whiny, unhappy day I take it all on my shoulders and think, "I must be a horrible mother." It makes me sad and angry that my children aren't happy all the time, so I often don't deal with it well.

I am trying to not feel responsible for her every emotion. I also try to remember all the times she is a happy little girl (at least 80 percent of the time). I try to figure out what might be wrong. She could have been up late last night, her father may have been working a lot this week, or she may have eaten too many sugary foods. Even if I contributed in some way (by letting her stay up too late or making the sugary foods available), I can face it and try to do better to prevent these moods from coming.

Beth T.

 I find that whining can usually be stopped before it even starts. I've noticed whining most often when my daughter is hungry, tired or hasn't been getting enough attention from me. When we're at home, it's usually not too hard to stop the whining by fixing a snack, encouraging quiet activities like reading together or watching a movie (if tiredness is the key), or making a point to stop whatever I'm doing and devote my full attention to her.

It can get a little trickier out in public, but whining in

public can often be avoided by not over-extending our-selves with shopping trips or other activities, and making sure that she gets plenty of downtime at home. It always helps to bring snacks, little trinkets in the diaper bag, or have fun games stored away in my head for those times most likely to induce whining: waiting in a doctor's office, long car rides, and big shopping trips.

Amy N.

Whining was one of my blind spots for a very long time. I never seemed to notice it at all. I started to focus on it after a friend bluntly asked me if I really wanted to encourage my son's whining by rewarding it. Gabe had learned to be a champion whin-er at four years old, and that wasn't exactly his fault. I'd let him.

He was rather shocked the first time I told him that until he could ask for something in a polite voice, I wasn't going to get it for him. He stood there with his mouth hanging open for a moment before he re-gathered himself for another whine. There were days when I had to stop, get on his level, look him in the eye, and say, "You can use a polite voice if you want something, and I will not get it for you until you do."

Despite the years of training to the contrary, he did get the point, and it was far easier to keep my temper when I'd stated it to him, as well. It helped keep me from sighing and giving in, even when I was tired. He still whines auto-matically at times, the result of three years of letting him do so without stopping him. But all it takes now, at almost seven years old, is a skeptical look and a raised eyebrow before he gives me a rueful grin, and uses a polite voice instead.

Heather P.

My daughter started whining around 20 months and continued until she was about four. Generally, I would ask her to speak in a voice that sounded like mine (I needed to be calm while saying that one) and I would immediately ask her to prac-tice with me. The best thing, though, was humor. I would cover my ears in horror and say, "Ow! I think someone must be whining because my ears are hurting! Owie!"

When she started laughing, I would immediately take my hands away from my ears and say, "Ah, much better. Did you want to ask me something?"

Sometimes I would imitate her, being careful to do it in a gentle way. I never did it with a mean tone to my voice or a sarcastic expression on my face. I would smile and say "Maaaaaaaadddy" every time she would say, "Mooommmmmy" until she "got it" that she needed to speak in a regular voice.

Jessica K.

 Mostly I do well at trying to stop the whining politely. I am really working to respect my children in a way I was not respected as a child. I say, "It's hard for me to understand you. I can't understand when you're talking like that. Use your strong voice."

When the situation gets tense, I'll burst into song. It seems to shock my kids into a less heavy place. We listen to the Rolling Stones and if they're wanting this and wanting that, I sing the whole chorus of "You Can't Always Get What You Want."

Sometimes I hear my daughter singing that song to herself and her dolls. It makes me laugh. I am glad that we can laugh about intense stuff.

Casey D.

Rudeness

 It's easy to react harshly to a "fresh" mouth. Punishment, time-outs, or whatever else will do nothing to stop my child's fresh mouth. In my experience, the negative emotions within my child will still be the same and likely much worse. Sometimes I tell her how it makes me feel when she speaks to me this way, but I don't dwell on it.

Instead I try to focus on the larger picture and believe the best about my child. She would not speak to me this way unless she was truly feeling out of sorts, and she desires a peaceful relationship with me.

The key is to get to the emotions behind her behavior. How is she feeling when she speaks this way? Irritated?

If they're wanting this and wanting that, I sing the whole chorus of "You Can't Always Get What You Want."

Annoyed? Angry? Frustrated? Sad? Lonely?

When I help her identify such feelings and acknowledge and validate them, I see the behavior subside.

Alecia I.

 Sometimes my three-year-old son is rude to me, in the sense of saying contrary things no matter what I say. This was my conversation with him as I was putting dinner on the table this evening:

HIM: What are we having to eat?

ME: Mexican pizza.

HIM: I don't like Mexican pizza! (He's never even had it.)

ME: You don't like Mexican pizza. (A statement, not a question.)

HIM: No, I like Mexican pizza. What's on it?

ME: Chicken, salsa, black beans, veggies, and cheese.

HIM: I don't like cheese, or beans, or chicken. They're yucky!

ME: You don't like cheese, beans, or chicken.

HIM: No! I like it.

He takes a bite. Makes a face. Leaves table. Comes back and eats another piece. Makes another face. Repeat. Repeat again until pizza is gone from plate.

This can be an all day marathon and can also disappear for days at a time. Just when I think we're beyond it, he brings it back for good measure and as much as I know it's not the truth, it feels as though he's doing it just to drive me nuts. At any rate, I just try very hard to not let it drive me nuts and to not take it personally.

I find if I can just be non-threatening about it (i.e., I avoid coaxing as much as possible and just roll with whatever he's contrary about), he usually comes right around. But if I so much as say something like, "Hey it's good, just try it!" we're likely to have a big power struggle.

Mary Beth K.

 Sometimes my six-year-old expresses his anger to me rudely. An example would be when I ask him to brush his teeth at night and he doesn't want to. He would turn to me with his fist clenched and scream, "I'm not going to brush my teeth! I hate getting ready for bed!"

When he starts to speak to me rudely I immediately stop him and say, "I want to listen to you, but you need to speak to me respectfully." Then I wait and do not respond to anything else he says until it's said kindly and calmly.

It does work, but it's hard not to respond to the eye-rolling, arm crossing, ranting little boy in front of me.

I realize that if I argue with him or yell, then I am being just as disrespectful to him as he is to me and that does not teach him anything. So I am calm, quiet, and respectful of him and I wait to speak with him until he can do the same.

Lauren K.

 I've spent the past week thinking, "We never would have talked to my parents like that!" whenever my four-year-old daughter has been cheeky to me.

Just today at lunchtime, she knocked her (empty) cup onto the floor and told me, "You can pick that up whenever you feel like it."

I told her that it upset me that she would deliberately throw things on the floor to make more work for me.

She ignored this, but then two minutes later asked for some bread and butter to go with her soup. I told her that I was still quite upset about the cup being on the floor and that I didn't feel like helping her make bread and butter at that moment. She got the message, picked up the cup, and we made her bread and butter.

She keeps doing this kind of stuff, even though I don't tolerate it. It's easy to forget in the heat of the moment, but my goal is to help my child learn to act and express herself appropriately. It's age appropriate for her to not always get it right at this stage.

Carolyn J.

 This was a very, very brief phase. I had to recognize that she didn't intend to be rude. Manners are learned, not inborn. They are learned in several ways: through modeling, respectful teaching about them, and having consistent expectations. Rudeness is also defined by culture, society, and different generations; what one person considers rude may not seem rude to others.

An example of what I consider to be rude behavior is when my daughter speaks to me in a demanding way or yells to me from a different room. When she does this I speak to her directly (not in a "wounded way") and tell her that either her tone or her choice of words was not acceptable and I would not expect her to find it acceptable if I spoke to her in that way.

If she demands, "Get me some milk!" from three rooms away, I go to her and say, "I know that you would like some milk and I will get it for you when you are able to ask me in a polite way." I use concrete examples of how she could ask for something or express her anger in a way that is respectful yet effective. When she was younger (she's four now) and just learning about good manners I would practice with her. I also used positive reinforcement for good manners. Now my daughter often points out to me that she is polite by making a request and then saying, "Hey! I used my good manners!"

Jessica K.

 Our three-year-old sweet girl has started saying things like: "I don't like your stupid words!" and an occasional, "I hate you."

I think I've just been so upset to hear words like that in our house that I've been overreacting. The fact that I've been hurt by it gives her power. When I impose a consequence for her actions (either I don't talk to her or I take her to her room), it seems to turn it into a power struggle that just keeps going on.

I find it helpful to try not to let it get to me. We have taught her the word stupid is not nice. I try to stay calm and tell her I'm sorry she feels that way, that I love her, and that I still need her to cooperate. She first picked up the word "stupid" from a friend a few months ago. At first, we tried to completely ignore it. It was gone in a week or two. Maybe if I ignore her new experiments they will go away as well.

Amy P.

My daughter (now three) has been talking back a little. For instance, once she said, "Don't tell me what to do, it's stupid." I'll say something such as, "I know you're frustrated and angry and that's fine, but you still have to put your toys away." Or "You can be as angry as you'd like to be, but you still have to be a good listener." We also say things like "If you'd like me to listen to you, you have to find a new way to talk to me." Or "You have every right to be upset or angry but that doesn't mean you can be unkind."

Megan C.

 I noticed a lot of rude behavior that my two-and-a-half-year-old picked up from television and movies—even from "The Lion King," her favorite. She started calling everyone "Murderer!" (How do I explain that one to a two-year-old?) When she seems to be imitating a story rather than being rude, it gives me the opportunity to discuss why it isn't nice to say these things to people, and that not everything we see on television is okay. Lately, she's started the "I wants" due to the commercials pushing products for Christmas. I can't protect my child from being influenced by other's behavior. The best I can do is to explain and teach right from wrong. At least with television, there is an option to be there and to discuss it at the time.

Sheri J.

Running Away in Public Places

 My three-and-a-half-year-old son starts running and won't stop. He is very conscious of cars, though, so I don't think he would ever run past the curb. Nevertheless, it is worrisome and annoying behavior. I used to freak out and really express my fear (as Martha Sears recommends) but this just doesn't work for us. For a while he may have been trying to push my buttons. So when I freaked out he got what he wanted and did it again. If I react calmly, he doesn't get what he wants so he stops doing it.

What did work was immediately, calmly, and firmly putting him in the stroller and telling him he could either walk safely or he would have to ride in the stroller. No fuss, no getting mad, no emotion whatsoever.

Liz C.

I've found that the phrase, "Listen to mommy," at least for us, is highly ineffective. I would define it more clearly: "When you hear me calling your name, I need you to look at me." "When I call your name, I need you to freeze like a popsicle."

Jesse M.

My younger son was nearly two years old when we went camping in Vermont, with family. With all the family about, we sometimes would lose track of where he was, exactly, for a few minutes at a time. Once, we looked up and saw his little blond head bouncing away in full trot into the woods. Alone. Yelling got his attention, and he didn't like it at all. But yelling, I knew, would not stop that from being a repeating problem. I'd just be yelling a lot.

Instead, we bought a small cowbell at a local souvenir shop, and attached it to his belt. Now, if we lost visual contact for a moment, we could still hear where he was. He was thrilled with the idea. It made a loud noise, and he enjoys loud noises. In addition, with the bell on, he was enjoying more freedom of movement than before! He could range in certain directions farther than we'd permitted without the bell, because we could hear him. A year later, he still loves to wear the bell when we're out, for the same reason. We love it because we can hear not only when he's getting too far away, but also when it becomes silent for longer than we'd expect. For us, this is a very useful tool.

Heather P.

I use a toddler tether and it's great! It's like holding hands but with longer arms. You both have both hands free. So my child can still touch, skip, pick up leaves, or whatever, and still know where I am in relation to him. I love it.

I never used one until I was in university and babysitting. One of "my" moms liked using it, so her kids were used to it. It was perfect for walks. Holding hands means you each have at least one hand you can't use and your child doesn't really have much range of motion. I always wonder if their little arms must get tired of being up in the air all the time.

I know people look at them and think, "leash." However, I think of it as being the same as holding hands, but with more freedom and less struggle. My child is unwilling to hold hands, but enjoys the tether because he still has freedom of movement and some independence.

Nicole D.

 I am a former New Yorker and I go back there often. I do so much walking there that I cannot function without a stroller. I insist that my three-year-old daughter be in it for her own safety and for the fact that it's too much walking for her to be expected to do. I let her get out in the park. Kids are very impulsive and although she might mean to listen, there is just so much noise and energy in the city and she might get distracted.

Jessica K.

 If I think my three-year-old daughter is in a running mood, I always try to prevent it with a firm hand around the wrist. If she's pulling away from me, I just say firmly, "I need to hold your hand right now so that you're safe."

Elizabeth B.

 When my son was almost three, he tried running away from me. We were leaving a playgroup where he was having a lot of fun, and he just was not ready to leave. Getting in the car was facing a truth (that our fun was over) he wasn't ready for. When I ran after him, he took off running farther away. We were in a quiet neighborhood and he is careful about roads, so it wasn't too bad. When he was quite a bit away and had turned a corner, I yelled for him to stop. He did not.

I finally caught up to him and put my hands around his torso to stop him. I was really shaken up and told him that he had really scared me and that he should never go where I couldn't see him or run off like that. He had a small tantrum and then dissolved into tears. I carried him back and just kept telling him that I was so afraid and worried and that he should never do that again.

As we drove home I reached back to hold his hand and he said, "I love you, Mommy." I love when we can reconnect after something like that!

Betsy S.

Car Seat Avoidance

 It is very important to me to let my two-year-old get in the car the way he wants, and in the seat the way he wants. He does not want me to do it for him. I try to allow extra time and energy for it. Giving him a special toy or a snack to hold sometimes works. Sometimes I use a silly song or a joke to distract him.

Betsy S.

 It really helped when we started calling it his special big boy seat. There is Mommy's seat, Daddy's seat, and Hunter's Special Big Boy Seat. He loves to be a big boy and loves to sit in the seat.

Kate S.

 Once my daughter stopped falling asleep all the time in the car seat (at about 16 months), she quickly learned that she did not have my full attention, and could count on not having it the whole time she was in the seat. This meant that if she was hungry or thirsty, I would not be able to help her out. At first, I didn't realize what was going on.

Now I plan ahead and bring lots of snacks, juice, and toys. I allow time to snuggle before loading her up, make sure her diaper is fresh, and her clothes aren't wrinkled beneath her. I sing songs and talk with her as I drive. I keep extra supplies in the front with me in case she drops hers. So if she asks, I can hand her something.

That said, if she's tired, she's going to be mad, because she wants me. I put her in the seat as gently as possible, buckle her in, and know that she'll be asleep in a few minutes because she is tired.

Jen M.

 We have a pretty simple rule in our family. The car doesn't move until everyone is strapped securely into their seat, including the grownups. We've always stressed how important this was to keep all of us safe. My children have seemed to test this limit most during the early toddler years. Maybe their newly discovered ability to walk makes them hate being strapped down.

Sometimes it helps to promise a snack and sippy cup after being strapped in. Other times I surprise my children with a favorite toy that wants to ride in the car seat with them.

Once my son got old enough to fasten his own seatbelt, he firmly refused any help. Unfortunately, he was still very slow at getting the task done. No matter how many times we stressed that putting on the seatbelt was the first thing he should do when he climbed in the car, he always distracted himself with something else. We found that encouraging him to race against us helped. Could he get his seatbelt on before I strapped in both of his younger sisters? How high could I count before he finished his seatbelt? Could he beat yesterday's number? Could he get his seatbelt on before I came back from the mailbox?

Carissa D.

 Here are some ideas I have used when I needed to go somewhere in the car, but my baby did not like the car seat:

- Let my baby get used to the car seat in the house first.

- Use a mirror to maintain eye contact with my baby.

- Sing while driving.

- Reach back to touch my baby when I could do so safely.

- Offer a pacifier.

- Find a place to park and offer to nurse.

- If someone else is driving, I try nursing while my baby stays in the car seat and I have my seatbelt on. (Dr. Sears describes how to do this in *The Baby Book*.)

- Minimize time in the car or go out alone while my baby sleeps.

- If my baby persists in crying despite my best efforts, I remain calm, speak softly to my baby, and go home as quickly as possible.

With an older (and mobile) toddler, I use these options:

Explain the trip before we leave the house. I offer to let her carry the keys while we go to the car, get into the car seat, and fasten seatbelts. I tell her I will trade a special toy for the keys so she has something to play with. Then, when we return home, she can explore the car. (This works nine times out of 10 for us.)

Sometimes, I allow my toddler to explore the car first. However, with my very persistent child, we just get in and go. It is better for us to simply tell him that we are going and that he can play in the car when we come back.

Genevieve C.

 Brendan was fine with car seats except once on a long car trip, he screamed, arched out of the seat, and generally made his displeasure known. On that trip, the car seat wasn't the real problem; it was the two-hours-on, almost-two-hours-off travel, for 10 hours.

It took a good 15 minutes to get him into his car seat. I think he felt that he was alone in how he felt. Once we explained that the seatbelts and seats were uncomfortable for mommy, daddy, and his big brother, too, but we still had to use them for safety, he settled down a lot more. He often seemed to feel better when he knew he wasn't alone, that even the grownups had to do things they'd rather not do. He disliked car seats for months afterwards, but would comply again (most of the time!) when reminded that everyone had to wear seatbelts, not just him.

Heather P.

 When my son was between one and two years old, he frequently avoided getting into his car seat. Usually it was so he could climb into the front and sit in the driver's seat, but sometimes he wanted to play with the door handles or just whatever was in the car.

I fumed at the beginning, but made up my mind that it was pointless to get angry.

Instead, I tried to make sure we were leaving the house half an hour before we needed to, and used it as an opportunity to have fantasy play with him. Sometimes I was the police officer asking to see his license, and sometimes I was the drive-through attendant, and so on. Other times, I used the opportunity to clean the car out, which probably hadn't been done since he was born.

Of course, sometimes I just didn't have the time for this, but the problem miraculously became easier over time. I think because I was usually allowing him all the play he wanted in the car, he was more willing to go along with me.

If I suddenly said in the house, "Oh! We have to rush now. How quickly can we get going?" he would start running to the door.

When none of that worked, I would think of a fantasy play that would involve having to drive the car: "Hey, would you like to be my master, and I'll be your chauffeur driving you around the capital to show you the sights?" At the time, he had no idea what either a master or a chauffeur were, but because I put on a different voice, he sure wanted to know. All I had to do was point out every landmark and give it a posh-sounding name.

Heidi O.

I struggle 90 percent of the time when it comes to getting my son (almost two) into his car seat, the other 10 percent I'm just in shock that he was being cooperative. I know why my son doesn't like the car seat. He's really active and doesn't ever like being restrained. With that in mind, I limit my outings with him to one place so I don't have to get him in and out more than once.

If I were to ask him to sit in his car seat, he never would. He loves playing in the car. So I have to heave him into his seat and either sing a song while I put the straps on or hand him something fun to hold.

Now this works only if he wasn't crying about getting into the car to begin with. If he was already crying, I just try to get him into his car seat as gently and quickly as possible.

It can be hard. I wish there were a better way of doing it so he and I would both be happy. But he's better if I just get it done as quickly as possible. If I give him time to play around before getting in, it just makes it take longer. He's fine once we're driving and singing songs.

Sohee P.

Cleaning Up

 Most of our toys are kept in baskets or bins, so it's easy enough to turn picking up toys into a game of toy toss–seeing who can put the most toys in the basket.

Sorting the laundry is lots of fun, too, because you can toss the clothes into the washing machine while at the same time learning how to divide dark and light clothes.

There are really lots of things my children (ages five and two) like to do to help around the house: sweeping, watering plants, putting away laundry, and loading and unloading the dishwasher.

I try to make sure that I don't complain about these things. I want them to look at keeping house as something that can be fun and isn't just another thing to finish before moving on to the good stuff. Playing music that we all enjoy makes it much more fun.

Amy N.

 I try to remember to tell my four-year-old daughter to clean up in the same way I would want my husband to tell me respectfully. I also try to be very clear and specific. Instead of saying, "Clean up this room," I might say, "Please put your clothes in the hamper and put the toys on the floor into your toy chest."

If she is having difficulty getting started, I may give an incentive such as offering to take a walk together after the task is done. If the task is very overwhelming, I will help but I give specific instructions on what she needs to do ("I'll put the yellow blocks away, and you put away the blue ones").

If she doesn't clean up, the result is that I then have less time to spend with her. It also helps if I ask her what she thinks she can do and what she would like me to help her with. If she really doesn't want to clean up the paints, she will often be happy to sponge down the table and put the brushes away after I have washed them. By asking, I am showing her that her opinion is valuable to me. By acknowledging her contribution, I am showing her that she is an integral part of the family structure. By complimenting her, I am encouraging her to feel good about herself.

I try to keep in mind my daughter's age-appropriate abilities. When she makes her bed, it looks about as messy after she finishes as it did before she started. But I acknowledge her contribution and her pride in her work without any criticism of the way it actually looks. The results are secondary to the effort.

Jessica K.

If Meara is not willing to help me clean up what we previously were playing with, and things are getting too messy for my comfort level, I explain to her it is time to stop playing. I tell her that I don't want to be the only one cleaning up, and that families pitch in and help each other. Sometimes, she will ask me to close my eyes, and she will do what I have requested her to do while I'm not looking. I believe she does this because it makes her feel as if she has some power in the situation.

Maureen C.

We had a family meeting to address cleaning up. Since I want a clean living room at the end of the day, I am willing to pick up the toys, but I will pick up each toy just once. If I have to pick it up, it goes into a box where it stays until I feel willing to pick it up again. My kids will actually assess whether a particular toy is worth putting away once they are done with it. I found this appalling until I realized that they were completely inundated with toys. It took several weeks of taking toys away before they really noticed. We decided we would offer to bring back one toy each day if they could name one that they wanted. I found that they were quite unaware of what they owned and missed very little. Of course, certain special toys are exceptions.

Bonnie A.

 I feel like my kid's job is to learn and explore and my job is to facilitate that. Therefore, part of my job is set-up and clean up.

If my son (nearly three years old) wants to help, that's great. But I think the only way he will really want to help is if I model that it is fun and a normal part of life.

Someone suggested this to me and it helps me a lot. It diffuses my grumpy attitude and helps keep me from alternating between punishing and rewarding in an attempt to get him to change. If I don't want to clean up and I'm the one who wants a clean house, then why would a small child want to?

Betsy S.

 I went through the toys and donated many of them to charities. We have a charity that comes once a month and picks up used toys and clothing, providing a great incentive to simplify our lives. I keep a box handy to hold potential donations.

I have a spot for everything. I find my toddler is much more likely to help pick up if she knows where things belong. It makes it easy to say: "Take this to your drawer."

We clean things up before we move on. I cannot tell

you how much this has helped my sanity. We used to just do a nightly sweep but I ended up (resentfully) doing most of it.

I teach my child how to clean up. I give specific directions, like: "Put the blocks in this box," showing her and telling her how.

I taught my daughter how to ask for help instead of pitifully wailing "it's too hard." I gave her a script: "Mama, can you help me, please?"

I help right from the beginning, by saying, "I'll pick up the red ones while you pick up the blue ones."

There are some times when she's just too tired, too overwhelmed, too frustrated, or just plain too out of cooperation. In these cases, everything is going to be a struggle, so I go ahead and pick things up myself. I feel no need to drive the lesson home all in one day; we'll be cleaning up a lot, and my need for a clean floor is still being met.

Meghan S.

If I don't want to clean up and I'm the one who wants a clean house, then why would a small child want to?

 I've told my four-year-old that her room doesn't have to be clean all the time or spotless ever. But I also point out that I have to come in her room to put away laundry and things like that. I need to be able to walk through her room without tripping on or stepping on toys. She herself has stepped on or tripped on toys countless times. She also has more fun with a particular toy when her room is orderly and she has ample space to play.

We're on a pretty good schedule that every night before stories we straighten up her room together for about five minutes. If I just ask her to help me clean up she'll often whine and resist, but if I say "I'm going to pick up your books and you can put away stuffed animals." Or if blocks are all over, I'll say "Pick two colors of blocks you want to put away and two colors for me to put away." Giving her a really specific task or letting her have a say in who does what makes her much more willing to pitch in.

Jenna D.

 In our house (we have a seven-year-old and a toddler), if a child does not clean up their mess in a communal area, then the next time the child wants to do whatever activity made the mess, it needs to be done elsewhere, usually their room. I feel that their rooms are their own, and messes in there aren't my problem. My goal is not to teach them a lesson about tidiness; it's to find a solution to the problem that's acceptable to everyone. This really goes for everyone in the house. Even my husband has a couple of areas that are his own. They're filthy by my standards, but I don't need to care and everyone's needs are met.

Courtney C.

By about the time each of my daughters was four years old, if one of them refused to clean up a mess she had made, I would kneel down, touch her arm gently, and speak softly: "You need to help me clean up." If she still refused, I would go ahead and clean it up by myself, maybe shaking my head a little in disapproval. Then when I was done, I would speak calmly yet firmly: "When you make a mess I expect you to clean it up. I did not like that you did not listen to me and did not like that you did not help clean up. Next time I expect you to do it."

That's it. No punishment. No escalation. Just my expectations clearly stated. This works for us.

Maya S.

> I feel no need to drive the lesson home all in one day; we'll be cleaning up a lot, and my need for a clean floor is still being met.

My kids are still young and I can tell they are still learning to control their impulses. Prevention is my friend. I have locked up and childproofed many areas in my house to control the chaos. Only things that are easy to put away and can stand the abuse of kids playing with them are left in family areas. I put only a few toys in reach at one time. I put clothes that are still clean enough back into drawers and hang up the rest. I remind myself that it won't always have to be this way.

I set the precedent that my things can only be used when I am around. Baking, cooking, washing clothes, and washing dishes all involve pouring and mixing things together. Sometimes their involvement makes small messes, but I am right there with them. I try to take the time to

invite my kids to help me so that they are less inclined to try to "play" with these items when I'm not there.

Putting things back where we got them can be an extension of their play rather than an end to it. It requires reminding them beforehand and then doing it together so it becomes a habit. Toys can go home to sleep. Clothes thrown about can be catapulted back into their drawers. We can see if we can beat the clock or our best time for putting things back in their packages. Or we may even pretend we are lions carrying things back to our den in our mouths. Of course, this type of play does take a little extra motivation and creativity, but it makes things easier sometimes.

Lisa P.S.

Bedtime

 We hit a point at about two years where our son's sleep needs changed and bedtime had become a nightmare. What has worked for us is to go "back to basics." We let him determine when he needed sleep. We tried to override those societal tapes in our heads that say he should have a bedtime and his own bed and that he needs to learn to fall asleep on his own. We had to trust that our son would go to sleep when he was ready and trust our own instincts that it is okay to respond to our child's needs just as we did when he was a baby.

Some nights he nurses to sleep while my husband and I stay up watching television or reading. It's great for Daddy to get some toddler snuggle time. And sometimes he stays up until we all go to bed. In both scenarios, he is able to fall asleep with security and respond to his body's cues.

Betsy S.

 Our bedtime routine can be a struggle, but we persist because Julia needs to get to bed at a decent time in order to wake up for preschool in the morning.

If we start the bedtime too early, we end up in bed

with a restless child wanting to read books and jump around for an hour. If we wait too late, we enter the danger zone where Julia (three) is overtired and just breaks down. When she gets like that, she gets so out of sorts that she can't even brush her teeth, get in bed, or even understand that she's tired.

However, even on the days when we time it right, Julia can take forever to go to the bathroom and brush her teeth. One thing we're trying that I suppose falls into that "natural consequence" category is to say, "It's 7 o'clock now and we have time for four stories. If it takes a long time to get ready for bed, we'll only have time for three stories." We're trying to get her to understand that there is a given amount of time before bed and she can either use it struggling about tooth brushing or she can use it in bed reading stories.

We're trying to help her see that brushing teeth and going to the potty before bed just happen each day, whether we argue about them or not.

We've also trimmed the bedtime routine down quite a bit. Every night Julia asks if she has to wear pajamas and every night we tell her the only two things she must do are to sit on the potty and to brush her teeth. Sometimes she chooses to wear pajamas, and sometimes she just wears what she wore that day. I think she finds comfort in knowing that the decision is hers. She does have some control over the bedtime preparations.

Karen K.

 The hardest times for me were bedtimes. Our three-year-old daughter was up until all hours. I was getting very tired at night with her up, which meant I would get snappy and closer to "the edge." It wasn't healthy for anyone.

Eventually, I learned to just go with the flow. That helped me tremendously in terms of discipline. Sometimes discipline is giving up your position instead of holding it. At some point I decided I just wasn't going to fight her over bedtime; if she didn't fall asleep within 15 minutes or so, then we would play some more and try again later. Before that, I was rocking her while she cried and cried. I would just get more and more frustrated and feel less and less connected to her. Learning to go with the flow instead of trying to force bedtime really helped our relationship.

Beyond that, maintaining a very regular routine is what worked for us. Sometimes it's actually harder for my husband and me to keep the routine going than it is for our daughter to conform to the routine. It's worth the effort though. Our routine is: a snack, bath, pajamas, brushing teeth, stories in bed, holding Monkey (her beloved stuffed animal), and lying down together with lights out until she is asleep. Even with our routine, she still cries sometimes when we turn off the lights. I stay to comfort her while also describing what's going on. "I know you don't want to go to sleep, but it's time for lights out. Let's lie here quietly together. I'm right here beside you. Monkey is here too." Eventually she quiets down and falls asleep.

Elizabeth B.

> **Sometimes it's actually harder for my husband and me to keep the routine going than it is for our daughter to conform to the routine.**

 I think that having parents who are truly present at bedtime can be helpful in getting children to go to bed willingly. Ruby, my 20-month-old, still nurses to sleep in my arms each night. I snuggle with Kaylee, my three-year-old, while she falls asleep. She likes me to hold her hand or rub her feet. I give her kisses and tell her how much I love her and how proud I am of her. It's relaxing for me to see the deep peace that comes over her as she drifts off beside me. My husband usually curls up with Keithen, our five-year-old, to read to him before bed each night.

Sometimes Keithen will reappear to request some snuggle time with mommy after I've put his sisters to sleep. We burrow under his blankets together and talk about the good things that happened that day or what we'll do the next day. He loves to have me rub and scratch his back to help him relax. It's nice to have that close time with him, since growing boys don't often slow down for physical affection. I think having these kinds of rituals helps our children know how much we value them. It allows them to unwind and slumber peacefully. It also helps to form an open line of communication that I hope stays strong as they grow older.

Carissa D.

 When my preschooler has had problems settling at night, it helps to get her up very early the next day. Then we make sure we go out and do something physically active during the day. Tiredness is a good thing!

Carolyn J.

 At bedtime, my boys have their own alarm clock that is set for the time the routine needs to start. The kids hit the "snooze" and have eight minutes to complete the next phase of the routine. When they get distracted, they are pulled back to task by the alarm when it goes off again. *Voila!* Mom doesn't do any nagging or reminders. When everything is done on time, there is enough time for an extra story.

Bonnie A.

 When our four-year-old first transitioned to his own room, he often wanted to stay up all night. No one could ever force me to sleep, so I wouldn't want to do that to my kids. But I don't think it's unreasonable to say that it's time for quiet time at 8 PM.

The compromise we came up with is this: He can play quietly or read books as long as he wants (with the lights on) until he's ready to sleep. However, going to his bedroom at 8 is non-negotiable.

At first, we had problems with him staying up until late at night. Now, most days he plays or reads for a couple of minutes to wind down, then goes right to sleep. Occasionally, he'll fall asleep with a book or toy next to him in bed. We come in and turn the light off when we go to bed ourselves.

Ann C.

My daughter stopped taking daytime naps before she was 18 months old and often sleeps only ten hours at night, with no ill effects for her. Accepting that she just doesn't need much sleep was half the battle for us.

We now have a routine, a later bedtime (9 PM), and predictable responses to her behavior. If she's not sleeping or going to sleep in 20 to 30 minutes, we get out of bed and take a 15 to 20 minute break doing something quiet. Then we swap parents and do the routine again. This is more for our sanity than anything. The most important thing is for us to wake her up at the same time every morning (7:30 AM).

We also make sure she does not nap during the day—not even in the car. She will often ask to go to bed on her own by 8:30 PM if we have been keeping this routine. Sometimes it gets mixed up by weekends, teething, colds, or other changes. As long as we go back to no naps and waking up at the same time each day, she falls back into it.

Jen M.

 We have trouble getting our three-year-old son to go to sleep at night. It takes quite a few hours of reading and being quiet and lying down. He hates to admit to being tired at bedtime. Even this morning, he came running out of his room and announced himself in the kitchen with, "But I don't want to go to sleep!" He didn't realize he had just slept the whole night.

Nipuna D.

 From the time my daughter was born she has only fallen asleep in the car or in a stroller. She wouldn't even nurse to sleep. If she did, it was such a light sleep that she would wake at the slightest sound or movement.

I read and heard all the theories about routines and timings. It didn't make a bit of difference to my daughter.

In fact, she still doesn't wear pajamas, but goes to bed in whatever she is wearing. The whole routine thing just set us up for stress and resistance, so we learned not to do it. Those books were not written for my daughter.

So I just started to trust my own judgment, day by day, and not worry about it. Some evenings, my husband would take her for a walk in the stroller and come back in five minutes with her sound asleep. We learned it worked best to leave her in there until we went to bed, rather than try to move her. But other nights, he'd walk for miles and she'd be wide awake when he got home. On those nights, we'd get into the car.

We learned to arrange our lives so that we'd often do errands that required driving in the evenings: getting gas in the car, buying groceries, or picking up mail. Once we accepted this routine, it was much less stressful.

She outgrew all this at around three years of age. She is four now, and we can lie down on the bed, cuddle up, and she goes off to sleep, often within minutes. I never thought I'd live to see the day.

Nicola C.

Roughness with Pets

We have two cats and sometimes my three-year-old daughter gets a little rough with them. I tell her: "That's not okay. Mishi cat is much smaller than you are. Her squeaking is her way of saying that she's not happy. Listen to her sounds to see if she's okay with that. It doesn't sound like she's okay with that. Please be gentle with her." Sometimes I need to show her the gentle behavior while I talk to her about it. "Mishi likes to be patted like this. Can you do that? Yes, see, she likes that!"

Elizabeth B.

I remember explaining to him when he was about two-and-a-half that he didn't get to decide how the cat felt about something. Only the cat was able to decide how the cat felt.

 Initially Gabe liked to stick his face right against his cat's or to lie on top of it with a huge toddler hug. I remember explaining to him when he was about two-and-a-half that he didn't get to decide how the cat felt about something. Only the cat was able to decide how the cat felt. Just like I didn't get to decide how Gabe felt about something, and Gabe didn't get to decide how Mommy and Daddy felt, either.

Because he had started to grasp that his feelings belonged to him, and were not to be dismissed or denied by anyone else, this made complete sense. He was a bit sad for a few days, because he really wanted the cat to love getting hugs. But with a little guidance, he learned to express his affection for the kitties in appropriate ways. Now, years later, one of the cats that he'd formerly harassed sleeps with him by preference and cries when he's away.

When our other son, Brendan, was one year old, he didn't care whether the kitties liked what he was doing or not. If he thought it was a good idea, it simply was a good idea. It worked best to let him learn through natural consequences that if he made the cats nervous, they ran away and stopped coming back to play with him. That natural consequence, plus very brief time-outs for any behavior that was directly threatening, got the point across. We guided him toward behaviors that kitties like and told him that only the kitties could decide what they liked. It didn't take long for them to lose their avoidance of him, and he now delights in their spontaneous "kitty hugs" (when the cats rub against and around him).

Heather P.

 My parents' dog, Pooh, is a tiny but highly excitable creature. My three-year-old can't keep her hands and feet off Pooh sometimes. She tries to squeeze Pooh too hard, she chases him around the house, and she attempts to kick him. We tried everything from not reacting to over-reacting.

One thing that has helped was to sit down with Julia and make a list (with pictures that made sense of the words) of what Pooh likes and what Pooh doesn't like. Pooh does not like being chased, being picked up, or being kicked. Pooh does like retrieving a toy, treats, and space. Having a list on the refrigerator to point to helped remind

Julia that she had already agreed to these terms. We could say, "I see that you are chasing Pooh. Let's look at our list. Does Pooh like being chased?" She'd run to get the list and say, "No, he doesn't like it." Having identified things that the dog likes helped to frame things in the positive and give Julia something concrete to do: "Pooh likes getting treats, but he doesn't like being kicked."

That said, there are times when it's just too hard for Julia and Pooh to co-exist despite our best efforts. We've just learned to keep Julia and Pooh away from each other during those times. Our own dog, Zoë, has a more mellow personality. But there are still times when the kids get too rough with her and we send her outside with a special treat for a while to give everyone a break.

Karen K.

 My son is 15 months old and at this age, it's next to impossible to stop roughness with animals in our house. All we can do is to be vigilant. We put a baby gate in the door of our den to help keep the cats safe. We put their food bowls on top of the file cabinet in one corner. We also bought a carpet-covered box for the litter box and placed it across the room. We put their climbing "tree" in another corner. They can jump over the gate to escape if they really need to.

Sandra V.

 When my son was two, he tended to be rough with the cats. First, we found a place for our cats to be where they could be safe: on top of the dryer in the laundry room. We put a couple of snuggly beds up there and that way they always have a place to go.

We found it extremely useful to get to our son before he touched one of the animals. I made sure to keep an extra close eye on him with the cats. If he began to approach, I would assume by my tone that he was going to be gentle, "Oh, you're going to give Cat some love. I know she'll really enjoy that!"

This approach really turned things around for us. First, I broke my son's attention for a moment by commenting. This may have helped him a bit with his lack of impulse control. Second, he knew I was monitoring and that he already had my attention, so being rough with the cats for attention's sake wasn't necessary. Whenever possible, I stopped what I was doing and approached the cat with him and we both played with her gently.

I had to remind myself to hang in there with him, and to bear in mind that just because something is not working today doesn't mean it won't work tomorrow or the next day. In any corrective action I take with my son, I always make sure not to look for results right away. Kids need time and many repetitions sometimes to really absorb and change their behaviors. Eventually, he learned to be gentle with the cats.

Mary Beth K.

 My son (nearly two) would sneak up on the dog while she was sleeping and poke or hit her. He didn't mean to hurt her, but she would jump up and run away. I'm not sure what was so enticing about it. I feared that eventually she would bite him if I couldn't teach him to stop.

The dog did have somewhere she could sleep safely, but she wanted to be with us. I can't blame her. When my son was younger, I made the dog go sleep in the bedroom whenever he felt the need to bother her. I think that as he neared two he was old enough to learn to control his behavior around her, for the sake of his own safety.

He definitely knew what would happen each time he poked the dog. He also knew that it wasn't allowed. He was at a stage where he purposefully did things that weren't allowed and made sure I was paying attention. He was looking to see what I was going to do about it and I didn't know what to do.

We hadn't used any kind of time-out for my son, but I began considering it just for this situation. I resolved that if time-outs didn't work in this case, I would stop. But if they did work, it would solve a very big and potentially dangerous problem. This is what I chose to do. And it actually worked.

First, I dropped all emotion and dramatics about the whole thing, because my son was clearly enjoying my reaction to hitting the dog. The more upset I got about it, the more he was hitting.

Then, I explained the concept of "time-out" to him. I told him "we don't hit," and if he hit the dog, he would sit in time-out.

When he did hit her, I reacted with no emotion, just reminded him of the rule, escorted him to his time-out spot, and set the oven timer for two minutes.

At first, he liked the novelty of it, but after two or three boring time-outs, he stopped. For about a week, he had time-outs about once a day, and then it stopped.

Whenever he showed interest in the dog, I reminded him of all the appropriate things to do with her. "Do you want to pat her? Look she likes it!" "Do you want to give her a biscuit? Oh, look how happy she is!" That seemed to help and made her a little less skittish around him.

Tina P.

Getting Out of the House

Giving my daughter a measure of control has gone a long way to building a harmonious relationship with her. I try to remember that in trying to get out of the house, I am working on my time-line and schedule. Since she is only four, she doesn't understand these concepts. To make outings run more smoothly, I need to spell out the routine simply. I have used several methods.

I made a chart with pictures that show the different things that need to be accomplished in the morning, such as use the potty, brush teeth, get dressed, and eat breakfast. My daughter loves to check off each thing as she finishes. It gives her a great deal of satisfaction and she feels as if she has important input to the morning structure. She even helped me make the chart by finding pictures in magazines that demonstrate her morning chores. I do not give her a material reward for completing tasks, rather I am teaching her the self-satisfaction that is derived from accomplishment.

I minimize stress by preparing some things ahead of time. I lay out my daughter's clothes, make her lunch, and pack her school bag the night before. The less stressed I am in the morning, the less stressed she is.

I tell my daughter what I expect her to do and give her a time limit coupled with an expectation. For example, I will tell her that after she gets dressed she can play with the dog for 10 minutes and then it is time to go.

Jessica K.

 I find that if I start the process of getting out of the house much earlier than we need to go, it goes much more smoothly. I think the extra time helps me feel less rushed. Then I can give Clio (three years old) plenty of time to do things herself. Also, I keep my eyes open for any naturally occurring break in her play and then swoop in.

Cheri R.

 Cole, my two-year-old, becomes excited anytime we go some place at this point. Accalia, my five-year-old, has her moments when she's not eager to make a trip somewhere, and if it's not a necessary trip, we usually put it off until everyone is eager to go. I find it helpful to give them plenty of warning and time to prepare for the transition. Accalia has gotten in the habit of asking what we're going to do each day or where we're going to go, so I can tell her right away in the morning if we have anything scheduled.

Amy N.

 My son started afternoon kindergarten a few months ago. Either we walk or I drive him to school each day. I discovered that getting him ready to go and still having time to eat lunch was a bit of a battle. I eventually set an alarm to go off 45 minutes before we need to leave each day. That alarm is his signal to stop playing, eat lunch, and then find his shoes, jacket, and backpack. Letting the alarm interrupt his play has worked far better than any verbal reminder I could have given him.

Carissa D.

My son used to get up and eat without clothes on. If I remembered to remind him, he would brush his teeth. But then getting dressed was a big ordeal because he would be busy playing and just really enjoying being naked.

When he was almost four, I tried a new approach. I found that having him use the bathroom, dress, and brush his teeth before we go to the kitchen to eat has worked well. He usually wants to eat so that is his motivation for completing the tasks.

Sometimes I use a crazy accent and pretend to be a goofy "crocodile dentist" who scrubs crickets, swamp grasses, toads, and old tires out of his mouth if he is having a slow-moving morning.

My husband plays a different game that he calls "Olympic High Step Dressing Team Practice." He uses a goofy accent and says, "Hello, it is time for Olympic High Step Dressing Team Practice. You practice and get better!" Then he holds his pants up really high and has our son just try to get his foot in, while he says, "Oh, higher, higher, just a little more," and so on. It is crazy. We all laugh. He tries so hard to get the clothes on!

Our son was often frustrated when we started adjusting to new routines. We have kept it up for about six months and it is now automatic.

Jessica C.

Tantrums

To me, a tantrum is a complete loss of self-control. My daughter, who is almost four years old, used to have them regularly. She did all of the things you read about in books: threw herself on the floor, screamed, flailed, and banged her head (not too often and not for long thank goodness). Tantrums usually lasted half an hour to an hour. She was like a tinderbox for hours afterward. She could be set off again very easily.

When she is in this state, my daughter does not want to be touched and touching her enrages her more. I would sit close by and empathize as much as possible—mostly to provide a gentle stream of conversation that sounded reassuring. I would ask my daughter if she wanted me to help

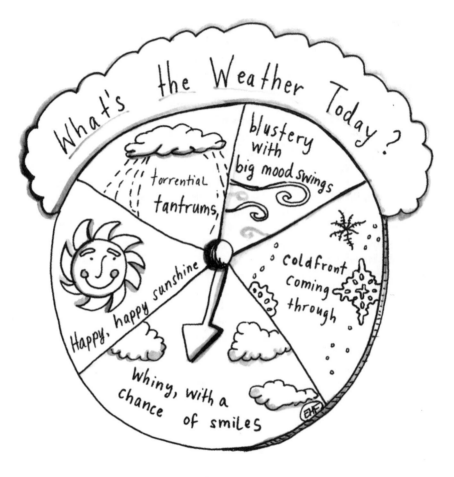

her calm down. Eventually she would be ready to take that step.

I find that if my child feels that her feelings are being validated, the tantrum lasts a shorter time and she will be able to control herself more easily in the future. Her tantrums are born out of frustration. I give my child fewer reasons to be frustrated by teaching her coping skills. Now her tantrums are diffused more quickly and occur less frequently.

Jessica K.

We have a highly sensitive toddler who experiences disappointment very deeply. If Sam has an expectation that something is going to be a certain way, and it is not, he is very likely to have a tantrum. For example, one time when Sam was about 18 months old, my husband put a waffle in the toaster and Sam completely lost it. He sobbed and pointed at the toaster, trying to talk but not making much sense. We stopped what we were doing, got down to his level, reassured him, and waited for him to be able to communicate. He finally got it out that Daddy had put the waffle in the wrong slot of the toaster. Apparently, I (the primary waffle toaster) had routinely used the slot closest to me while my husband used the one in the back. No one but Sam noticed this, and it bothered him enormously. So we switched the waffle to the other side of the toaster and reassured him that we simply hadn't known and we were glad he was able to tell us what his need was.

We don't view the tantrum as something that needs to be stopped, but rather as a cry for more connection and support and that's what we strive to respond to. I firmly believe that helping and supporting him through these struggles builds our attachment and models empathy, problem solving, and trust.

Betsy S.

 When my three-year-old son starts to throw a tantrum, I say something like, "I cannot understand you when you are freaking out. Breathe. Breathe. Breathe. Now tell (or show) me what you want." I want him to learn to speak up for what he wants in a loud but very clear way.

Valerie P.T.

 We just had to stay consistent. When a tantrum would come up, we'd let him "ride it out" but only as long as he wouldn't hurt himself. I learned to shut myself off from it so I wouldn't feel embarrassed or become distraught about it. (The looks people used to give us were appalling!)

We'd tell him, "Go ahead, scream, kick, cry, yell, hit the ground, whatever you need to do. I'm here. Go ahead and let it out. But this isn't the way to get what you want." We'd wait as long as it took. Then he'd tire himself out and get hugs and he'd be fine. Sometimes though we found it was better to distract him (i.e., just pick him up and start swinging him around, something he loves doing and that always makes him laugh).

When it gets really bad and I just want to scream, I try to remove myself mentally from the situation. I visualize a field of flowers (or something else that makes me happy) until the worst of his tantrum passes. That way, I stay calm enough to help him, and he has the time he needs to deal with his emotions.

Beverly E.

Yesterday, my two-year-old had a meltdown in the checkout line at the grocery store. She wanted to unravel all of the plastic bags and I was busy bagging my groceries and couldn't tend to her. I tried to get her to stop and come stand next to me, and she threw herself on the floor, screaming at the top of her lungs.

At another point in my parenting journey, I would have lost it. I probably would have abandoned my bagging and dragged her out the door, or just let her have her way with the bags.

Instead, I tried to talk to her calmly. When that went nowhere, I put her in the cart and finished bagging, letting her scream until she noticed I wasn't listening.

The big milestone here was that I didn't lose control. I maintained my patience and my composure and didn't give in to her.

Later, in the parking lot, a woman came up to me and said, "I just wanted to tell you, it does get better." I smiled. I know it does.

Sheri J.

I used to think that when my child would throw a tantrum, he was simply out of control. But as my son got older, I started to say at the start of a tantrum, "Now look at what you are doing." I say this in a gentle voice. I believe this helps him understand that he can be angry, mad, upset, and still able to think about his actions.

And it works. He is now seven and will say he is getting angry. We will set up a space for him to kick, scream, yell, and fight. I am with him each second so he does not feel alone or get left alone to cope by himself. Now he knows that as soon as he hurts me, or breaks something, I am done. The "session," as we call it, is over. I do not want him to think it is okay to lose control.

Simone H.

 My daughter (age three) has had some big tantrums. The kicking, thrashing, screaming "Get away from me!" kind that eventually end with her curled up in a ball of heaving sobs.

Here is my strategy:

I focus on prevention. I keep the limits simple, necessary, and consistent, so she learns that some limits remain no matter how outraged she gets (car seats would be a prime example). I am proactive by responding with playfulness, finding ways to say "Yes" as often as possible. I seek her suggestions for a compromise when my answer has been "No." My daughter has gotten very good at compromise. She will suggest compromises when I am too tired to think of one, or when I am resisting the idea of compromise because I just want my way. It will so often be a brilliant idea that I would have never thought of. Her creativity makes me feel so proud. It makes up for all of the kicking and screaming!

When we are getting into a struggle, I try to head it off before it becomes a tantrum. I make eye contact and physical contact, saying, "I'm listening. Tell me about your point of view." We try to work it out. Usually, this is the end of the episode.

If she continues in the direction of a temper tantrum, then there is usually an aggravating factor such as fatigue, over-stimulation, or hunger. At that point, it is clear to me that she needs to get out of the situation. Giving in is not going to help! She will just be melting down about something else soon. So then, I move to empathizing strongly, but remaining firm. Screaming is not reasonable behavior.

Kicking and hitting are not reasonable behavior. So we move from reasoning to damage control, and work on calming the tantrum.

Her outbursts frustrate me, infuriate me, sometimes embarrass me, and always break my heart. But they are just emotions— an overflow of negative emotions. She's "getting it out." Sure, I want it to stop as soon as possible. It's miserable for all parties! I try to help her (as much as she will let me), but I am not desperate for her to stop. Therefore, I don't act desperate for her to stop.

We talk a lot about her finding "peace in her heart." She knows what that feels like; she will tell me when she finds it. It is sweet, really.

I stay close for when she is calm enough to be comforted. (Some days just really, really stink, and I handle it badly. Sometimes I walk away from her and close a door behind me because I just can't stand the screaming. But then I count to 10, come out, and try again.)

After she is calm, if she wants to "try again" or suggest a compromise, that is fine with me. But screaming will not change my mind. I know that at times she does not have the patience or capacity to reason. Goodness, she is only three! But "giving in" doesn't seem to help the situation. For us, it only delays the inevitable meltdown.

Rebecca K.

 In our case, my son escalated his tantrums if I tried to comfort him physically or even if I stayed very close to him. One time, I said to him, as calmly as I could, "I'm going to go sit on the couch. When you're ready, you can come sit with me." (You could see the couch from the kitchen, but the couch faced away from the kitchen.) Honestly, I did it for myself that time, as I was afraid I was going to yell at him, shake him, or do something I would later regret very much. (Ten years later, I can perfectly picture that room in that house—which we moved out of six years ago—and I remember how desperate I felt. This is not a good memory.)

As soon as I walked away, he started to calm down. He was still in a tantrum, but it was as if he went over the top of the hill and started coming down. Soon, he came to sit next to me on the couch. We talked about how scary and sad it is to feel like he did when he was lying on the kitchen floor.

Next tantrum, I tried the same thing, with the same result.

What I eventually figured out about my kid, by trial and error, is that he is very easily over-stimulated, even by his Dad or me. I had suspected that about him as a baby and his toddlerhood only confirmed it. Even now, as a pre-teen, he needs much more alone time than his father or I do, and more than the parents of his peers say their kids need. He still occasionally needs our help to process things, but for the most part he goes to his room and shuts the door or walks around our yard (it's enclosed by trees for privacy) and talks it out with himself.

Once I figured out the "key" to my child (his over-stimulation issue), parenting got much, much, much easier.

Kathleen C.

 Around here, I do my best to prevent tantrums, but if it needs to happen to restore equilibrium in my child, I'll do my best to avoid adding negative energy to it, or try to end it. If it gets to that point, I just tell my four-year-old to "get it out, get it all out, I'm right here when you're ready." I am there, nearby, if not holding (one likes holding, one doesn't) him. Neither of them likes me talking, humming, or adding anything to the moment. They just need to get all that anger and frustration out so they can have the ability to be rational again.

Once I looked at my role in dealing with tantrums, I realized:

I am not afraid of tantrums.
I am not embarrassed by tantrums.
Other people's perceptions don't concern me.
Tantrums don't sway me.
My role is one of support and comfort.

The depth of feeling pouring out of my tiny child always affects me. I want to help him work through it, and pick up the pieces afterwards. I don't want him to stuff all that emotion inside. I want him to feel like he still has dignity when he is done. I don't want him to feel ashamed for "losing it." I want him glad I'm on his side, not cowering from me, feeling like he didn't live up to something I want-

ed in him. I want those moments to prove I am there for him, no matter what. No matter how loud he yells, screams, or cries. I am there to support him, not take control of the moment, but support him through the moment.

Anna W.

I remember one time Holly was being out of sorts. She was four, and very upset about something. I don't remember if it was my idea, but she started taking out her frustration on her stuffed animals. She tossed them all around her room for about 15 minutes, and then all of a sudden she started picking them up, kissing them, and putting them back on their shelves. I guess she had gotten whatever was bothering her out of her system, and reverted to her peaceful self. I watched her have her little tantrum and recovery, while I sat silently nearby, nursing her sister.

Dee R.

> I've found that one of the worst things I can do when my five-year-old is having a meltdown is to leave her alone.

My daughter (18 months) can throw a pretty good tantrum. I believe these are normal and important for a child's development. I usually will sit with her and tell her that I understand that she is angry and sad and wants to play with XYZ, but that it isn't safe. I tell her to let all of her anger and frustration out. That she'll feel better. I stay near her (she won't let me hold her during these) and when she is ready, she comes over for a hug. I find this is much more productive and allows her to explore her emotions much better than if I yelled or tried to make her stop.

Nancy W.

With both my two-year-old and five-year-old, taking them away from the situation to a quiet place where I can be with them and help them calm down is the most helpful. I've found that one of the worst things I can do when my five-year-old is having a meltdown is to leave her alone. I know this isn't the case with every child, but my daughter feels as if I'm abandoning her if I go somewhere else.

My two-year-old is still at the point where meltdowns can be ended fairly quickly by suggesting a new activity or showing him a new toy. Since he's less verbal than my five-year-old is, it also helps a lot to help him verbalize his feelings (i.e., "You must be feeling very mad that the blocks fell down." "Are you feeling sad because the puppy walked away?")

Amy N.

 I address temper tantrums with my toddlers by first getting my own annoyance under control. Then I go to physical touch: nursing (back when that was available), cuddling, back rubs, or a hug. I realize that in a sense "this is not my child." I pull them close and try to figure out what is not right. Usually it is either hunger or fatigue. If they've just eaten, and just woke up, it's harder, but also rare. I pull out something (healthy) to eat and drink and offer it. Sometimes they eat it; sometimes they cry louder, sometimes they throw it. Anyway, it does send a message that I am trying. If they are tired, I try to go up to the bedroom and lie down with them. They usually go to sleep right away.

I do what I can to avoid public tantrums. I plan our outings for their good times of the day. I know better than to plan a playmate for my toddlers at 1 PM, or right after preschool or a birthday party. They always have food and a drink before we go, and I take snacks. Also, for some reason, they find comfort in taking along one toy. Sometimes it is a stuffed animal, sometimes a truck.

Brooke S.

 I found the best way to deal with temper tantrums is to try to avoid them when I can. I know what pushes his buttons and what he can't handle.

We don't take long car trips, ever. We don't make Gabriel sit still for a long time, including trying to avoid television as much as possible. We almost never eat out, and if we do, I take Gabriel outside the restaurant to run around while everyone else enjoys the meal. If I see him

"losing it" in a La Leche League or Attachment Parenting meeting, we leave early or go outside to play. We make sure to play outside every day. I always give him a warning countdown when we need to leave the playground or play-group. "Five minutes. Four minutes." and then, "Last time." Then we say goodbye to the toys and the kids. I try not to force him to do anything. If he has to do something that he doesn't want to do, we try to make it fun. For example, for a while he hated baths and would have a temper tantrum at bath time, so we bought him a new bath toy and then he loved baths again.

If Gabriel does have a temper tantrum, I hold him and tell him it's okay to cry and that I know that sometimes it feels good to cry. I tell him, "Mommy's here for you and you can tell me why you're sad." As he's gotten older, he usually will come to me crying and say, "I'm sad" instead of having a temper tantrum. Then I can ask him why he's sad and he can tell me about it. I always make sure to thank him for using his words to tell me his feelings. We don't always give him what he's crying for, but I make sure to validate his feelings and tell him that I understand why that makes him sad.

I remember having temper tantrums as a child, and my parents would send me to my room. I grew up in a family where it was "bad" to cry. I felt so unloved and I remember that I just wanted someone to hold me and listen to me, not even to give me what I was having a temper tantrum for. So I always make sure to tell Gabriel that it's okay to cry and tell me that he's sad, as long he doesn't kick or scream.

Beth C.

Hitting and other aggressive behavior

Sometimes I think my toddler (20 months) gets overexcited and hits, so I rein her in with our "gentle touch" game that positively shows her what to do instead. We take turns naming body parts on each other and pointing to them. She knows she has to be gentle when playing this game.

Suzanne H.

I have been at my wits' end with my daughter, who is just about two and a half. She has changed from a sweet loving child to a monster this past two weeks. She now hits, throws massive temper tantrums, kicks me, and seems to be contrary about every little thing. By the end of the day, I am wiped out. Earlier today, she was hitting me and I swatted her on the leg. I explained to her that hitting hurts. She started crying and said, "Mommy hurt me," which broke my heart. Less than 20 minutes later, she hit me again! It seemed obvious to me that this approach did not work with my child. I felt terrible.

Then a friend reminded me that kids act right when they're feeling right. She said that when her son is going through a rough patch, the most useful thing is to spend more focused time with him.

I cried. It's exactly what's going on, and as usual, it's about me and not about my child. I have been taking on a huge workload lately and have been very busy and not spending the quality time with her that I did before. In addition, she is turning two-and-a-half. She is growing like a weed, and I moved her into her own bed. She's next to our bed in our room, but that's still a big change all by itself. She doesn't know how to express how she feels.

I know what I need to do.

Be there.

I love that at this age they are so articulate. She "told on" me for hurting her. So we talked about it and I said I was sorry for hitting her, that hitting is wrong, even for mommy. I said, "I am sorry I was mean to you" and she says to me, "No, you not mean, you nice mommy." I started bawling. Kids are so forgiving and sweet.

Cheryl L.

This month, we have had a breakthrough! In the last few weeks, I have started helping my son (two years old) practice "gentle hands" before social situations. Then, when we're with other children if I see him about to act aggressively, I will say, "Parker, gentle, nice hands." He has started going up to the other child or adult and touching them gently.

Today at the beach, his little friend—who is now 18

months old and used to be the brunt of his pushing—has started her own pushing stage. He just looked at her and said, "No Ella, gentle!" He yelled it, but he didn't hit back. I breathed a sigh of relief. It took a long time, but being gentle with him and showing him how to be gentle has paid off.

Heather M.

When my son was around two, he went through a phase of hitting. It was very frustrating.

I tried putting myself in his place. I would imagine what it is like to need or want something but be unable to communicate it to the people who will help you get what you want or need. Imagine how hard the world of a toddler must be, where you are learning so much every day but are unable to express yourself verbally. I did what I could to work with him on it, and in a just a few months, he stopped hitting. At the same time, he went from having a very small vocabulary to speaking in sentences. I think the hitting had to do with frustration of needing to say much more than he could.

Patricia S.

I give him alternatives for hitting such as beating on his drums if he feels a need to hit.

My son is three and currently going through a new hitting phase. He talks a lot about being a "not nice guy" and is trying out some "not nice guy" behaviors. He does have a reputation for being the sweet and sensitive boy among several more aggressive playmates; I wonder if he's trying out the not-so-greener grass on the other side. Luckily, it seems to be passing as quickly as it came on.

My way of dealing with it is to try to stop his arm before it hits me (or another person), and tell him it's not okay to hit people. I tell him it's okay to feel grumpy or "not nice" as he puts it, but that it's not okay to hit. I tell him he can use his words to tell people how he's feeling or if he's upset, but that it's not okay to hit people.

I stay calm, try not to react too strongly and again, move on. If I make a big deal about it, it seems to fuel and perpetuate the behavior ("Wow, Mom really lost it. This behavior turns heads!").

I give him alternatives for hitting such as beating on his drums if he feels a need to hit. In all, I try to validate the emotion, give him an appropriate way of dealing with it (words) and also a suggestion for an alternative kind of "hitting" if he really feels the need.

Sometimes I've told my son that I won't let him hit me and left the room to do something else. When people are hit, they generally don't stick around for more. So to me, that's a pretty natural consequence.

Mary Beth K.

 At times when everyone is calm and happy, we talk about and role-play things to do when someone grabs your car, knocks down your tower, or is in your space. Not just five minutes later, but the next morning when everyone is snuggling in bed, or when we are driving in the car. I think that talking about how a body feels when it's hungry or tired helps, since I think that they are most likely to hurt when they are feeling bad. So we talk about how helpful it can be to just sit quietly and notice how your body is feeling.

Mallory P.

 Most of the time, I get out the crayons and construction paper and ask my son, who is three-and-a-half, to draw me a picture of how he feels. A friend of mine had suggested this technique. When I first started using it, I didn't think my son would be able to communicate what he was feeling through drawing.

The first time we tried this, he was taking a break because he pushed his sister down. He drew a picture of himself lying on a bed. He said he was tired. He wasn't going to admit that he needed to rest until he had an outlet to show me.

Other times he has drawn dark circles and has said that, "Sister is driving me nuts!" Even if he doesn't get an emotion out, whatever was bothering him usually subsides when he can take a break from the situation and calm himself down.

Susan L.

I think that talking about how a body feels when it's hungry or tired helps.

When Keithen was four years old, a little boy at some of our parenting group meetings was pretty aggressive. The two boys frequently tested their limits against each other, ending with both of them resorting to yelling, throwing toys, pushing, hitting, you name it. It was apparent that the other boy's mother had very little control over her child. When he got out of hand, she seemed helpless and if she tried to step in, he was very disrespectful to her. After several of these confrontations, I was determined to help my son avoid getting into another battle of wills with this little boy. Before going to the meeting, we talked about how Brian sometimes got rough. We discussed the appropriate way to react if Brian did something that Keithen didn't like. I suggested ways that he could use his words to help keep the situation from escalating, such as telling the other boy, "Brian, you need to calm down," or "Stop! I don't like that."

Preparing him for the situation really worked. Instead of letting his anger and frustration build when Brian started chasing and playing rough, Keithen put his arms out in front of him and loudly declared, "Brian, you need to calm down!" Brian was also much more willing to listen to his peer tell him that his behavior was out of control.

Carissa D.

My son (almost three years old) has been hitting, kicking, head butting, and even biting lately. I've had a bit of a light-bulb moment. The last time he was this aggressive and "out of control" was when he was about 18 months old and we were unknowingly giving him all manner of foods he was allergic to. We have recently introduced a new food and he has a large spot of eczema on his arm. Why this didn't occur to me before is beyond me. It's like the first thing on the checklist: Has he eaten anything new? Is he tired? Is he hungry? Is he overwhelmed? Is he bored?

Betsy S.

We're currently going through a hitting and biting phase with my three-year-old. She bites in the guise of being a doggie. This has been a real struggle for me to deal with, because being bitten is a big hotspot for me. My child only bites me, not anyone else. I can't say that I always deal with it gently. I try to remember to talk to her as if she's really a dog, saying firmly, "No biting, doggie." She usually responds with a "ruff," which is okay with me.

I also make up fairy tales about incidents. I really feel this talks to her on an unconscious level. My daughter always loves the fairy tales and asks for them over and over, adding elements herself. It becomes interactive with us. I made up a story about a princess who lives in a castle and wants to be a doggie. A fairy godmother comes and turns her into a doggie. The only condition is that she must not bite anyone or else she will turn back into a princess. She is so happy because she has a beautiful doghouse, sleeps under the stars, and gets to lick people. Then a big giant hears about the doggie and comes to steal her away. The doggie does clever things in order to escape from the giant without biting him so that she can remain a doggie happily ever after.

My daughter and one of her friends sometimes start hitting each other. His mother and I try to react consistently. As much as possible, we try to anticipate hitting and prevent it. Usually they will start screaming at each other before they hit. So at that point, we try to de-escalate them by reflecting their feelings and describing what's going on. "You want your friend to move over. He's not moving over. Yes, I can see that it's making you sad and frustrated. Maybe you could move over instead. Maybe you would like to come help Mommy make cookies." Something along those lines usually works.

If it does escalate to hitting, then each of us first comforts our own child. Then we talk to them about the impact on the other child. "Look, your friend is crying. He's very sad, because you hit him. It hurt him. Does it hurt when you get hit? Yes? He's hurting too now. Maybe we could help him feel better." Helping the other child feel better is optional, never forced. Usually the child will come up with a solution to helping the other child feel better too. I try to wait and see if they do before I suggest anything like a hug.

Elizabeth B.

The first time my son hit me, at 18 months old, it threw me straight back into my own childhood. I remembered my fury at being told to be nice to my brother, when as far as I was concerned, my brother deserved the wallop I'd given him. Seeing my son's anger in context with my own memory, I knew I had to find another answer than "use nice touches." I improvised, "Gabriel, we don't hit when we're angry. We scowl (demonstrated), or we cross our arms and stand like this (demonstrated), or we use our words and say 'I'm angry!'" How I wish someone had said that to me when I was a child! I'd needed a way to express my justifiable fury without getting in trouble for it.

He took about a week to get the idea, but he came to understand that his automatic reaction to his anger (hitting) wasn't the only possible reaction, and that other responses that communicated his feelings might work without getting him in trouble. He decided not to use any of the options I gave him for how to let us know he was angry. He chose, instead, to stomp. He needed something loud, physical, and dramatic to express that emotion. My husband and I decided that stomping was acceptable (for then—we've modified it as he's gotten older), and Gabe was thrilled to have discovered, on his own, a way to get his point across. I was thrilled to have taught him that he was entitled to be angry, but just wasn't entitled to hurt anyone because of how he felt.

Heather P.

We have some phrases in our house that we say over and over so our son can remember them. One of them is, "We don't hit; we talk about what makes us angry." Whenever he hits, I take him aside and remind him we don't hit. I ask him, "What do we do instead?" And he'll say, "Talk about what makes us angry." Then I'll ask him what made him angry and I listen to him.

Now that we've been doing this for a while, he usually will tell me, "I'm angry!" instead of hitting. I make sure to praise him for using his words to express his feelings and then I listen to him while he tells me why he's angry. It really works!

Beth C.

Part Four

Personal Essays

The previous parts of this book have explored the basic components to gentle discipline, the importance of bringing gentle discipline to ourselves, and short examples from various families telling how they put these ideas into practice. This final section brings in the voices of parents who share their real-life gentle discipline stories with you. Some will resonate with you, while others may not fit. You, too, will have your own journey, with your own challenges and breakthroughs.

Ditching Stepford Mom

by Bettina Lanyi

We'd had a horrible week. The whining, the crankiness, the vast intake of candy just to achieve emotional stability.

And that was just me. My toddler was a wreck, too.

"Mommy I want…I want…I want…" eyes searching around the kitchen.

"No sweetie. We're all done with chocolate for today. Let's have another snack. I know, I'll make you some apples and cheese."

"No! I want chocolate. I want my choc choc choco choco choc. Mooommmmy!"

"No, no more today. It's time for an apple and cheese snack."

"I want chocolate. Moooommmmyyy. Choc. Choc choc choc choco-choco-chocoEEEHHH!!"

"You need to stop. Whining. This very instant. Now!"

Bettina Lanyi, a former health policy analyst, is an at-home mom of a daughter, age three, and a son, three months.

She burst into tears. I almost cried along with her.

"Sweetie, I'm sorry." I knelt next to her and took her in my arms, my heartbeat pounding in my ears. I never spoke to her that way; never permitted myself to. What was wrong with me?

What had happened to us? My sweet, affectionate child had become a Jekyll-and-Hyde creature, whiny and clingy one minute, imperious and demanding the next. I was trying so hard to stay calm, to treat her like the good person I knew she was inside, instead of a two-year-old candidate for an insane asylum.

But I was slipping. That edge crept into my voice more and more often, a new sharpness that hadn't been there before. Several days ago, I had come close to losing it when Chloe kept pulling our dog Bella's tail. She knew how to treat her gently, but on that day she was clearly testing me, grabbing the dog's tail over and over after we had the discussion on not to do it. She had a glint in her eye I'd never seen before—mischievous, and—was I imagining it?—almost sadistic. She grabbed the tail again and held on tight. The dog froze, miserable. Suddenly the words poured out of me in an angry rush. "Chloe, I'm Bella's mommy, too. It's my job to take care of her, and I won't let you hurt her. Next time you grab her tail and hurt her, I'm going to hurt you." I grabbed her wrist and squeezed, hard; she let go. She didn't cry that time, just looked chastened and a little shocked. I was shocked too—by my strong desire to swat her on her little butt. I had never felt that before, never thought I would even want to spank her. But I felt the fury rising up in me; I was frightened. What would happen the next time I felt that way?

She got the message; for a while we were both on our best behavior. But it felt all wrong; I never wanted her to learn anything that way. I don't want my baby to be a bully, I thought. By threatening her with my physical strength, that's what I was teaching her, just as I felt spanking would. I was falling back on the patterns I knew, the angry words that came out of my mouth like second nature.

My parents loved us, but believed in enforcing discipline through spankings or, more often, the looming threat thereof. I can't remember for the life of me what I was ever spanked for or what lessons were being imparted at the time. I do clearly remember several spankings themselves, the anger that was transmitted to us, the humiliation of being hit, the frustration of

> My parents loved us, but believed in enforcing discipline through spankings or, more often, the looming threat thereof.

being so very small in such a big world that didn't seem to have the time to stop and listen to my feelings, which seemed so very big, too big to manage. I knew spankings didn't teach me anything about what to do about those.

I wanted something different for us, for my child. My husband and I found a path through attachment parenting, breastfeeding on demand, extended breastfeeding, co-sleeping. We believed that fostering a strong attachment with our child would help create a foundation of loving discipline for years to come. And it seemed, if not always easy, then certainly natural to us. We never had to agonize over letting Chloe cry; we would always pick her up, keep her near us. It might have been intense, but in many ways it was blissful, harmonious. For a very long time we weren't worried about discipline, and secretly felt it was less of a problem for us because of our parenting practices.

Now, after more than two years, I faced a real challenge. The night of the tail-pulling incident, I ran down my mental checklist for reasons Chloe and I were having a tough week. Was she teething? Sick? Napping less? Eating more sugar? What more could I possibly do that I hadn't done yet?

Then I realized what I hadn't done. I was so busy trying to be gentle with Chloe that I wasn't being gentle with myself.

While I held her to the standard of reasonable behavior—not expecting her to do more/ behave better than she was capable of—I was placing impossible expectations on myself. I was supposed to be always patient, constantly understanding, and never express frustration. In fact, I found it difficult to say "no" to her in many other circumstances, as when I was requested to read a book for the millionth time or give the umpteenth piggyback ride of the day. Petrified of subjecting her to the anger of an adult, I expected myself never to express any negative emotions whatsoever, to be up for anything, always.

In short, it was as if I were expecting myself to sit up straight and be good all day long, putting myself in a straightjacket in order not to express my feelings—something, I was horrified to realize, I would never expect of my young child. As a result of the past week of full-time caretaking with my testing two-year-old, I was feeling like a tamped-down volcano of emotions about to blow. No wonder I was scared of my own feelings, of what I might do next. If my real feelings had a chance to come out, she might not get spanked—she might actually go sailing through a window.

I was overcorrecting for the way I was raised, for harsh hands and voices, and when the pressure built, I just reverted. I didn't know any in-between. I didn't know how to say I was angry without scaring someone else. I forgot that so much of teaching discipline is practicing self-discipline, and if I wanted to practice gentle discipline, then the voice that governed myself must be gentle, too.

I was supposed to be the designated adult here. Instead, I was Stepford Mom—my real self hidden behind a blandly patient façade. But I had forgotten my first role—to show her how to act by example. How could she learn that bad feelings were okay, weren't overwhelming, if she never saw me dealing with them myself?

So we made some changes around our house. I practiced expressing my feelings in a calm way, in words that my toddler could handle. And it does take practice—not to mention creativity, a dash of humor, and always a deep breath—when it's not something that comes naturally. I told myself it was okay to let Chloe know I was frustrated if I explained, not exploded. We have some stock phrases, trite perhaps, but handy in times of stress:

- "It's hot, we've had a long day and done lots of things, and we're both tired and cranky. Let's pull the car over and take a break for a second." (Our version of "time-out"; sometimes this means silence, sometimes a break and a story, or a song.)

- "I'm a little preoccupied right now. That means I'm thinking of a lot of different things at once. Let me finish what I'm doing so I can focus on you properly."

- "I know you really want me to do that with you right now. Sometimes we just have to wait until someone else is ready to play with us. I'm not ready now, but I will tell you when I am."

- "I think I'm getting close to my patience limit. Let's practice having a quiet moment right now and then I'll feel better."

- "My energy tank is running a little low right now. I'm going to take a moment to refuel."

If I wanted to practice gentle discipline, then the voice that governed myself must be gentle, too.

Phrases like this help me create a small, desperately needed breathing space for myself during a difficult day—just enough for me to keep that cool, peaceful center that tells me I am doing okay, that I can be that calm, reasonable adult my daughter needs me to be, that I need myself to be. That I am going to make it. They were also the first step to helping me learn to set boundaries for myself. I worked hard to make sure I respected my child's feelings and personal space; now, I was starting to teach her to respect mine, a new step for us, a new understanding of the concept of discipline, and a crucial one.

We also use a lot more words to talk about feelings. Feelings can be like big, galloping horses, but you can take a deep breath, hug yourself, and wait for them to slow down. Then it's easier to use your words and tell someone, an adult, what you're feeling. People think it's cute when Chloe explains herself: "When that woman tickled me I was startled. I don't like that." "I cried at summer camp because I was nervous. But then it was okay." When I hear her articulating her feelings, it makes my heart fill with the hope that she can manage her feelings, as big as they are, that they are not bigger than her ability to handle them. And if they are overwhelming, she has her mom and dad to help her name them and tame, but always accept, them.

Maybe now she's lost something—her angelically patient mother, that Stepford Mom, who would put up with anything. Now she's getting a mom who has big feelings like she does, but tries different ways to handle those feelings. There's a new mom in town. I think I like her better. She laughs more. And she's a lot more at home in my skin.

Yes Days

∿∿∿∿∿∿∿∿∿∿∿∿∿∿∿

by Ginger Carlson

Ginger Carlson, writer and educator, lives, loves, and laughs with her husband, Raphael, and their son, Zeal, in Eugene, Oregon. They continually look for ways to say "yes" to one another. Ginger also works as an educational and homeschool consultant and serves as adjunct faculty at the University of Oregon.

"This way, Mommy! Do you hear the rocks crunching under my feet?" My son darts past me on the walking trails near our home. We spend the morning snooping in the bushes, snacking on only the plumpest berries that drop effortlessly into our palms, and sprinkling "fish food" (crumbled Autumn leaves) into the creek. Today is a "Yes Day," a day in which I consciously choose to say yes to my child, to honor his spirit, his desires, his choices. Today there is no "We need to…," "Time to go…," or "One more minute…," and (practically) anything goes. Days like today fulfill us, bring us closer together, and help us release the struggles long enough to see the wonder in the world through our shared eyes.

I am a stay at home mom who redirected my life (aka quit my successful profession to work at home) in order to soak up this time with my son. Still, I find myself often feeling directed by the places we should be. Many of these "should be's" are places we actually have to be or things that indeed do need to be done in order to make our lives run smoothly; meetings, errands, or household chores. Many are my own omniscient-parent "have-to's"—outings we go on for his benefit: library story times, playgroups, community activities, or visits to parks and playgrounds. It's easy to get tied into having self-imposed time limits on our day, our week, our life. I find myself comforted by having a plan, a time frame for it all.

Disturb the comfortable. Isn't that what they say? What would life be worth if there wasn't a little discomfort now and then? So I've tossed my "plan" aside for the day. And what a gift it is when I take the moment to stop and evaluate it all. I realize that letting go of these have-to's, if only for the day, is how we are able to really build the deep connections I sought after when I made the decision to stay at home with him. Through the simple things we do today, like collecting the knobbliest sticks and then finding things to measure with them, we are learning to understand each other better. That, it seems, becomes the key to nurturing a confident, passionate, creative, and valued human being.

As we enter this very freeing day, my heart reminds my head that saying "yes," affirming my son as a human being, is a gift to both of us. I watch closely as my son's eyes light the pathways to the soul that is fed by his choices being honored, not having time limits or have to's for once. I feel my own soul swelling as I inhale his pleasure in these simple moments and take the time to truly draw in his joy, something we often forget to stop and do in our hectic world. I affirm to myself that the world I am creating for my son will directly affect the world that he will help create as I attentively listen to his movements, his explorations, his problem-solving techniques. As a joyous gift from him, I gain insight into his world.

Like the lightning bug he is, my son takes a quick unbridled left turn down the road less traveled, through the bramble toward a swell of stones that seem to be calling his name. I follow his path, the one he is creating for himself, away from schedules, away from siblings, away from pressure. Just one on one time with Mommy that helps us recognize the way this puzzle really does fit together so nicely.

It's easy to get tied into having self-imposed time limits on our day, our week, our life.

I feel my own soul swelling as I inhale his pleasure in these simple moments and take the time to truly draw in his joy.

In so doing, we are learning to question agendas, getting past reflexively saying "It's time to go," or "one more minute." I now grasp that imposing my agenda on him to go somewhere he will enjoy (even if that means entering into a power struggle that leaves both of us exhausted) is only training him to look to others for direction rather than gaining sovereignty over himself. I witness him finding strength in the love he feels from me as he is given control over his situation.

So here we are in the eyes of our shared day, viewing the world as it is and as it should be, through each remnant egg shell we discover, each ripple we create in the creek. We are learning to say "yes" to each other, to the people we interact with, to the ebb and flow of the world. Perhaps these "yes days" are only training for us to live a "yes life." Even more so, perhaps our "Yes lives" will be the impression left on our children that in turn creates a "yes world."

But for now I am content to accept the joy we both get from our simple "yes days" and even the tiniest of "yes moments" when carving out a whole day just seems too impossible. Because there is only one thing I could say when my three-year-old circle-danced atop a stone mountain in the forest, arms outstretched as if he were tickling the sky, and I caught up in time to ask, "Tell me about your dance," and he responded, "I'm changing the world, Mommy."

"Yes, honey, you certainly are!"

O Captain, My Captain

by Jody Mace

When Kyla and Charlie first started climbing out of the windows of this house, I found it strangely charming. We had just moved to England to live for one year while my husband worked on assignment. I had worried so much about the children being homesick that when they came up with a hide-and-seek game that involved swinging the many downstairs windows open, climbing out, and racing through the back yard (or, I should say, "the garden") and back inside, I was happy that they were making themselves at home.

For a while I observed this activity, casting a blind eye on the hazards, until finally my mommy brain kicked into gear, and I informed them that climbing out of windows was not allowed.

"Why?" they asked.

"Because you might fall on something sharp."

"We'll move sharp things out of the way," they countered, reasonably.

Jody Mace's permanent home is Charlotte, North Carolina, where she lives with her husband, Stan, their daughter, Kyla, and their son, Charlie. Her essays about family life have appeared in many magazines. "The Captain" was originally published in *Brain, Child: The Magazine for Thinking Mothers*.

"Because the window might break."

"We promise we won't break the window," Charlie solemnly said.

This was the kind of logic that you can't debate. Such a promise is unenforceable, but I can never convince Charlie or Kyla of that. They can promise to try to not break the window. They can promise to not intentionally break the window. They can promise to take great care with the window, to treat it like a magnificent, ancient piece of glasswork. But the window might still break. Broken windows have little to do with intent, and much to do with the physics of unexpectedly falling bodies.

I pulled a new rabbit out of my hat.

"The captain wouldn't like it."

The captain isn't some character I made up; not exactly. Right on the lease agreement, it says: "Landlord: Captain Timothy Brown." This pronouncement had just the effect I had hoped for.

Kyla asked, "Who is the captain?"

"The captain," I explained, "is the person who owns this house. He does not want people climbing out of his windows. If he found out, he would not be happy."

Kyla and Charlie immediately acquiesced to the absent captain's authority.

They were in awe of this stern figure. I had to wonder why it was that the captain, whom they had never met, inspired such respect while I had to reason with them about why it's not a good idea to climb out of windows. Why were his wishes so honored? Was it his rank, his uniform?

In truth, I didn't wonder about it for too long because I was starting to love the captain. When the kids took food into the living room, I informed them, "The captain doesn't allow food in the living room." Later on, the captain made an exception for fruit that was eaten at the coffee table, by people leaning over the plate, and who remembered to throw away the remnants of the fruit so that bugs were not attracted into the captain's living room.

When Charlie lay on the back of the couch, like a cat, smashing down the cushions, I informed him that the captain was quite attached to his sofa and would not be happy to see the cushions flattened. Charlie immediately rolled off the back of it

In truth, I didn't wonder about it for too long because I was starting to love the captain.

and stared at me with wide eyes.

I was thankful that my children never bothered to read the lease agreement, which actually said nothing about food in the living room, or boys on the back of the sofa, but said much about the holes that I had drilled in the wall to move phone jacks around and the satellite dish I had installed on the roof. I used the captain as I wished. He wasn't there to speak for himself.

The more I invoked the authority of the captain, the clearer his picture became in my mind. He was a captain in the British Navy, I decided, in his late forties, with jet black hair and a crisp London accent. In my imaginings, he was always in uniform, even when mowing the lawn or making love.

But there were problems with my idealized captain, details about the house that challenged the picture I had of him. The carpet was cranberry-colored, and the walls in some rooms were violet. Most disturbing were the pink walls in the bedroom. What captain worth his salt would be caught dead with a pink bedroom? And worst of all, there were images of cats everywhere: kitty mugs, cat paintings in the bathroom, and a cat plaque by the house number on the outside of the house. I could think of nothing less captain-like than an affinity for cat memorabilia.

Maybe the captain wasn't at all what I was imagining. Really, there was no way to know the first thing about him. I didn't even know for sure that he was in the military. Could just anybody call himself a captain? (Captain Kangaroo, Captain Underpants, Cap'n Crunch, Captain America, Captain and Tenille …) Sometimes in my more dreamy moments, I imagined Captain Jean-Luc Picard, of the Starship Enterprise, with his elegant manner and gleaming head. When I told the kids to clean their rooms, there was Jean-Luc, behind me, intoning: "Make it so!"

But usually I was able to keep my mental image of the British Navy Captain clear in my mind. I chalked the pink walls and the cat pictures up to his wife, Helen (I knew her name because it was on the cat mug). Perhaps the captain was just the flexible sort when it came to décor. Maybe he was just that much in love with Helen.

With the captain's help, I was enjoying authority of a different sort with my children than I'd experienced in the past. Kyla and Charlie were apt to question me. I didn't see this as a negative trait. I had encouraged them to think things through, to learn to solve their own problems, to speak their minds. And for the most part, I was pleased with the results.

They were very self-disciplined for kids their age; they behaved about as well without supervision as they did with it. And they were willing to come to me to talk about anything; I can't remember either of them really lying to me. They were trustworthy. I believe that children who learn to think things through will grow to be responsible adults. But they sure didn't see my instructions to them as infallible words of wisdom, carved in stone.

So it wasn't surprising that the times when, out of frustration or impatience, I'd told Kyla, "Because I said so," she thoughtfully answered, "That doesn't sound like a very good reason."

And she was right. If I couldn't conjure up a reasonable answer, then why was I insistent on having my way? Why shouldn't Kyla rearrange her furniture at will? Why couldn't Charlie wear just underwear all day if we weren't going anywhere? Why? I didn't know. I couldn't think of one good reason.

But how much simpler it must be to have children who didn't question so much and just did what they were told. Imagine telling a child to put on a coat and him doing it—without walking outside to check the temperature. When Kyla and Charlie unquestioningly obeyed the captain, I experienced what it would be like to be one of those parents whose "because I said so" signaled the end of the conversation, rather than a thesis on my faulty reasoning.

But authority, even when it's borrowed from a phantom captain, is addictive. I found myself tempted more and more to abuse this authority, in ways that made less and less sense. Sure, the captain might object to cookies in the bedrooms, but would he really care if Kyla straightened her room or not? Would he actually become agitated just because the sofa pillows were piled on the floor? Was the captain really that petty?

It was becoming clear to me that my "captain" technique was a short-cut, a kind of quick-fix parenting. Instead of taking the time to teach them the reasons why they should take care of

> I believe that children who learn to think things through will grow to be responsible adults.

belongings, and getting them to own the responsibility, I was just using fear to control them. I've never wanted my kids to fear me, but here I was, regularly inspiring fear to get the results I wanted. The only difference was that it wasn't me that they feared. But, regardless of whom they feared, the problem with abusing this kind of authority remained—it was only effective if they thought that they would get caught. Would my thinking, self-disciplined kids become the kind of kids who only behaved well when an adult was watching?

And I even found myself longing to use the captain's authority with other people. When the rental agents were slow about repairing a lock on a door, I caught myself before I warned, "The captain wouldn't like it!" I was heady with borrowed power.

I knew that I was relying too much on the captain. If there was something that I wanted the kids to do, and I had no logical reason for it, at least I should take the heat myself, instead of pinning it on the absent captain. So I tried to refrain from overdoing it, and just saved him for the biggies. But I couldn't give him up completely. He was too useful to me. And besides, my days with the captain were limited. Before I knew it, we'd be moving back to America, leaving him behind. And then I'd have to fend for myself on the parenting battlefield. O Captain, my Captain. How I will miss you.

Epilogue:

One day, Charlie accidentally did some minor damage to a wall, and he said, "Oh no. The captain will be so sad." His voice was filled with concern, not fear. And it struck me that even as I was guiltily trying to use the old-fashioned fear-based parenting, the kids had been, at least partly, interpreting it a different way. They were worried about the captain's feelings. Not because he was a scary authority, but because he was a human being. I found it heartening that Charlie was motivated by caring, not by fear. Despite all my blunders, I guess this ship is in good hands.

Sibling Afternoon

by Krista Minard

Krista Minard is the editor of *Sacramento* magazine, a monthly lifestyle publication covering California's capital city. Her daughters, who earlier this year decided to share a bedroom, continue to use "the solution" to help them resolve conflicts peaceably.

When seven-year-old Anna asked if she could purchase a horse poster at the end-of-the-year school book fair, the realization that I had no cash in my wallet hardly fazed her. The fact that she had no money in her allowance jar didn't worry her, either. "Melissa," she said, turning to her four-year-old sister, whose allowance jar held five precious dollars, "Can I borrow your five dollars? I'll pay you back. The poster I want is $3, and if they have something for $2, I'll buy it for you."

Happy to help, Melissa dug out the money and gave it to Anna. Then the three of us hopped on our bikes and rode to school. It was a bright sunny day, which brought happy thoughts of the impending summer break from school—in just a few days, school would be out and we'd have entire days to fill with unscheduled activities: art projects, swimming, bike rides, reading. We could hardly wait.

After Anna locked up her bike, Melissa hugged her goodbye and said, "Don't forget to buy me something."

My daughters had made deals like this many times. Not yet in school, Melissa didn't have access to the book fairs and other sales that took place on campus at lunchtime. When Anna used her allowance money to purchase something, she usually bought a little trinket for her sister as well. Melissa never got the joy of making the selection, but she was always thrilled when Anna surprised her with an eraser, a pencil, or a miniature notebook.

On the day of the book fair, Melissa and I rode our bikes back to school to pick up Anna that afternoon. We parked in the bike compound and walked to Anna's classroom, expecting to see her emerge any minute with the horse poster and whatever she had found for Melissa. Anna burst out the door and said, "Come on, let's go to the book fair!"

"I thought the book fair was at lunchtime today," I said.

"No, it wasn't. It's after school," Anna replied, charging ahead. Melissa followed eagerly, reminding Anna that she was going to buy her something.

We got to the book fair, which was held in a stuffy classroom across campus, and I knew immediately that we were in trouble. At $3, the posters were the cheapest things in the place. I hadn't brought my checkbook, so between us we had $5, total.

Anna rifled through the posters while Melissa eyed all the beautiful, glossy books. Books with covers of kittens, horses, and puppies. "Mommy! Look at this! Ooh, I want this! Is this $2?" Every book she saw was more than $2, but Melissa grew more and more frantic to own one.

Anna couldn't find the horse poster she wanted. The heat in the crowded classroom was stifling, and I found myself becoming increasingly irritated with kids who brushed up against me, stepping on my toes. I grew tired of saying, "No, that's too expensive," to Melissa while we waited for Anna to go through those infernal posters. Finally Anna announced that they seemed to be out of horse posters. I seized the opportunity and said, "Okay, then let's just go."

Melissa said, "But I want to get a book!"

Anna said desperately, "Wait. I'll find something else to get."

"No," I said firmly, heading for the door. "Come on. It's too hot in here, we don't have enough money for both of you to get something, let's just go."

Outside, Anna said, "Mommy, they had a dog poster I liked. I'll get that."

"Then what can I get?" Melissa asked, a whine creeping into her voice. She clearly wasn't going to be able to handle watching her sister get something if she didn't.

I said, "You know what? This isn't working today. Five dollars isn't enough for you both to get something. Let's just go on home."

"But I want to get a poster!" Anna said, and I heard a rare conviction in her tone. Normally a very calm, agreeable kid who can "go with the flow," Anna would only occasionally put her foot down and fight hard. I sensed this was one of those times.

"If you get a poster, there won't be enough money leftover for Melissa to get anything," I said, ruing the fact that the book fair hadn't been held at lunchtime. At least if it had, Anna could've gotten her poster and Melissa might have been disappointed, but she wouldn't have been left empty-handed while surrounded by all these lovely and tempting books.

Melissa burst into tears.

"Look," I said, remembering something. "Tomorrow they're having a big book fair over at another school, to raise money to save the school library program, and how about we go to that? I'll bring my checkbook and you each can choose a book."

I thought it was a great idea. Melissa agreed, and stopped crying. But as we walked toward the bike compound, Anna began to cry loud, angry tears. Typically a reserved child, especially at school, she was oblivious to the stares of other children as she stomped along the corridor, sobbing.

"Melissa ruins everything!" she raged. "Everything, everything, everything! I just wanted to get a poster today, and she had to ruin it!"

I stayed quiet, embarrassed at the public display, but sensing that anything I said would not help the situation. I was beginning to think it was going to be a very long summer indeed.

Melissa stuck her thumb in her mouth, a sign that she was really distressed.

Anna, red-faced and full of self-pity, continued her rant. "She ruins everything! Every time I want to get something.

Every time I want to read by myself. Every time I want to play by myself!"

I've never had much patience for absolute terms—words like "always" and "never" are rarely accurate—and I worried that her tirade was demoralizing for her sister. I said, as calmly as I could manage, "Anna, come on. Get your bike and let's go."

Anna continued to sob as we straddled our bikes and started up the hill toward home. Listening to her, I did not feel at all sympathetic. The whole incident seemed so selfish: Borrow money from your sister, then have a tantrum about not being able to spend it. I began questioning my whole parenting philosophy. Maybe we're just way too easy on these kids, letting them express their feelings so openly. I could practically see my own mother, pursed lips, muttering about who's boss and who ought to shape up unless they're cruising for a bruising. After all, when I was a kid, I never would have behaved like Anna. I wouldn't have dared.

I questioned other parenting decisions as well. Maybe these girls shouldn't get allowance. Maybe we shouldn't go to the book fair at all—to heck with the drive to save the school library program—because the last thing these kids need is more stuff. And perhaps we ought to just throw out all the toys and books in our house because my two ungrateful beasts couldn't appreciate their good fortune.

Anna cried all the way home, then slammed into the house, racing up the stairs to her room. Hearing her gulping sobs, I knew she was on her bed, thumb in her mouth, baby blanket wrapped around her head. She had come completely undone.

Listening to her cry, I began to feel sorry for her. Not because she didn't get to buy a poster, but because she was alone. Alone with these feelings that had exploded and become so big that she couldn't pull herself together. I got Melissa settled downstairs with a snack, then knocked on Anna's door and asked if I could come in. She said "yes."

She continued to sob and shake while I rubbed her thick hair silently, just like I'd done when she was a little fuzzy baby. When she finally calmed down, I asked if she could tell me why she was so upset. She said she wasn't sure. I asked her if she was angry with Melissa and she said "yes." I asked her to tell me about it. In explaining herself, Anna never once mentioned the horse poster or the book fair, but instead brought up old resent-

> I stayed quiet, embarrassed at the public display, but sensing that anything I said would not help the situation.

ments—the time Melissa barged in on her play date, or when Melissa violated a safety rule at the park and we all had to leave, or when Melissa interrupted her while she practiced piano. Anna's eyes shifted nervously each time she tested out some new, potentially shocking statement. "Melissa always bugs me." "She's going to bug me all summer, every day, no matter what." And finally: "Sometimes I don't even like Melissa."

This last line was delivered in a tone laced with guilt and regret, almost like she was horrified at her own admission. As the younger of two sisters, I felt an odd hilarity creeping into my throat, at the same time as tears stung my eyes. I wasn't bothered by Anna's expression of dislike for Melissa—good grief, we all know little sisters can be annoying—but I felt deep sympathy for my older child, who so clearly felt bad for feeling resentful. No seven-year-old should have to carry that load alone.

"Honey," I said, gathering her lanky body onto my lap. "It sounds to me like you could use a break from Melissa sometimes."

"Yeah," Anna said, so relieved that the tears started again. "Sometimes I just want to read by myself."

I continued to hold her for a minute, then said, "I think we could come up with a solution."

"How?" Anna asked. "Melissa will never leave me alone."

"Well, let's all of us talk about it and see what we can come up with," I said. "Can I go get Melissa?"

Anna agreed, so the two of us went downstairs to the table, where Melissa was quietly coloring. She'd heard Anna's harsh words on the way home, and seemed to sense that it was a good time to keep a low profile. I asked Melissa to go into the kitchen and get me a note pad, and suggested Anna locate a pen. Both girls looked at each other, intrigued, and collected the items.

"Okay," I said, when we were all seated around the table. "We have a problem and we need to come up with a solution. Anna needs some more time to herself and she feels like Melissa interrupts her alone time too much. How can we solve this?"

Anna spoke first. "I could tell her I want to be alone."

Melissa said, "Okay." I wrote down "Tell Melissa," as Melissa said, "Maybe she could hang a Keep Out sign on her door."

"Yeah!" Anna said. I wrote down "Sign on door."

As the girls worked through the problem, I prompted them

> She was alone with these feelings that had exploded and become so big that she couldn't pull herself together.

only slightly, with statements like, "So … how much alone-time does Anna need?" or "What shall Melissa do while Anna has time to herself?" For 20 minutes, the girls delivered suggestions, fine-tuned the list of possibilities, and, full of smiles, reached their solution: Together they would create a Do Not Disturb sign (friendlier language than "Keep Out," they decided), which Anna would hang on her door every afternoon for an hour while Melissa colored by herself or read books with Mommy. And if Melissa continued to bug her, Anna's time alone would be extended by the same amount of time Melissa spent interrupting her.

Now it's August, the end of a very peaceful summer. The Do Not Disturb sign has gone up a few times, but mostly, Anna and Melissa have played together happily and Melissa has wandered off agreeably when Anna has chosen to curl up with a book. In two weeks, they'll both start school—Anna's off to third grade, Melissa will start kindergarten, and our time together will be significantly shortened. Yesterday, the girls created a new Do Not Disturb sign; the one they made in June got closed in the door too many times and they felt it was time for a new one. As they sat together at the table, amiably cutting out flowers to decorate their sign, Anna remarked, "Hey, this sign worked really well." Melissa replied, "Yeah, that was a good idea I had, wasn't it?"

Back on that June day, I had felt a touch of a thrill that I'd been able to help my daughters help themselves. But it wasn't until yesterday, hearing the pride in my girls' voices, that the lessons I learned that day truly sank in. By resisting the urge to command Anna to shape up after that book fair, I'd allowed her to feel the full effect of her emotions. And by listening to her carefully and silently in her room, I'd been able to discern the root of her unhappiness and help her recognize it. It wasn't about a horse poster; it was about needing time to herself. And by guiding my daughters to solve the problem themselves, I let them discover their own power to work through their squabbles in a manner that satisfies them both. One of the phrases heard most often around our house these days is, "We need a solution." Someone runs for pad of paper, another grabs a pen, we gather at the table.

Is this gentle discipline? I don't know. I've never been able

By guiding my daughters to solve the problem themselves, I let them discover their own power to work through their squabbles in a manner that satisfies them both.

to accurately define gentle discipline. In my mind, it has something to do with guiding my children to make good decisions, without forcing my opinions down their throats or stomping on their spirits. It's about realizing that they're young and inexperienced, and about respecting their solutions, which are often different than mine would be—and trusting that theirs will work. I'm not always a successful gentle disciplinarian—impatience often generates a tone too sharp or a directive too authoritarian—but when I feel that irritation rising in my throat, I often think of that day in June, when a sunny day turned dark for a few hours, and we all worked together to make it bright again.

Have Mercy on Yourself

by Kristen Hanley Cardozo

W hen I found myself pregnant the first time, I knew I wanted to practice loving discipline, and looking back, my ideas of what this meant were gloriously vague. I would allow this child gestating in my womb to be a whole individual. I would offer respect and wise counsel to my child; never treating the little one as an inferior, merely as someone less experienced. I would give my child free rein to make creative choices, and to fail when necessary, at which point I would sail in as a bastion of support and love. The more specific ideas I had were strangely irrelevant. I'd allow a child to get any haircut he or she could desire. I'd make sure that we had a pet to develop a relationship with animals and respect for nature early on. I would limit the toys in our house to make sure that my child was never overwhelmed with possessions.

Gabriel arrived, and I felt instinctively that I would never be

Kristen Hanley Cardozo is a writer and mother. Of the two, she'd say that mothering is the more constantly challenging, and offers more chances at humiliation and ecstasy. She lives in Northern California with her husband and children.

able to yell at him, that I would always be able to step in reasonably and calmly to solve together whatever problems we might have. Of course, a child as perfect as Gabriel would never create any serious problems. How could he, the itty wee snoogums with the bitsy little toes? In other words, I was still delusional from the birth.

There was a barrage of parenting advice coming my way, which could at times become overwhelming. Here I was, a newly minted mother, and it turned out that the baby hadn't come with an instruction book. Luckily, plenty of experts were happy to fill that gap. I read voraciously, and in time began to find a path that worked for me. I took anything that felt right and discarded the rest. I read those who agreed with me that children should be treated with respect.

Nearly five years and another child later, the rose-colored glasses are off. Not just off, but buried in the bottom of my purse, the lenses scratched and stained from a constant barrage of crayons and interesting rocks and shells. Oh, I still believe in the basic tenets of my ideal discipline, but I understand more about the day-to-day frustrations of parenting. It's not all cute little toes and baby snuggles, as it turns out. There's a lot of aggravation, caused both by the beloved offspring and the all-knowing parent. I don't remember the first time I yelled at Gabriel, but I know I swore it would never happen again. I was wrong about that, as well. I've never come to believe that yelling is acceptable, but I've had to learn to forgive myself some small transgressions and move on.

Here's a little secret, though, which none of the books mentioned. No matter how much we love and respect our children, we live with them. Living with people, no matter how much you love and respect them, is conducive to conflict. Living gentle discipline means messing up on occasion, and finding it in you to apologize and move on. What ultimately is most harmful to everyone is dwelling upon mistakes as failures and taking each example of human fallibility to be a unique example of your own personal inability to parent.

Forgiveness is a big part of how I parent. A child makes a mistake, and I try to remind myself that that is all it is, a mistake. Empathy for the child is a big part of it, too. I try to get behind his eyes and see where he's coming from. Why, then, is it

> Living with people, no matter how much you love and respect them, is conducive to conflict.

so hard to extend this same courtesy to myself?

I don't remember the point at which I realized that my own parents were winging it. Parents are so wise, so capable, that even when they admit mistakes, a child knows that everything is well in hand. And yes, there does come the realization that parental imperfection is the reality, but somehow, it all disappears when we begin to parent our own children. We forget all the times that our own mothers thought they were losing their minds. Perhaps we never knew how often that happened.

As soon as I had my own little bundle of humanity, I suddenly lost the sense that all parents are confused and frightened. It seemed only to be me, holding this tiny little mass of potential, who was incapable of thinking of the next step. My first few days of motherhood were spent wondering how a mother ever showered or went to the bathroom when all of the books and pamphlets I had said never to let a newborn baby out of sight or arm's reach. I dragged a bassinet after me wherever I went, and hoped for the best. It worked out just fine, though the bathroom door wouldn't close when I pulled the bassinet in there. Gabriel survived this worried incompetence without a scratch.

Many of the phrasings of positive discipline still don't come easily to me. I know mothers who can say, "Your body is full of energy. Let's find something for you to do," naturally and automatically when a child is throwing toys. For me, it's still a struggle to find those words, more of one to say them without feeling silly and awkward. Part of me is there in the background, sneering, "Your body is full of energy! How disingenuous!" I'm having to forgive myself this sniping and move on. As long as I continue to practice, the wording becomes easier.

I wonder why I'm programmed to think that anger is the only genuine emotion. Anger is a secondary emotion, and describes nothing of its cause. Anger comes after frustration or irritation or fear. We are not taught by society to identify this primary emotion, nor to look for it in others. Anger is so real to us. I'm trying to learn to look for the primary emotion in my son's anger, and yet, it remains elusive in my own. Perhaps because it is myself, I get so caught up in the feeling of anger that I neglect what brought this powerful feeling on. I forget to ask if I am feeling scared or threatened, or simply irritated to the point of anger.

> Many of the phrasings of positive discipline still don't come easily to me.

I also find myself struggling to find ways to phrase directions positively. It is so much easier to say "don't" than it is to say "do." Don't is the easy way out. We, the parents, do not have to think of what it is that the child should or could be doing. We don't have to engage in a dialogue. We leave that all to the child. We just tell him what it is that he must stop doing, now.

The good news, for me, is that while my bad habits are hard to change, they aren't impossible to change. I am learning, however slow the curve may seem to me. I find certain discipline books immensely comforting in this respect, because the authors share their own struggles with learning about discipline. In at least two of these books, the authors mention that several of their children were teenagers before they changed their parenting. It wasn't too late.

No change is instantaneous, either from adult or child. As my parenting improves, we still suffer many setbacks. My children resist the change sometimes, and sometimes their behavior gets worse before it gets better. But the boys and my husband and I are in this one together. As my children are learning to be human beings, Daniel and I are learning to be parents. The only job training we have for this task is the observations we made of our own parents, people we might or might not wish to emulate.

I think I'm probably doing my best discipline when I don't know it. When I drop everything to read a story, or when I help a friend, or when I say aloud that I'm having trouble, but finish a task anyway; those are probably the times I'm parenting the best. I never know when those moments may be, but with two young children developmentally programmed to observe, I have no doubt those moments are getting through.

Until I became a mother, discipline was a synonym for punishment. Discipline was something bad that happened to you, not restraint imposed from within. When used as a verb, discipline usually is intended that way. I see nothing positive in the statement, "He got disciplined." The dictionary is more comforting. Punishment is the fourth definition down; the first two are "1. Training expected to produce a specific character or pattern of behavior, especially training that produces moral or mental improvement," and "2. Controlled behavior resulting from disciplinary training; self-control."

I have a lot of books on discipline, and I read them fre-

> I think I'm probably doing my best discipline when I don't know it.

quently. At some point it occurred to me that what I was reading described how I'd like to be treated, and how I'd like to treat everyone, regardless of age or need for outside discipline. I started using some of the phrasings and ideas when speaking to my husband and it was eerie to see how well the techniques worked on adults. Awkward though I may feel, when I can use positive methods of communication, I am behaving toward others in a way that seems ideal. Moreover, it works. People respond well to being listened to and understood. This may not be news, but it is a revelation when we realize how rarely most people make the effort, and how difficult it is to learn.

Every day as a parent, I fall far short of my goals. Every day I do or say something I regret. But every single day I let my boys know how loved they are. Every day I find something new and wondrous about being here at this exact time in this place with these people. The best lesson I've gotten from parenthood is to take one day at a time, and to find the things I did right that day, even if there was just one little thing.

We try to parent our children the best way we know how, but unless we allow ourselves some of the nurturing we're offering, we can't do our best work. Our children are everything to us, and we are their whole world. A world that is deserving of some gentle discipline as well. I've had to learn to tell my sons that Mommy makes mistakes, and is sorry for them. And ultimately, being a less than perfect parent is probably teaching them more. Every time I can stop and think, "Would I expect this of an adult?" I am parenting the way I want to.

On Losing My Cool

by Lynn Siprelle

Lynn Siprelle is mama to Josie, age seven, and Louisa, age four. They homeschool in a big old house with the help of their daddy/husband, John, in Portland, Oregon. When not counting to ten, Lynn is the editor and publisher of (thenewhomemaker. com), a secular support site for stay-at-home parents and caregivers.

I am the mother of two girls, a seven-year-old and a three-and-a-half-year-old. I don't spank. I remind myself I don't spank at least a dozen times a day. Sometimes the reminder doesn't take and I yell, or worse, smack one on the butt. I lose my cool.

Cool is an elusive quality for a mom some days, at least for this one. My cool starts to slip on the days when I can't even answer email for two minutes without the small one hanging upside down from my shoulders, sharp little elbows digging into my sides. The days when the oldest decides making a layer cake from an entire loaf of (expensive, health food store) bread and chocolate syrup is a great idea. The days when the two of them are at each other tooth and nail for hours, over everything from who gets to sit closest to the heat vent to who gets which of two identical dolls. Or when they both think that Mama is actually talking to herself when she tells them not to do things like lick electrical outlets.

On these days, my cool can dive deep into hiding. I have no

idea where it is or how I can get it back before I smack these two kids senseless. I haven't smacked them senseless yet, so apparently I've been successful. How do I do it? Good question!

Now that I think about it, getting back my cool is just part of the way I've decided to parent, which is as gently as possible. Note the "as possible." Show me a mother who says she is 100 percent gentle, 100 percent of the time, and I'll show you a mother in deep, deep denial, and probably passive-aggressive to boot.

When I was a child, I knew my parents loved me, and I loved them, but I was also scared to death of them. I'm betting that's true of a lot of you. My daughters are not afraid of me. I have no idea why, truthfully, and in some ways it works against me; I can't rely on that murderous glare or certain tone of voice that my parents could. Sure, I still try those tactics now and again, and sometimes they even work, but my girls usually flash their sunny smiles at me: "Oh, Mama, you're so funny." Over time I've learned that threats—which is what those glares are—only have power if you're willing to back them up, and I'm not. Okay, sometimes I am, but I consider even getting to the point of threats to be a failure of my parenting skills, so that should let you know how I feel about letting myself get to the point of carrying through.

My consolation is that while my daughters aren't afraid of me it also means that they find me approachable. It means I don't have pretend I'm perfect and always know the right thing to do; I can make a mistake, back up, apologize, and try to set things right. It means my daughters can (and do) call me on stuff when I'm clearly in the wrong (and vice versa). It means we can work out ways together to get out of our current difficulties. And it means my girls get an honest model of how human relationships are and can be, that people get mad at each other and can forgive and move on, often a dozen times a day. This is what living with other people is about.

My oldest, Josie, doesn't tolerate wheat well, and so of course she loves it. I decided I would try making noodles for her out of non-wheat flour, because, of course, I am a perfect mother who would do that for her darling child. Ahem. Long story short, the experiment was not going well to put it mildly, and the girls were displaying that peculiar childhood talent of getting on a

> Getting back my cool is just part of the way I've decided to parent, which is as gently as possible.

parent's absolute last nerve. Lou was alternately poking the dough with a fork or using it to sculpt robots, Josie was trying to feed it through the pasta maker backwards. No amount of redirecting ("here's a piece you can play with over there, honey") or outright scowling was working. I yelled "Little girls out of the kitchen right now!" Scurrying feet to the living room, followed by stealthy feet back to the kitchen door. More flying flour, more yelling, more dough sticking to everything in its path.

Finally, I sat down on the little milking stool that puts me right at Louisa's eye level, just the right height to give Josie a really big hug. I pulled them close and said, "Look, I'm sorry I'm yelling. Mama's not having a very good day."

"No, you sure aren't!" said Jo. "What's wrong?"

I explained about the dough not working out and all the time I'd spent on it, and how I really wanted it to work because it was for her, and how frustrated I was. And it's not helping, I said, that two small girls wouldn't let me finish the work, but it's also not fair that I was taking my noodle frustration out on them, and could they please go keep themselves busy until I was done. Josie said, "It's okay, Mom, we forgive you. C'mon, Lou, Mama's having a bad day. Let's go play." And I got two hugs. It didn't help the noodles—they turned out truly awful—but it did help how the rest of our evening went.

How could I have avoided my little meltdown? I could have tried to make the noodles earlier in the day when we all weren't so tired. I could have set Louisa up at her own table with a piece of dough before she saw what I was doing in the kitchen. I could have let Josie crank the pasta machine. I could have just gone to the health food store and bought some non-wheat noodles. But I didn't. So in the end I was left with what I have found is often the most effective method: Being honest and working out the solution together with my daughters.

I'm not saying it always works, or that I always do this exactly the right way. I'm saying it makes it easier to coax my cool out of its hidey hole. In the end, what I rely on the most is the old advice that longtime married couples have given newlyweds since time out of mind: Don't go to bed angry. We family bed at our house, at least for going to sleep (and sometimes waking up). It's literally impossible for me to go to sleep angry at my kids when they're curled up on either side of me. How can I stay angry at Louisa when she yawns "Night, Mama, I yuv you," even if she's taken scissors to the clothespin bag, dumped out all the Lite Brite pieces and refused to pick them up, and insisted on hanging onto my leg most of the day? How can I stay angry at Josie when she's just sung me a lullabye, even if she's dumped all the clean laundry out of the basket so she can use it for a ship— over and over and over again?

On the really bad days, when it seems as though I've yelled myself hoarse and I just haven't been able to remember that I'm the grownup, at the end of the day I rely on that bed. We go to bed early (because always on those trying days one or more of us is tired and cranky). We read a little story, turn out the light, and snuggle up under our thick down comforter. The last thing we say to each other every night is always, "Good night, sleep tight, I love you." Then I've got so much cool that I feel as if I just might have enough left over for the next day.

Not Easy

by Melissa Ridge Carter

Gentle discipline is easy when you bring three well-rested, contented children into the grocery store. It's easy when the sweet little blue-haired old lady behind you in line gushes over your four-year-old's curls and he, in turn doesn't growl at her. It feels especially easy (and perhaps slightly superior, although it's best not to let that thought fully form) when, as the cashier comments on your beautiful, well-behaved family, you hear a mother in the next aisle hiss thinly veiled threats at her screaming child.

It's a heckuvalot harder when your child is the one screaming and you're desperately biting back your own thinly veiled (or not so thinly veiled) threats.

My husband and I never discussed children. We'd started dating when we were children ourselves and I don't think it occurred to us to plan beyond the inevitable, eventual appearance of a baby. We told

Melissa Ridge Carter is a homeschooling mom to three beautiful children. She is a freelance writer in her "spare" time.

everyone we would have one child and have, so far, ended up with three.

I have a dog-eared copy of the "What to Expect…" book that has now been shoved out of sight because nothing it told me to expect actually happened and what did happen apparently wasn't expected. We tried "Ferberizing" our first child for approximately three minutes because our kindly old pediatrician told us she needed to cry it out in order to sleep through the night. We then secretly co-slept for years because those three minutes of crying were too traumatic for all concerned. And we had always assumed that corporal punishment would be a part of our discipline plan.

We were both raised by the traditional rod. My husband picked out his own switch on more than one occasion and my father once broke a hairbrush on my tush. (Of far greater concern than the spanking was the loss of my favorite brush.) Both of us will claim we weren't irreversibly scarred, that it was simply a method of discipline. We learned from those spankings and we understood why each one occurred (usually because they were punctuated by "Didn't…I…tell…you…not…to…!"), but, for some reason, that particular method isn't part of our parenting.

Did everyone have that list as a child, the one I kept meaning to write down? "Things I Will Never Do To My Own Daughter" or "What I Will Do Differently." I may have even started the list a few times. I have no copies of it and only vague memories of the incidents that inspired the lists, but I do remember a common theme: listening. Every time I felt wronged by parents, it was because I felt ignored. I felt as though I wasn't heard. I also believed, at those times, that my parents had forgotten what being a child was like and therefore no longer had the ability to listen and to understand and were only able to control and command.

So I entered parenting with only three clear goals: to love, to cherish, and to listen. And I found out that the desire to control and command may just be genetic.

I hear myself sometimes. "Why?" I snap, "Because I said so!"

It's my mother's voice resonating out of my wayward mouth. The same sharp, shrill tone exposing the same desperate floundering for control. Whenever my patience wanes and one of my kids spills his water or calls, "Maaamaaaa!" one too many times, I feel that tension bubble to the surface and I forget how much I love being Mama and that water really is just water and I start doing a slow intense burn that leads to…my mother. And I cringe. Does my commanding voice work? Um, no. It's about as effective as my in-laws' directive: "Well, if you don't, you better!" My husband is still trying to figure that one out.

> So I entered parenting with only three clear goals: to love, to cherish, and to listen.

But the futility alone isn't my greatest concern. My mother's parenting seemed painfully dismal. It lacked the incredible joy I feel when I look at my children. It lacked a warmth. I never doubted my parents' love but I never sensed the intimate bond I seek with my own children.

In order to best raise my children, I must know and understand them. In order to understand them, I must communicate. I must, I've learned, be able to sit down and gaze into their eyes and see them and listen.

Gentle discipline is easy when, after surgery (in my case, two cesarean births), you're floating from the effects of Percoset. It provides a different level of escape, a suspended reality, a happy little place that I'm planning on pursuing—drug-free—with yoga. Or meditation.

Gentle discipline is hard when you're writing, trying to be creative, trying to define yourself outside the realm of motherhood, and a persistent whine for attention reminds you too harshly that mothering comes before writing.

What Percoset taught me was to defer my anger. Push it aside, numb the effects, until I'm able to sort it out without exploding. My children, with their tiny missteps, don't deserve my adult-scale frustration. They don't think like adults; they don't reason like adults, and I need to understand their child-driven motivations and honor their perceptions.

> And we try to talk to our children, not at them.

Sometimes, though, when my husband and I are tired, when the bills outweigh the bank account, when our four-year-old can't stop asking questions and our nine-year-old wants to analyze the tiny details of life, our minds simultaneously combust and we explode. Then, we need a few minutes to gather the pieces and, eventually, to talk.

And we try to talk to our children, not at them. We try not to toss around imperial decrees over their heads; instead, we get down, eye-to-eye, and talk. And listen. Our daughter is thoughtful; she'll pick up the intent of a rapid command said in rage or frustration and understand the purpose beneath the anger. Our four-year-old son, however, will hear only the angry tone—and he'll respond in kind. He's a tightly bound, intense bundle and he pushes our patience and challenges our intentions—but he needs gentle discipline. He thrives on it.

When the anger or frustration is too much, my impulse is to explode, but that just leaves all of us sad and cranky and disconnected. Instead, I've learned to get down on the floor with them and look at them and explain my feelings. If I do snap, I backtrack. I apologize for yelling—but, I don't apologize for my feelings.

It's very different than how I was raised and I've never been certain how my mother interpreted my choices until recently. My grandmother passed away and it was shocking and awful and our emotions were spinning out of control. My patience had gone out the window, and my mother was, truthfully, a mess. She looked at my four-year-old son bouncing around her kitchen and barked at him to stop. Then, she paused.

"Langston, I'm sorry."

I blinked.

She continued, "I'm sorry. You weren't doing anything wrong. I'm feeling sad and angry; I don't have any patience. But, I shouldn't have yelled. Do you think you could be very calm for a little while?"

And he nodded and gave her hug. And was very calm (for a little while).

Effective discipline doesn't occur just during a crisis. It's a constant. It's the entire climate that envelops our family and shapes our responses. It is, I hope, a sense of unconditional love and security that will allow my children to communicate freely and respectfully. It's an atmosphere of trust woven in such a way that my desire to celebrate my children overrides my learned impatience.

Usually.

It's not easy. It requires a focus, a commitment, an energy that sometimes I don't have.

To maintain sanity, we carve out personal time. For my husband, it's a nap. For me, it's a good book after the kids are asleep, sometimes as late as 1:00 in the morning. It's survival. Parenting isn't about losing yourself; it's about expanding yourself to encompass your family.

And, to me, gentle discipline isn't about squishy, touchy-feely warm fuzzies. It's about embracing your children, heart and soul. It's about respecting who they are and honoring those individuals. It's about valuing their thoughts and feelings and guiding them to make the best (not necessarily the most convenient) decisions—not for us, but for them.

It's not easy.

Perfect Parenting

by Rebecca Jacobson

Rebecca Jacobson is a mother of two beautiful children. She lives with her childhood sweetheart and now husband, Mark. Rebecca strives to give her children a happy and balanced upbringing. She is also a teacher and budding freelance writer.

I was the perfect parent. When Mother Nature was handing out maternal instinct, she evidently gave me a huge double helping. Obviously I'd been to a few parenting classes, read a few magazines, and it did help that I was on a first-name basis with a few parenting experts (my mum and my mother-in-law). But in general when it came to parenting, I excelled. And I had Isaac to prove it. My sweet, angelic, never threw a tantrum in his life, toddler. While my friends struggled to maintain their sanity and reason with their tiny tyrants, I spent my days sipping tea while my angelic charge played contentedly with his Play Doh.

I would take Isaac out shopping and he sat so patiently in the supermarket trolley that total strangers offered to buy him treats. I took him along to important functions, like weddings and work dinners; no one even noticed he was there. While parents around me were going into lock down, in a last desperate bid to salvage any precious ornaments, my cupboards remained lock free. My knick-knacks never migrated to higher shelves. And at Christmas time my finely adored tree remained as picture perfect throughout the season as the day I put it up. Sure every now and then Isaac would wander over and play with the decorations. But he was always so gentle. A far cry from the 24-hour security guard and iron clad fences that my friends had custom ordered to protect their Christmas trees.

Of course, I never blatantly flaunted my supernatural parenting abilities in front of other mothers. I may have occasionally offered suggestions to parents whom I thought needed a little guidance. Okay, truthfully, I was like some sort of obsessed parenting guru. I thought all mothers the world over should gather in huge temples and listen to my teachings on the fine art of child rearing. I saw at least several potential book deals and perhaps an infomercial or two on the horizon. I held up my son like some kind of sacred token, an example of the miracle parents could create if they simply heeded my advice. I brushed aside comments made by obviously, insanely jealous types about my luck not being so good the second time around.

When Isaac was two and a half I discovered that I was pregnant. An ultrasound revealed that I was having a baby girl. I was elated. I was home free; everyone knew that little girls were easier to handle than boys. I was certain that I would be able to do it again, to mould and shape the perfect child. And after two perfect children I was destined to be a "Mother of the Year" nominee. I was on cloud nine. And then I gave birth to Charli!

Charli looked deceivingly like any other baby at birth, but within a few days, I realized that I had a baby dynamo on my hands. She screamed constantly and demanded constant attention. She didn't slowly and methodically reach the milestones like Isaac had, she flew through them. At seven months, she developed this ability to drag her body around the floor, like a wounded soldier. Although it looked awkward, she moved at lightning speed. Charli would lie in wait and then attack passing ankles. By nine months she was walking. At ten months, Charli ran for the first time. She has not stopped since.

Now at 20 months, Charli leaves me emotionally and physically exhausted by mid-morning. She can empty the entire contents of the kitchen pantry in the time it takes me to answer the

> I was certain that I would be able to mould and shape the perfect child.

telephone. Charli has all the skill of a trained spy; she can come from nowhere and attack without warning. She wears enough grime on her face to camouflage an entire armed service. She recently beat her eight-year-old uncle in a wrestling match. My beautiful, petite little princess is more at home in a pair of jeans than a frilly party frock. And she is a veteran temper tantrum thrower. If she doesn't get her own way she turns into a miniature hurricane that destroys all in its path.

Amidst all this Charli has the most amazing personality; she can put a smile on the most reserved face. People are instantly drawn to her. When she smiles her whole face lights up, and she has the most gorgeous dimples. Charli is incredibly inquisitive and has the ability to retain knowledge like a thirsty car guzzles gas. She also has the kindest heart. She delights in giving strangers kisses and hugs. And although I have never cried so much in my life as I have these past 13 months, I have never laughed so much either.

Up until recently the term "discipline" meant saying no to an extra serving of chocolate pudding after a meal. Nowadays it means staying one step ahead of my little cherub. I would estimate that 95 percent of Charli's mischief is curiosity based. She wants to know how everything works and she often has accidents caused by her overzealousness. I have a lovely brand new dinner set courtesy of Charli's penchant for holding tea parties with my good china. I don't believe in punishment for accidents. If she is not harming anything or anyone and is in no great danger, I usually just turn a blind eye. Other times I join in and help guide her in her play. People underestimate how much fun it can be to create fashion accessories with tin foil and kitchen utensils. Distraction is the best thing when behavior becomes really inappropriate. I will often bring out something interesting, such as the Christmas decorations, to divert Charli's attention.

I really only have two rules; no angry yelling and no physical violence. These rules apply to adults as well as children. Having a no smacking policy in our house has made it easy to teach the children that we never use any part of our bodies to hurt anyone else. The adults aren't allowed to break the rules. When the children break one of them, I use quiet time. Both Isaac and Charli have a little couch that they use when watch-

> I really only have two rules; no angry yelling and no physical violence.

ing television and reading. Quiet time means sitting on your couch for a few minutes, I use a minute per year of life as a rough time length. So Isaac sits for longer than Charli. The key to the success of quiet time is not overusing it. My children know that they must have been really naughty when they are asked to sit on their couch and stay there. And neither likes thinking that they are in trouble. After quiet time, I usually get the child to apologize to the appropriate party. And that's it; the incident is forgotten and never mentioned again. I think it is important that once the time has been served, so to speak, that the child knows everything is right in the world again. If one of them gets off the couch before the time is up, I have them spend the rest of the time-out in their bedroom. In my experience this usually only happens once as children prefer to be in the same room as everyone else.

So although for now, I'm leaving the book-writing to the real child experts, Charli has taught me a few new truths. Even though Charli is not what I would have once considered an ideal child, she is perfect. She's taught me that there is no definition of the ideal child—that each of us is perfect in our own individual way, and we should celebrate these differences. I've realized that children should be allowed to be children and childhood should be about fun and adventure. Rules and responsibilities are the domain of adulthood and will come around soon enough. I've learned that perfect parents only exist in Disney movies. And even those parents struggle at times. All we can do as real parents is seek out advice, ride through the rough patches, and above all else follow our hearts.

Starting Over

by Sarah Martin

On a good day, all three of my kids are bathed, dressed, fed and the older two have had their teeth brushed twice. I can head off impending arguments, keep the baby content and occupied, and find time to read a stack of library books to each child. On a good day, everyone is in bed by 9 PM without complaint. Sometimes it seems like good days are few and far between here. Today was not a good day.

This morning, three cups of orange juice were spilled on the carpet. The older two ran outside in the rain and trailed muddy footprints through my dining room and kitchen. The baby is learning to stand unaided and managed to hit her face on the hardwood floor; her top lip is now roughly the size of a walnut. My son and daughter have been at each other's throats, arguing over how to correctly assemble their dinosaur puzzle. Still, for a bad day I managed to make it over the biggest hurdle of all; I didn't yell.

To say I'm an unconventional parent is putting it mildly. I'm much more laid back than most of the other parents I know,

Sarah Martin is a freelance writer and mother. She spends her days trying to sneak in some time at the keyboard amidst the chaos. She lives in Western New York with her three children and husband.

which often makes me feel like a fraud. The art of discipline eludes me. In the beginning, I tried on all sorts of different parenting hats: "Non-coercive" parenting, "positive" parenting, "natural" parenting. With each new addition to our family, though, the dynamics and expectations changed and approaches that seemed reasonable with one child were difficult with two and nearly impossible with three.

Impractical expectations had me trapped, constantly feeling like a failure. I was angry with myself for losing my temper, angry with my children when a parenting method didn't seem to "work," and feeling defeated all around. I finally came to the conclusion that theory alone wasn't going to work for me. Each of my children has a unique personality and a unique set of disciplinary needs. I threw away the labels and decided to just focus on mothering my children, taking each situation as it came to me.

I'm usually pretty good at finding common preferences— picking an activity everyone would prefer, rather than forcing anyone to compromise. It involves a tremendous amount of creative thinking, but is not as hard as it seems once you get the hang of it. For example, my daughter attends a local Waldorf class for homeschoolers once a week. Yesterday, when we brought her to class, my son saw all of the neat toys in the classroom and wanted to stay. Obviously, that wasn't possible, so we found a common preference—something both Sagan and I preferred instead of staying in the classroom. During the time my daughter was in class, we went to the zoo. He was happy, because it was time he was able to spend with me at a place he loved and I was happy because the zoo is a place I enjoy and I was able to pass the time with a happy child instead of a screaming, crying three-year-old. Both of us found this activity more agreeable than staying at the school and interrupting the class.

The difference between a "common preference" and a "compromise" is that in a compromise, everyone gives a little of what they want in order keep the peace. With common preferences, the result is choosing an activity that everyone finds more pleasing that the original idea. One of our favorite common preferences is a trip to the playground or library. It seems that my kids always find those things preferable to whatever games, toys, or activities they have been arguing over. I still haven't figured out how to make it work in every situation. There are times when I just don't have the energy left at the end of the day to find a creative solution to everyone's problems, but for the most part, the theory of common preferences has worked well for our family.

Of course, this method is a lot harder to put into practice when the kids are already hysterical and the baby is crying. That's when I'm closest to my breaking point. I've discovered that theory only takes me so far, because there will always be a situation that requires a unique approach, something that I've never thought of before. It's a lot easier to think these things through in advance than to try tackling the problem when everyone is already upset and frantic.

It's the screaming that sets me off. One child crying I can usually handle, but it never fails that as soon as the crying child lapses into howling, someone else will begin whining. Not to be outdone by louder siblings, the third child will chime in, usually with completely unrelated tears. I'm not sure what small part of my brain thinks that adding my voice to the already cacophonous symphony of dissatisfaction will actually benefit anyone, but sometimes I find myself yelling just to be heard.

This is when detachment comes in handy. If I can separate myself from the situation, if I can pretend that I'm an impartial observer, watching a mother who actually knows what she's doing handle the tantrums, then I can find my moment of Zen. I can glide through my day with a sense of inner peace and a calm demeanor. On a bad day, it's difficult to differentiate between Zen and catatonia. Sitting on the sofa and staring blankly out the window might mean that I've found inner peace or that I've had a complete breakdown.

But if I can reach that space in my head that detaches me from the flood of emotion, I can turn it over to Fantasy Mom. Fantasy Mom is my inner parenting guru. She can speak calmly to an hysterical two-year-old for hours while bouncing a teething, screaming baby and making lunch for the preschooler. Fantasy Mom has an unlimited number of distractions and educational craft projects at her disposal and is always up for an impromptu trip to the zoo if anyone needs a change of scenery. Unfortunately, most days Fantasy Mom is missing in action and I'm stuck here in her place.

Having three children under five years old makes for a hec-

> It's a lot easier to think these things through in advance than to try tackling the problem when everyone is already upset and frantic.

tic household and a myriad of bizarre parenting moments never discussed in the books. I keep a running mental tally of statements I never thought I'd hear myself utter, my current favorite being, "Get your shoe out of your sister's soup." There is a lot of noise in my house most days, and that leads to a tense and potentially explosive mother. When I'm close to losing it, when I feel as if one more wailing cry is going to snap me completely, that's when I remember my grandmother telling me, "This too shall pass," and I try to make the conscious decision to start over. When in doubt: start over, start over, start over.

The little ones are much more forgiving of my mistakes than I am. When we decide to start over for the day, I'm the one who has a hard time forgetting my earlier parenting blunders. Children are adaptable, far more so than we adults tend to give them credit for. They understand the concept of making mistakes because they do it all the time. They also have greater comprehension of moving on. Children don't hold grudges. When the moment has passed, they are happy to begin again. I try to remember that when I'm facing a sink full of dirty dishes and a brood of whining, hungry kids. There's always time for a fresh start, no matter how far I've fallen from my parenting paradigm.

I don't have many static rules. Aside from the unyielding rule of no abuse of any kind, I try to give myself room for mistakes. Holding myself to an unattainable standard, like expecting that I'll never raise my voice, or threaten to send them to their rooms if they don't stop fighting, is unrealistic and self-defeating. Acknowledging that I'm going to mess up and offering sincere apologies when I do have helped me keep my sanity.

I know that I haven't hit the hard part of parenting yet. My eldest is not yet kindergarten-age and I'm well aware that the trials my friends face with their school-aged children are out there waiting for me. I know that I'll change my technique a thousand times before my children are teenagers, but for now, we're getting through each day one new beginning at a time. And I think we're doing all right.

> Children are adaptable, far more so than we adults tend to give them credit for.

Index

A

ADHD 51

Anger (**see** Emotions)

Apologies 138, 223-24

Attitude 143, 160, 219, 233

Authority 133, 139, 178, 187, 316-19

Autism 51

Autonomy 57, 61

B

Bedtime, encouraging 96-100, 224, 278-283 (**see also,** Transitions)

Boundaries

bodily 94-96

definition 76-78

"no," saying 108, 120-25, 132-35

safety, of child 4, 21, 41, 48, 59, 148

spirited child 64-65

(**see also,** Prevention; Rules; Transitions)

Breastfeeding, as discipline tool 27, 31, 143, 271, 278, 280

C

Capabilities (**see** Developmental stages)

Car seat avoidance 38, 228, 269-73, 293 (**see also,** Transitions)

Childish 56-58

D

E

Email lists 237, 332

Emotions

> empathizing with child's 104, 113-16, 126-29, 146, 254-55

> helping child express 36-40, 84-85, 163-65, 300-04, 323-25

> helping child identify 116-17, 262-66,

Empowering child 12, 19, 37, 118, 139

Expectations

> realistic, of child 32-34, 56-58, 60-70, 72-74

> unrealistic, of child 81, 90, 189

F

Family members

> disagreeing with 242-47, 249-53

> supportive 170-71, 240-42, 254-55, 339

Feelings (see Emotions)

Flexibility 70, 72-73, 134-37, 176 (see also, Develomental stages; Temperament)

Follow-through, (see Consistency)

Food

> additives 27, 49-50

> allergies 50, 302

> struggles, avoiding 95, 114, 263

> (see also, Needs, food and/or drink)

Forgiveness (see Compassion)

Friends

> disagreeing with 243, 247-49

> supportive 65, 170-73, 200, 231-37, 254-55, 299, 301-03

G

H

I

L

M

N

V

Village, it takes a, (**see** Family members; Friends)

W

Well-being (**see** Needs)
Whining 260-62

Y

Yelling 182-83, 198, 201, 210, 212, 216-17, 220

Photo Credits

Back cover, Ben Flower

Pages 9, 20, 109, 143, 147, 169, 170, 197, 207, 244, 303 David Arendt

Pages 13, 263, 287, 295, Aaron Molnar

Pages 18, 30, 42, 75, 101, 105, 161, 165, 191, 231, 233, 267, 278, 282, Karen Levy Keon

Pages 19, 25, 35, 72, 145, 149, 248, 274, 336, Hilary Flower

Page 41, Keri Haskins

Pages 43, 158, Sheree Young

Pages 55, 57, Donna Young

Pages 63, 131, Kim Cavaliero

Page 87, Mary Lofton

Page 93, Angela Boicheff

Page 95, Rolland Oselka

Page 103, Dylan Keon

Page 114, Clay Stroup

Page 259, Judy Torgus

Page 269, Paul Torgus

Page 307, Rahyab Lari

Page 312, R. Raphael

Page 315, Stan Mace

Page 320, Krista Minard

Page 327, Daniel Cardozo

Page 332, Kraig Scattarella

Page 340, Mark Jacobson

Page 344, Rebecca Swinton

About La Leche League

LA LECHE LEAGUE
INTERNATIONAL

La Leche League International is a nonprofit organization founded in 1956 by seven women who wanted to help other mothers learn about breastfeeding. Today La Leche League is an internationally recognized authority on breastfeeding, with a mother-to-mother network that includes La Leche League Leaders and Groups in countries all over the world. A Professional Advisory Board reviews information on medical issues.

Mothers who contact LLL find answers to their questions on breastfeeding and support from other parents who are committed to being sensitive and responsive to the needs of their babies. Local LLL Groups meet monthly to discuss breastfeeding and related issues. La Leche League Leaders are also available by telephone to offer information and encouragement when women have questions about breastfeeding.

La Leche League International is the world's largest resource for breastfeeding and related information and products. The organization distributes more than three million publications each year, including the classic how-to book, THE WOMANLY ART OF BREASTFEEDING, now in its seventh edition. Look for it in bookstores, or order from La Leche League International by calling 800-LALECHE, 847-519-9585, or 847-519-7730 weekdays between 9 am and 5 pm Central Time. Or fax your order to 847-519-0035 or order online at www.lalecheleague.org/

In Canada, call 800-665-4324, or write to LLLC, 18C Industrial Drive, Box 29, Chesterville, Ontario.